DOCTRINE

—— *according to* ——

GODLINESS

DOCTRINE
— *according to* —
GODLINESS

a primer of Reformed doctrine

Ronald Hanko

REFORMED
FREE PUBLISHING
ASSOCIATION

Jenison, Michigan

Scripture cited is taken from the Authorized (King James) Version

The Reformed and ecumenical creeds are found in *The Confessions and the Church Order of the Protestant Reformed Churches* (Grandville, MI: Protestant Reformed Churches in America, 2005)

The Westminster Confession of Faith and its Larger and Shorter Catechisms are found in *Westminster Confession of Faith* (Glasgow: Free Presbyterian Publications, 1994)

Reformed Free Publishing Association
1894 Georgetown Center Drive
Jenison MI 49428-7137
616-457-5970
www.rfpa.org
mail@rfpa.org

Cover and interior design by Erika Kiel
Typesetting by The Composing Room

ISBN 0-916206-84-X
ISBN 978-0916206-84-0 (hardcover)
ISBN 978-1-936054-24-4 (ebook)
LCCN 2004094080

DEDICATED

—— to my parents ——

Herman and Wilma Hanko, who taught me
these doctrines from a very young age and who
instilled in me a love for Bible doctrines by their
teaching and by their living witness to them.

If any man teach otherwise, and consent not to wholesome words, even the words of our Lord Jesus Christ, and to the doctrine which is according to godliness; he is proud, knowing nothing, but doting about questions and strifes of words, whereof cometh envy, strife, railings, evil surmisings, perverse disputings of men of corrupt minds, and destitute of the truth, supposing that gain is godliness: from such withdraw thyself.

—1 Timothy 6:3–5

CONTENTS

PART 6

THE RETURN OF CHRIST AND THE LAST THINGS

FOREWORD

One of the challenges encountered in mission work is to present the gospel and the truth of God's Word clearly and simply, to expound the doctrines of Scripture thoroughly yet briefly. We live in an age when many who confess Christ wander in confusion, are poor in scriptural knowledge, and are led astray by every wind of doctrine that blows through the church. Much of the knowledge of the faith once delivered to the saints has been lost by those who should know it. A missionary today must also address the Word to those who do not know Christ and have not heard the authentic gospel. He must speak to professing Christians concerning the faith and call the unbelieving to repentance and faith in Christ.

At a time when reading of solid material has declined and attention spans are short, these limitations of readers set before the pastor or missionary a difficult task. Materials are hard to find that are sound in doctrine, address these difficulties, and are truly useful. In the 1940s Rev. Herman Hoeksema met the need for short messages in his radio sermons, some of which were later compiled in book form. His *Wonder of Grace* is an excellent example of this. Another book, written by Rev. Ronald Hanko and Rev. Ronald Cammenga and titled *Saved by Grace*, more extensively develops the sovereignty of God and the five points of Calvinism from the Scriptures.

Doctrine according to Godliness continues in the line of such efforts to explain doctrine in a simplified way. Rev. Hanko's book is the fruit of much diligent labor expended on the mission field. He developed most of the articles found in this work over a number of years as missionary pastor in Northern Ireland, where the Reformed faith once flourished among the Presbyterian churches.

Each brief yet thorough exposition is complete in itself and sets forth a basic doctrinal concept. At the same time, the author develops the line of the Reformed faith in its unity in each succeeding article. This gives to these doctrinal studies a twofold character. Each article, or several together, can stand as a brief development of a specific truth or doctrine, providing material to answer specific questions that are often asked. At the same time, the development of the articles, following the line of Reformed doctrinal thought, allows the work to be considered as a whole. In this latter aspect, *Doctrine according to Godliness* may well serve as a basic manual of Reformed doctrine or dogmatics.

Such an approach makes the material suitable not only for Reformed mission work, but also for study and discussion in the established congregation or in Christian education. The book in its entirety can serve as material for group study or discussion. Individual articles can be used topically as well. Those called to teach in various capacities—whether they are elders, parents, teachers, or leaders of Bible societies—will find here doctrinally sound resource materials to aid them in their preparation.

Reading these articles will equip the believer to be ready to give an answer for the hope that lies within him. For one who finds the weighty character of a dogmatics text somewhat daunting, the material covers the scope of Reformed doctrine in a way that leads the reader to the Scriptures and to further study.

Limiting each article to one or two printed pages in which the contents are both thorough and complete is a difficult format to carry out. It is no small accomplishment that Rev. Hanko has done this so effectively. Bringing the truth to bear on the Christian's life and walk, the author has also provided us with a useful devotional. By combining faith and practice, doctrine and life, truth and application, the articles both instruct in knowledge and edify for a walk of godliness. The title of the book is thus well chosen.

May the Lord continue to use the fruit of these labors in the cause of his kingdom and glory.

Rev. Thomas Miersma

PREFACE

This book has its origin in a series of approximately two hundred articles written for a study sheet that was distributed over a period of eight years as part of a mission work in the United Kingdom. The reception of those articles, as well as the encouragements received from many readers, are the occasion for putting the articles together in book form.

A few of the original articles have not been included, but about fifty new articles have been added to fill in gaps in the subject matter. Most of the original articles have been revised, and a few have been entirely rewritten.

The book follows the customary divisions of Reformed theology, and the six main sections of *Doctine according to Goldiness* are the six divisions of dogmatics, even though the traditional names for those divisions are not used.

When the articles were originally written as a mission witness, they were as simply written as possible, abundant Scripture proof was supplied, and an effort was made to show how the doctrines of Scripture apply to life. All this is retained, believing that it may be of further use in teaching the Reformed faith on the mission field and in the churches.

The articles are also very brief in the hope that those who know something of the Reformed faith will be encouraged to read further. It is my conviction that one of the things that has contributed to the decline of Reformed churches in the United States and elsewhere is a lack of reading on the part of God's people. I trust that these articles, easily read, will encourage deeper study of the doctrines of grace and of God's sovereignty in salvation.

May God bless these efforts and use them for good.

Rev. Ronald Hanko

INTRODUCTION

The Importance of Doctrine

Doctrine is not highly regarded anymore. In many evangelical churches there is such ignorance of doctrine that even the fundamentals of Christianity are not well understood. Even in churches that remain faithful in their teaching and preaching, there is often little interest in learning and understanding doctrine. The youth are, for the most part, bored by it, and their elders are content with a superficial knowledge of the doctrines of the Reformed faith.

Very often the symptom of this lack of doctrine is a constant agitation for more "practical" preaching and teaching along with a greater emphasis on liturgy and on the other parts of the worship service until the sermon is all but squeezed out. On the part of the preachers themselves, one finds less and less biblical exposition and more and more illustration, storytelling, and entertainment.

Symptomatic of doctrinal indifference in the private lives of God's people is complete disinterest in reading good Reformed books and periodicals. In some cases these are purchased and not read; in others there is not sufficient interest even to purchase them. If any reading at all is done, it is superficial, mostly of the "how-to" variety. Almost nothing of substance is read, and most would consider a book of doctrine too deep even though their fathers and grandfathers, who had far less education, not only were able to read theology, but read it widely and well.

If the church and the lives of God's people are to be rescued from superficiality, decline, and all the church troubles that afflict us today, there must be a return to doctrine. For proof we need look no further than the great Reformation of the sixteenth century. Above all, the Reformation was a return to doctrine—to the doctrines of justification by faith alone, of sovereign grace, of the church, and of the sacraments. Without an interest in or return to doctrine, we cannot even hope for revival and renewal in the church.

In 2 Timothy 3:16–17 the Word of God tells us that Scripture is profitable for many things, but for doctrine first of all. Indeed, if it does not first teach us doctrine, it is not profitable for reproof, for correction, and for instruction in righteousness. To all of these, doctrine is not only first, but also foundational.

Scripture emphasizes the importance of doctrine in other ways. We learn from John 17:3 that the knowledge of God and of Jesus Christ is eternal life. Nothing is more important than that. Doctrine, properly taught, understood, and believed, is that knowledge of God and of his Son. Scripture teaches nothing else. "Search the scriptures," Jesus says, "for they are they which testify of me" (John 5:39).

Let us, then, give heed to doctrine. It is the province not only of the theologians but of every one who desires life eternal. Let us not set doctrine aside in the interest of more "practical" matters, but understand that doctrine reproves, corrects, and teaches the way of righteousness. Above all, it brings us face-to-face with the living God himself, in whom we live and move and have our being. To be without doctrine is to be without God.

part 1

GOD AND HIS WORD

Revelation

One of the most marvelous of God's works is his revelation to us. Just the fact that he does reveal himself is a great and wonderful thing. He is sufficient unto himself, has no need of anyone or anything besides himself, and yet chooses to reveal himself in all the works of his hands.

Even more wonderful is that God reveals *himself* to us. We are only creatures, the work of his hands, less than dust before him. He is the Almighty, the infinite and eternal God, who cannot be comprehended. Yet he makes himself and his glory known to us.

Especially when we remember that he is, according to 1 Timothy 6:16, the one whom no man hath seen, nor can see, pure Spirit and forever invisible to our eyes, do we realize that revelation is a miracle. That he who is so great should speak in human language and in a way that the simplest of us can understand is almost unbelievable. Calvin spoke of God "lisping" to us as a parent lisps to his little child. That is the miracle of revelation.

Part of that miracle, of course, is that God makes himself known to *sinners* who have closed their minds and hearts to him. In this we see the connection between the miracle of revelation and the miracle of grace and realize that revelation has its ultimate purpose in the salvation of God's people.

That brings us to the different ways in which God reveals himself. The Belgic Confession of Faith, following Psalm 19, speaks of two ways, through creation and through Scripture,[1] but there are other ways as well. God also reveals himself in history, which really is "his story," in the conscience of every man, and in the Old Testament directly by dreams, visions, angels, and other means.

God's revelation in creation is described in the Belgic Confession as a "most elegant book."[2] Just as the work of a master painter or sculptor reveals something of the artist, so do God's works reveal something of himself. Nevertheless, that revelation, as well as God's revelation in history and in the conscience of man, is a terrifying book to unsaved sinners. The unsaved sinner can read nothing in that revelation but wrath

---

1. Belgic Confession of Faith, Article 2.
2. Ibid.

and judgment, and for that reason he also corrupts that revelation and puts it away from himself (Rom. 1:25).

Only in the Scriptures does God reveal himself through Jesus Christ as the Savior of his people. For that reason we think especially of the Scriptures when we think of revelation.

Having known God through the Scriptures, we can also profit from God's revelation in creation and history. As Calvin suggested, the Scriptures are the eyeglasses through which we are also able to read in creation something of God's love and grace. Scripture teaches us to see in sunrises and in lilies, in seeds and in mountains, evidences of the great God of our salvation and of his grace.

Let us learn to read that "most elegant book" of creation, but let us not neglect that greater book, the Word of God in the Scriptures. There we learn to know him who has so graciously revealed himself to us in his Son.

General Revelation

"General revelation" is the term often used to refer to God's making himself known in creation, conscience, and history. The term is used in distinction from "special revelation," God's saving revelation through Jesus Christ in the Scriptures.

General revelation is referred to in a number of passages, but most clearly in Romans 1:18–32. That passage speaks of God's making himself known in the things of creation (vv. 20, 25) and in the conscience of man (v. 19; notice the words *in them*).

This general revelation, however, has no saving power. It is not even a kind of grace, although many speak of it as an example of so-called common grace. Instead, as Romans 1 makes so clear, this general revelation is of the *wrath* of God and only serves to leave the wicked without excuse (vv. 18, 20).

Certainly, then, general revelation does not provide another way of salvation. The idea that the wicked can be saved by a moral response to this general revelation is wholly without ground in Scripture and is just another form of salvation by works and of religious humanism.

This idea that general revelation has saving value is flatly contradicted by Romans 1 itself. The wicked do see the "invisible things of God," particularly his eternal power and Godhead (v. 20). There is even an *internal* aspect to this manifestation of God. Verse 19 says that the things that may be known of God are manifest "in them."

This has important implications. The manifestation of God in the things that are made is the reason no one will ever be able to plead in the judgment that he did not know God. There is, as far as Romans 1 is concerned, really no such thing as an atheist. Therefore, the wicked who never heard the gospel can and will be condemned in the judgment day as a result of this manifestation.

Nevertheless, the only result of this manifestation of God, as far as the wicked are concerned, is that they refuse to glorify God, continue unthankful, and change the glory of God, manifested to them and in them, into images of corruptible things (vv. 21–25).

Put simply, this means that the idolatry of the wicked is not a seeking after the God whom they do not know or an attempt, however feeble, to find him. It is rather a turning away from the true God, *whom they do know.*

They are not, according to Romans 1, seeking truth, but suppressing it (v. 25). Their philosophies and religions do not represent a small beginning of truth or a love of truth, but truth refused and turned into lies. Confirming all of this, Scripture also makes it clear that salvation is only through the preaching of the gospel (Rom. 1:16; Rom. 10:14, 17; 1 Cor. 1:18, 21). There and there alone, Christ is revealed as the very power and wisdom of God unto salvation, so that without the gospel there is ordinarily no hope of salvation.

General revelation, therefore, only serves to increase the guilt of those who do not hear or believe the gospel. To teach otherwise is to deny the blood of Jesus Christ and his perfect obedience as the only way of salvation and to slander him and his cross.

The Word of God

God is so great that we cannot know him unless he reveals himself to us. He is so great that we cannot see him or touch him (1 Tim. 6:16), and so he reveals himself to us as our Savior and Father by his Word. We ought not to be surprised about that, since speech is the principal means of communication even among ourselves, who were created in his image.

Nevertheless, that God speaks to men is a miracle. It is a miracle, in the first place, that the infinite and eternal God should speak of himself and his own glory in our limited and imperfect speech and yet make something of himself truly known to us. It is *God* whom we know and with whom we have fellowship through his Word.

In the second place, God's speaking to men is a miracle because, just as with human language, that speech of God to us is more than just a means of communication. It is the means by which we have fellowship with God, know him, and love him. As a man knows and loves the voice of his beloved wife above all others, so really do we know and love God through hearing his voice (Song of Sol. 2:14).

In the third place, God's revelation of himself through his Word is a miracle because the Word is not mere sounds in the air, nor marks upon a page, but living and abiding (1 Pet. 1:23). It is a Word that we not only hear and read, but that takes on visible form and becomes a tangible revelation of the living and unseen God (1 John 1:1) so that though God is forever unseeable, we do see him in the person of his Son, the Word made flesh.

Finally, the Word is a miracle because it is an act of the greatest possible condescension and mercy that God should speak to us. Since we have fallen into sin, would it not be more fitting that he withdraw himself and hide himself from us? Yet he speaks, and speaks peace.

That God speaks in mercy as our Father and Savior is possible only because of the inseparable relation between the Word made flesh and the Word written and read and preached. Neither can exist without the other. Only through the written Word do we know the living Word; there is no other possibility, whatever those who speak of direct revelations may claim. Nor is the written Word understood and received unless one also knows and receives it through that living Word made flesh.

There are errors to be avoided on both sides. On the one hand, we must avoid all talk of knowing and believing Christ apart from the Scriptures, as though, now that the Bible is complete, we can have fellowship with him, hear him, and see him apart from those Scriptures. On the other hand, we may never forget that to read the Scriptures and *not* find Christ in them (John 5:39–40) is to read them without understanding and in vain.

So that these Scriptures may never be doubted or forgotten, they have been given to us in written form and preserved in that form by God from the earliest times. It is by these Scriptures alone that God is pleased to make himself known in and through our Lord Jesus Christ. "They are they," Jesus says, "which testify of me" (v. 39). Let us then give the more earnest heed to them (Heb. 2:1).

Scripture

Why do we need the Word of God in written form? Has not God in other times and places revealed himself in different ways and made himself known to his people? Did he not give his Word long before it was written? Is it not a form of idolatry, therefore, to suggest that the written Word of God is the only word to which we must give heed, the one rule for our faith and life?

The fundamental reason we do not have and should not want God's Word in any other form than the written form in which he has given it is that "All men are of themselves liars and more vain than vanity itself."[3] God's written Word remains as a testimony against all their efforts to deny, twist, and corrupt what he has said to them.

This is not to say that men do not still neglect and twist and disobey and refuse to hear the Word as it is infallibly written for us in the Scriptures, but its written record leaves them without excuse.

In the end they cannot really deny that the creation as told in Genesis 1 and confirmed throughout Scripture is the story of divine creation in six days. Nor can they deny that Scripture teaches that women ought to keep silence in the church. They may call this teaching time-bound and culturally conditioned, but what the Word says is clear. Denying it, they lose not only the Word of God, but also eternal life (Rev. 22:18–19).

Besides the fact that all men are liars and corrupt the Word of God to their own ends, we are by nature so corrupt and depraved that we would not get God's message straight if he had left us with only his spoken Word, whether through angels or prophets or directly. We would surely misunderstand and corrupt the spoken Word.

---

3. Belgic Confession, Article 7.

We would not even remember what God had said if he had not given us his words in written form. Who of us remembers perfectly the sermon he heard spoken last Sunday? Or who can be absolutely certain that he heard and remembered correctly? Ask two witnesses what someone else has said, and almost always you will get two different versions of whatever was spoken.

Also there are many things God has said that do not sit well with us—things that we do not like to consider or hear. There is always the possibility that we will put them out of mind and forget them, as we do so often, or that our hearing of them will be colored and interpreted by our weakness and sin. That men do this with even the written Word is proof that they and we would certainly do it with the spoken Word.

In his wisdom and mercy, therefore, God has given us his written Word, so that we cannot claim we never heard it or heard it incorrectly. We must, then, have the highest possible regard for the written Word and not seek elsewhere for the knowledge of God and of his will.

The Sufficiency of Scripture

Have you ever thought that your faith would be much stronger and your life more holy if only you could have walked with Jesus himself as the apostles did—if you could have seen his miracles, heard his teaching, and followed him around through Galilee and Judea? Peter tells us that we must not think this way when he calls Holy Scripture "a more sure word of prophecy" (2 Pet. 1:19). We have something better and more sure than the apostles had who were "eyewitnesses of his majesty" (v. 16). Think of that! Can you imagine any stronger statement of the value and sufficiency of Holy Scripture?

Let us look at what Peter says. In 2 Peter 1:16–18 he is talking about the transfiguration of Christ. Not long before his death Jesus was "transfigured" on a mountain in Galilee. You will find the story in Matthew 17:1–8, Mark 9:2–8, and Luke 9:28–36. The three disciples who were there—Peter, James, and John—not only saw Jesus and Moses and Elijah, but they also heard the voice of God himself testifying of Jesus. What is more, they saw Jesus in his heavenly glory, as we will see him when he comes again. That is why Peter speaks in verse 16 of seeing his "power and coming." What could be better than that?

Peter knew we would think that way. He knew we would ask, "But what about us? How can we know and be sure? We did not see him. We were not 'eyewitnesses of his majesty.'" Peter answers these questions before we even ask them when he tells us that Scripture is a *more sure word* of prophecy. It is more sure than being an eyewitness. That is part of what we call the *sufficiency* of Scripture. In Scripture we have everything we need for faith and life.

But do you know why Scripture is a more sure word? Peter explains that, too, by talking about the inspiration of Scripture: "The prophecy came not in old time by the will of man: but holy men of God spake as they were moved by the Holy Ghost" (2 Pet. 1:21). In other words, Scripture was not written because the authors of the various books wanted to write. They were not the ones, finally, who decided what to write and how to write it. In all their remembering, consulting of sources, planning, actual writing, and editing, the Holy Spirit "carried" them. That is what the word translated "moved" really means. They were carried! The real author of Scripture is the Holy Spirit.

The result is that Scripture is a light shining in a dark place. This world is the land of the shadow of death, a land darkened by the wrath of the Lord (Isa. 9:2, 19). Scripture tells us that there will be no night in the new heavens and earth, but on this earth there is no day. From a spiritual point of view, this world is all darkness. It is only, ever, night. And all around us the darkness deepens in these last days. In that darkness the light of Scripture shines, and until Christ the Day Star arises, it is the only light we have.

Take heed to the Bible, therefore. Its light does not shine when its covers are left closed. Read it daily. Study it with the prayer that God will make its light shine in your heart. Meditate on its precious truths. And follow it as a light on your life's pathway.

The Inspiration of Scripture

In some ways the doctrine of Scripture's divine inspiration is the most important of all doctrines. Every other doctrine and all instruction in piety and godliness come from Scripture. Without Scripture we cannot know God and Jesus Christ whom he has sent, whom to know is life eternal. All that God reveals of himself in Christ is there. Without Scripture we cannot know how to please God. Scripture is our only guide for holiness. If Scripture is not the inspired Word of God, we lose everything.

This doctrine of inspiration is taught in 2 Timothy 3:15–17. There God says of his Word that it is all "God-breathed" (the words *given by inspiration of God* are a translation of one Greek word meaning "God-breathed"). This is a very striking way of saying that Scripture is the work of the Spirit of God ("breath" and "Spirit" are the same word in Greek), and that Scripture is therefore the very speech of God's own mouth.

Because Scripture is the breath of God, it must be perfect and without error. To speak against Scripture is to speak against God himself. When we read the Bible, we hear the sweet voice and smell the sweet breath of him whose lips are "like lilies, dropping sweet smelling myrrh" (Song of Sol. 5:13). Who, then, dares to be critical?

Scripture in 2 Timothy 3 does not only teach *inspiration*, but also teaches *plenary* inspiration. The word *plenary* means "full" or "complete" and refers to Scripture's inspiration in all its parts, in all the different kinds of literature that it contains, and in all matters that it addresses. Not only in its doctrines, but also in matters of geography, history, science, culture, and life, it is God-breathed and therefore perfect and infallible. Even its grammar is God-breathed, a reason we must insist on a careful translation of Scripture and must not be satisfied with anything less.

Because the Scriptures are fully inspired, they are profitable in four ways: doctrine, reproof, correction, and instruction in righteousness (vv. 15–17). Without speaking in detail of each one of these, notice that there is a beautiful completeness here. The Scriptures are profitable for *everything* we need for salvation. They show us the way of salvation (the basic meaning of *doctrine*). They bring us to the way by convicting us of sin (*reproof*), without which we will never know our need of Christ and his cross. They keep us in the way by *correction*, thus restoring us when we are weak and wandering. They also nurture us in the way (the word translated as *instruction* is the same word that is translated as "nurture" in Ephesians 6:4). They lead us to spiritual maturity, perfection, and glory in Christ. There is nothing else necessary in the Christian's life! The Scriptures are able to make us "wise unto salvation through faith which is in Christ Jesus" (v. 15).

What more can we ask? Let us, then, receive the Scriptures as God-breathed and use them accordingly.

The Plenary Inspiration of Scripture

The word *plenary* means "full." We speak of plenary inspiration, therefore, to emphasize that Scripture is fully inspired.

That is a truth that needs much emphasis today because there are those who, while claiming to believe in the inspiration of Scripture, deny that *all* of Scripture is inspired. Perhaps they do not accept the creation story of Genesis 1–3, or what Paul says about the place of women in the church, or the testimony of Romans 9 concerning sovereign, double predestination. Perhaps they claim that Scripture is accurate in matters of doctrine and salvation but not in matters of geography, natural history, science, and history. They do not believe that *all* Scripture is given by inspiration.

Over against all such claims we believe in *plenary* inspiration, which means several things.

First, plenary inspiration means that all the books of Scripture (and no others) are inspired by God. There is no one of them that has any less authority or necessity than any other.

Second, it means that Scripture is inspired in the different kinds of literature in which it is given. History, poetry, letters, prophecies: all are "given by inspiration of God, and profitable" (2 Tim. 3:16).

Third, plenary inspiration means that Scripture is inspired also in all matters of science, natural history, history, and geography. Indeed, there are some remarkable examples of this. Scripture has always taught, for example, that the earth is round, even when men did not believe it to be so (Isa. 40:22). It taught the hydrologic cycle before it was understood by science (Ps. 104:5–13). The belief that God is the inspirer of Scripture and the great Creator absolutely rules out any possibility that Scripture should be incorrect, even in its smallest and most insignificant details.

Fourth, it means that Scripture is fully inspired in all matters that pertain to our own lives. There are no commands or requirements of Scripture that are time-bound or culturally conditioned. Though given through men, all that Scripture says comes from the eternal God and cannot be set aside as having no application to us.

Fifth, plenary inspiration means that even Scripture's grammar, vocabulary, and syntax are inspired. It makes a difference that God said *seed* and not *seeds* in Genesis 17:7 (see also Gal. 3:16). It makes all the difference in the world that we are justified *by* faith or *through* faith, but not *because of* faith. Every letter, every word, and every sentence is important and must therefore be carefully translated. Because of plenary inspiration we do not accept paraphrases of Scripture, or even Bible versions that are a compromise between accurate translation and paraphrase, such as the New International Version (NIV).

Our faith in plenary inspiration is tested by whether or not we give this teaching mere lip service or receive Scripture as the inspired and infallible Word of God in all things, not doubting, not setting aside any part, but submitting, obeying, and believing all that God has said, and doing so even though the whole world is against us.

The Verbal Inspiration of Scripture

The doctrine of verbal inspiration is closely related to the doctrine of plenary inspiration. It emphasizes that the very *words* of Scripture are inspired by God. Scripture is not only the Word of God, but also the *words* of God.

We teach and emphasize this over against those who piously prate about Scripture being inspired in its teachings and doctrines, but not in its words and details. Such teaching is, of course, simply nonsense, for it is impossible that Scripture be the inspired Word of God in its teachings and thoughts if the words in which those teachings are given are not themselves inspired and infallible.

A belief in verbal inspiration makes us as English-speaking Christians strong proponents of the King James (Authorized) Version

(KJV). One important feature of this version, found in few of the modern versions, is that it puts in italics those words that are *not* found in the original Hebrew or Greek, thus showing those who cannot read the Hebrew and Greek the actual words of Scripture as much as possible. It may be necessary to add words in order to get a competent translation in English or in some other language, but those who read ought to know that the italicized words were added by men and not, in fact, spoken by God.

The doctrine of verbal inspiration is taught in Scripture in passages such as Psalm 12:6, Proverbs 30:5, and Revelation 22:18–19, as well as the many passages of Scripture that refer to the *words* God has spoken and caused to be written (Ps. 50:17; Ps. 119:130).

There are many remarkable examples in Scripture of the importance of this doctrine—the exact words spoken by God are important. In some cases the word choices make an enormous difference.

If Genesis 17:7 said *seeds* and not *seed,* the difference only between a plural and a singular, it would not be a prophecy of Christ (see also Gal. 3:16). This reference to Christ is completely lost in the modern versions, which retranslate the word in Genesis 17:7 as "descendants."

Sometimes the words in the original language make it difficult to understand a passage, as in Hebrews 11:11. There Scripture says that Sara received strength to *conceive* seed. The Greek word is ordinarily used for the male and is translated elsewhere as "beget" or "generate." Since that is the word Scripture uses, our only obligation is to figure out why Scripture uses that word, and not to change the passage, as the NIV does, to bring it into line with our own thinking. The NIV says that Abraham was enabled to become a father, even though Abraham is not mentioned in the verse at all. Such changes, and there are many in the NIV, are a denial of verbal inspiration.

There are many more examples of the same thing, but the point for us is that we need to listen carefully to what God says. To be satisfied that we have gotten the gist of it, the general import of what God is saying, is not enough. We must make sure we have heard, believed, and obeyed him exactly and in detail. If he has taken such care to reveal himself, speaking to us by the written Word, who are we to take any less care in hearing, obeying, and believing that every word of God is pure (Ps. 12:6)?

The Organic Inspiration of Scripture

There are many who stumble at the fact that Scripture was given through men. Because this is so, they think that there is a human element in Scripture and cannot quite believe the truth that Scripture is fully and completely the Word of God, without error—that there are no contradictions, no imperfections, no faults, and nothing in Scripture whatsoever that can be ascribed to human shortcomings.

We do not deny that Scripture was given through men. But this is so unimportant that in twelve of the sixty-six books of the Bible, we do not even know who the human writer was. Even where we know the author, however, the truth of organic inspiration holds.

Organic inspiration means that the inspiration of a book of the Bible began long before any book was ever written. To take the book of Ecclesiastes as an example, organic inspiration means that God began the work of inspiring that book not by moving Solomon to write it (2 Pet. 1:21), but by preparing all the circumstances under which Solomon would write, and by preparing Solomon himself as its writer.

God began the inspiration of Ecclesiastes when hundreds and even thousands of years before, he arranged the circumstances of history so that all things in Israel and among the nations would be just as Solomon found them when he wrote the book. God began the inspiration of Ecclesiastes when hundreds of years prior, he established the Jewish nation and the twelve tribes, one of which was the tribe of Judah, which later included the family of Jesse. God was preparing for that book when David became king and established his dynasty so that Solomon became king after him. God was preparing for that book even when David saw Bathsheba bathing and committed adultery with her and connived at the murder of her husband in order to marry her himself.

God arranged all the circumstances of Solomon's own life in such a way that he was not only the wisest of all men living, save Christ, but also one who fell into grievous sins. So it was that the book of Ecclesiastes, when written, was the record of Solomon's repentance and a testimony to the vanity of life without God.

Ultimately, of course, the doctrine of organic inspiration takes us back to the counsels of eternity and to the fact that there is nothing that takes place, or ever has in all this wide world, that is not sovereignly foreordained of God and brought to pass by his sovereign and irresistible power. No more than we, tracing our salvation back to God's eternal decree, can claim to be the authors of our own salvation, even when we are repenting and believing and obeying, could Solomon claim to be the real author of Ecclesiastes, though he wrote the words and wrote them out of his own experience. It is the eternally decreeing and sovereign God and his Spirit who, through the living Word, are the authors of our salvation and of the books by which salvation is made known to us. What a great God! What a wonderful book!

The Infallibility of Scripture

Because Scripture is the Word of God, it is also perfect. To find error in Scripture is to find error in God. To receive Scripture as anything less than infallible is to deny the immutability and sovereignty of God.

John 10:35 clearly teaches the infallibility of Scripture. In that verse Jesus says, "The scripture cannot be broken." He uses the singular, *Scripture,* to show that the Bible is the *one* Word of God, though it was given through many different men and in many different times. Because it is *one,* any attempt to tamper with Scripture is an attempt to destroy it. No one can take away parts of it or deny that they are forever true without leaving only a ruin behind.

It is interesting that Jesus not only says that we may not break the Scripture, but also that it *cannot* be broken. He means to say that all the efforts of men to find error in Scripture or to throw off its demands are in vain. They are, when they find fault with the Scriptures, taking counsel against the Lord and against his Anointed, and he who sits in heaven laughs at them (Ps. 2:2–4). They, not Scripture, are broken on the unbreakable Word of God when they claim to find fault with the words or teachings of Scripture, for by such efforts they come under the judgment of God.

The context of John 10:35 is important, too, where Jesus quotes from the Old Testament in support of his claim to be God. He refers to Psalm

82:6, which calls earthly rulers *gods*. He says that if they can be called gods, then surely he who is sanctified and sent of the Father into the world ought not be accused of blasphemy when he says, "I am the Son of God." Without going into the question of how earthly rulers can be called gods, we should notice that this is a remarkable statement. We would not dare to say it if it were not in Scripture, and even then we probably find it difficult to understand. Jesus assumes that the statement must be true and an infallible guide simply because it is found in Scripture. Just the way he quotes and uses Scripture is a great lesson for us on the theme "The Scripture Cannot Be Broken."

It is significant, too, that Jesus refers to these words from Psalm 82 as "law." He means that all Scripture, because it is the infallible Word of God, is the divine rule for our whole life. There is nothing in Scripture that is not the will of God for us, nor is there any counsel we need that is not found in Scripture. History, poems, prophecies, letters—all are God's *law* for us. This is perhaps the most important point of all. It is not enough simply to say that Scripture is infallible and inerrant. We must also bow before it, submit to its teaching at every point, and receive it as willing and obedient servants of God. Otherwise, our confession of inspiration and infallibility is mere hypocrisy.

Do you believe that Scripture is infallible? Then ask yourself this question: "Is Scripture the *law* of God for me in everything I believe and do?"

The Authority of Scripture

Because Scripture is the inspired and infallible Word of God, it has supreme authority. There is no human authority that is greater, no man-made rule that can supersede its rule, and no teaching that can contradict anything it teaches.

It has authority in all matters of doctrine. This is implied in 1 Timothy 3:16, where doctrine is mentioned first. In that passage the authority of Scripture is not the thing being emphasized, but its profitableness. We must understand, however, that Scripture is of profit because it has authority: its teaching is always the "last word" in any matter, especially in matters of doctrine.

It has the same authority in all matters of practice and Christian living. That it was written thousands of years ago, in different cultures and to different people, makes no difference at all. Because it is the Word of God himself, who knows the end from the beginning and who does not change, the changing circumstances of life in this world do not destroy the authority of anything Scripture says.

Because Paul wrote about the place of women in the home and church in a different culture than ours does not make what he says invalid. It is not Paul who says it, but God himself.

Indeed, it is a reason for amazement to those who believe in the inspiration of Scripture to see how often Scripture, as the Word of eternal God, anticipates present-day false teachings and practices. A good example of this is found in 2 Peter 3:1–7, where the theory of evolution is undermined and destroyed by Scripture's repudiation of uniformitarianism, the assumption that all things continue the same from the beginning of time.

Scripture's authority is supreme even in matters of history, geography, science, or any other academic discipline insofar as it has anything to say on those matters. It does not have authority only in the area of theology and Christian living. So great is its authority that the believer must accept what it says even in the face of opposition from science.

We must understand that Scripture's authority is the authority of God himself. To say that Scripture is the Word of God is to say that it has *all* authority. To deny it is to deny God; to contradict it is to contradict God himself.

No one can say that he accepts Scripture's authority at one point and rejects it at another. He cannot say he accepts what it says about Jesus, but not what it says about creation. It is all God's Word, and all of it is crowned with God's authority. God and God's speech cannot be accepted or rejected at will. His Word cannot be broken (John 10:35).

It is one thing to confess Scripture's authority; however, it is another thing to bow to it. At every point in our Christian life, our submission to Scripture is tested. Nor is it easy to submit to Scripture's commands when they cross our wills, or to Scripture's teaching when it runs contrary to every fleshly inclination, as it usually does.

Only by grace do we obey. God, who gave Scripture, also gives us the necessary grace. We say with Augustine, "Give what Thou commandest, and command what Thou wilt."[4]

The Interpretation of Scripture

Because Scripture is the Word of God and the Holy Spirit its author, no one has the right to interpret it. People often speak as though they have this right. They speak of "my interpretation" or of someone else's. That is wrong (2 Pet. 1:20). Even in controversy there is only one acceptable interpretation of Scripture, and that is Scripture's own interpretation of itself. That interpretation is God's own, not man's.

One of the great principles of the Reformation was the principle that Scripture is self-interpreting. Though that may seem strange to us, it must be so, for only the author himself, the Holy Spirit of God, has the right and the power to tell us what he means. My own interpretation means nothing. Only God's interpretation matters.

This is taught in 2 Peter 1:20–21, which states plainly that no Scripture is of any *private* interpretation. This statement seems a bit out of place at first, because the emphasis is not on interpretation, but on inspiration. Nevertheless, the doctrine of inspiration, as taught in these verses, has this as its application: no one but God himself, who inspired the Word, has the right to interpret it.

The Holy Spirit does interpret Scripture, but not in some mystical manner—not by mysteriously and secretly revealing the meaning of Scripture to us by some private revelation. It is wrong to say, "God showed me," or "God told me," or "God revealed this to me." That, too, is a denial of Scripture, not only of its sufficiency, but of the inspiration of Scripture. The person who says these things is claiming that he has an interpretation of Scripture that God has given to him privately, apart from Scripture itself. The proper interpretation of Scripture is given when Scripture is compared with Scripture.

---

4. *The Confessions of St. Augustine*, trans. E. B. Pusey, ed. and condensed David Otis Fuller from Book X (Grand Rapids, MI: Zondervan Publishing House Christian Life Library Selection series), 122.

For example, if we wish to determine the meaning of a word in Scripture, perhaps the word *baptism,* we must look up the different passages in which the word is used and the context of each passage in order to determine what the word means in Scripture and how Scripture uses it. The proper interpretation of Scripture, therefore, requires careful study so that we may learn from Scripture itself what it means. The person who thinks he can turn to a passage of Scripture and understand it without study is very foolish and proud.

We must be careful, therefore, not to impose our own ideas on Scripture, but humbly and prayerfully to receive what it says. Learning the proper interpretation of Scripture requires grace, submission, and prayer.

There is no one, not even ministers of the gospel, who may claim to be above the Word of God. Every interpretation, every creed, every sermon, may be and ought to be subjected to rigid scrutiny in light of what God's Word says, exactly because no one has the private right to interpret Scripture. For this reason, even the preaching of the apostles was subject to careful examination and criticism (Acts 17:10–11). Even that preaching, as any other, had to conform to the Spirit's own interpretation of his own Word.

May God give us the necessary grace—much grace—to seek out and find that one interpretation and give heed to it (Heb. 2:1).

The Unity of Scripture

Because Scripture is God's Word and has one author, it is also *one.* God does not speak with sixty-six different voices. He cannot, because he himself is one in power, in purpose, and in being. Because he is one, his Word and revelation are one also.

That Scripture is one is of the utmost importance. For this reason Scripture cannot contradict or be at odds with itself. One book cannot differ from another, nor the Old Testament from the New. Scripture cannot teach one thing in the Old Testament and something opposed to it in the New, nor one human writer something different from another.

It is wrong, therefore, to speak of "the theology of Paul," as some do, suggesting that it differs from the theology of Jesus or the theology of Peter. Nor may anyone suggest that Jesus had different views from Moses or Paul or John on certain matters, such as divorce or the place of women in the church.

This doctrine of Scripture's unity is especially important over against dispensationalism, which sees no unity between the Old Testament and the New, between Israel and the church. Even the Baptist teaching that the covenant with Israel is a fundamentally different covenant than God's covenant with the church is a denial of the unity of Scripture. Scripture is one book and cannot teach two or more different and conflicting covenants.

If Scripture is one, there cannot be different revelations, different covenants, different peoples of God, or different ways of salvation. Our objections to the teaching of dispensationalism and believer's baptism, therefore, are not only based on passages that disprove specific teachings of these groups, but also on passages that teach Scripture is one and cannot be broken (John 10:35).

The notion that the Old Testament is not authoritative for New Testament Christians except where its teaching is restated in the New Testament is a denial of the unity of Scripture. What is written in the Old Testament was written for us as New Testament Christians as well (1 Cor. 10:11).

The unity of Scripture, as Jesus reminds us in John 10:35, is in himself. It is all, from beginning to end, the revelation of Christ as the Savior and of the grace of God that is revealed in him. As Spurgeon said, "Wherever you cut the Scriptures, they flow with the blood of the Lamb."[5] To find Christ in every passage must be our goal, and in doing so we will most certainly find that the Scriptures speak with one voice.

The doctrine of Scripture's unity is important not only as a defense against other teachings, but also for our *study* of Scripture. If Scripture is one, no passage of it may ever be studied, believed, or even quoted in isolation from the rest of the Word. Nothing we ever say or think from the Word of God may contradict anything else. And this means, of course, that we must be busy with the Scriptures so that we know them from beginning to end and are thoroughly acquainted with their teaching.

The doctrine of Scripture's unity means, then, that all Scripture is

---

5. Location of quotation in Charles Haddon Spurgeon's writings is not known.

necessary and important and that no part of it may be neglected. We must know, read, study, learn, and give heed to all of it. Do you?

The Perspicuity of Scripture

Perhaps you have heard the *perspicuity* of Scripture mentioned and wondered what that meant. It means that Scripture is *clear and easily understood.*

Perspicuity is part of the miracle of Scripture, especially since Scripture reveals God. That he, the infinite and eternal God, not only is willing to reveal himself to us, but also does so clearly and plainly, is a great wonder.

We do not deny, of course, that there are difficult passages in Scripture, even difficult books. The Bible itself teaches us this (Ps. 78:2; 2 Pet. 3:16). Nevertheless, we believe that every doctrine of the faith, and all things necessary for God's glory and our salvation, are clearly taught.

Psalm 119:105 teaches perspicuity: "Thy word is a lamp unto my feet, and a light unto my path." Scripture could not even be called a light if it was not clear, and this verse says that it is a light for our *path,* that is, for our whole life. It is a safe and reliable guide to bring us all the way along our life's path to glory.

Because Scripture is clear, it can be understood even by the unlearned and by children. It may not, therefore, be kept from them. It ought to be translated into the language of every people to whom the gospel comes so that they may read it and have its light with them always.

There are things we must understand about the perspicuity of Scripture lest we fall into error.

First, because there are difficult passages, we must always interpret such passages in the light of those passages that speak more clearly. No interpretation of a difficult passage, for example, may contradict any important doctrine of Scripture or any rule for thankful living that *is* clearly taught.

Second, Scripture is clear only to believers. Unbelief cannot understand Scripture, because the things that are in Scripture are the things of God, and they are spiritually discerned (1 Cor. 2:14). We should remember this when speaking to someone who denies an important truth of Scripture like the deity of the Lord Jesus Christ. When such a person cannot see from Scripture that Jesus is God, we should not begin to doubt that Scripture plainly teaches this important truth. The problem is not in Scripture. The problem is in that man's heart and mind. Before anyone can understand anything Scripture teaches, his heart must be opened and his mind enlightened by the Holy Spirit. Without that, proof texts, logic, and argument are useless.

Since Scripture is the clear light of God's own revelation, we must follow its light. The warning and the promise of 1 John 1:6–7 are for us: "If we say that we have fellowship with him, and walk in darkness, we lie, and do not the truth: But if we walk in the light, as he is in the light, we have fellowship one with another, and the blood of Jesus Christ his Son cleanseth us from all sin."

Bible Versions

There has been such a proliferation of Bible versions, especially in recent times, that one hardly recognizes the Word of God anymore when it is read. This constant production of new versions is no small matter. If Scripture is indeed the all-sufficient and inspired Word of God, it is very important that we use a good version of the Bible.

Before recommending a particular version, note that the proliferation of modern versions is one of the ways in which the Bible has very effectively been taken away from God's people. Because so many different versions are in use, a passage may no longer sound familiar when it is quoted or preached. Nor do children easily learn and memorize Scripture, since they are being taught from so many different versions. They hear one version at home, another in school, yet another in church, and still others in their fellowships and Bible studies, and they remember none.

It is also very telling that the many and varied versions have arisen in an age of modernism, apostasy, and doubt, not during a time when the church was strong and faithful to the Word of God. This in itself is a good reason to be suspicious of these versions. Many of them are not true translations at all but are paraphrases, such as The Living Bible, or something halfway between a paraphrase and a translation, such as the NIV.

It is probably obvious by this time that the only English version we would recommend is the King James Version (KJV), which is called the Authorised Version in Britain. We would recommend it for many reasons, the most important being that it is an accurate and faithful translation of the Hebrew and Greek Scriptures. This is so much the case that the English of the 1611 KJV is not really the English of the 1600s, as is sometimes charged, but "biblical English," the result of the efforts of the translators to be as faithful as possible to the original Greek and Hebrew. An example of accurate translation in the KJV is its practice of putting *in italics* all the words that are not found in the original Greek or Hebrew.

In defense of the KJV, it is not true that the modern versions are based on better manuscripts unknown to the translators of the KJV. They knew of other manuscripts, even though they did not have all of those that have been discovered since. These other manuscripts, though some of them are very old, are also very corrupt, having in them thousands of unique changes and omissions. The majority of manuscripts (80–90%), however, support what is sometimes called the "Received Text," the text on which the KJV is based.

The need for a good, faithful, and accurate translation like the KJV is expressed in the words of its translators: "Translation it is that openeth the window, to let in the light; that breaketh the shell, that we may eat the kernel; that putteth aside the curtain, that we may look into the most holy place; that removeth the cover of the well, that we may come by the water."[6] Let us, then, be faithful to the Word of God as he in his providence and grace has given it to us, and be satisfied with nothing less than the Word of God.

---

6. From the section "Translation Necessary," originally in the preface to the King James (Authorized) Version of the Bible, 1611. Quoted here from the booklet with modern spelling as "The Translations to the Reader" (London: Trinitarian Bible Society, 1998), 12.

Knowing God

The whole of the Christian religion is knowing God. Knowing him is the purpose of Christianity, its highest goal and endeavor and its greatest blessedness. As Jesus says in John 17:3, it is eternal life.

This knowledge of God is the only true knowledge. We cannot even know ourselves without him or apart from him. That is true not only because we are sinners whose hearts are deceitful and corrupt (Jer. 17:9), but also because we are created by God to live in relationship to him (Ps. 30:5). Apart from him we cannot know who and what *we* are.

Even our deeds are judged in relationship to God. One cannot know whether his actions and words are good or evil except by comparing them to the standard of God's own perfect holiness. That explains why there are few moral standards left in today's society. The majority, even of those who have religion of some sort, do not know God. Ignorant of him, they have no moral standard.

To know God is not merely to have a head full of doctrines or of facts about God, even if these are biblical facts and truths. That is not to say that the doctrines and teachings of Scripture concerning God are unimportant. Knowledge is part of faith, and without it faith is nothing. One cannot claim to believe in a God of whom he knows nothing. Yet the knowledge of God is more—so much more that it is possible for one to know intellectually what Scripture teaches about God, and to have been taught, perhaps as a child, the doctrine of God as it is found in Scripture, and yet not know him.

The knowledge of God is also something *experiential*. God is so great, one cannot know him merely by the activity of the mind or by intellectual endeavor. One must have met him, heard him, walked with him, and known him as a man knows his friend. Indeed, when Scripture speaks of knowing God, the word *know* is synonymous with *love*. Just as Scripture speaks of a man knowing his wife to describe the loving intimacies of marriage, so Scripture speaks of knowing God. Not to love him is not to know him—not truly.

To know God, therefore, is to delight in him, to enjoy him, and to obey him. So wonderful is he in grace, mercy, and majesty that it is impossible for someone who does not enjoy him and love him to say that he knows God. That person, even though he may know very well what the Bible says about God, is rejecting him, turning his back on him, hating him, and showing that he really does not know God at all. His mind is blinded and his heart hardened.

Do you *know* God in that true sense of the word? Do you show every day anew that he is your greatest delight and treasure? Do you love him and his glory with all your heart and strength? Do you enjoy him and obey him?

God's Names

One of the ways in which God reveals himself to us is by his names. It is for that reason that he has given us so many different names in Scripture. Those names are many because God is very great and his glory without end. Each name tells something about him, but all of them still cannot describe his infinite praises.

When we study these names, we must remember that God's names are different from ours. Our names are only labels that can be changed; and if changed, they do not change who and what we are.

God's names show us who and what he is. They are as unchangeable as God himself. To abuse and misuse those names, as some do in their speech, is to abuse God himself. That is the reason God will not hold guiltless the person who uses his names *in vain,* as though they are empty of meaning and holiness.

It is great sin to misuse God's names. That sin is forbidden and threatened with punishment in the third commandment (Ex. 20:7), but what we must remember is that it is an equally great sin *not to use* the names of God at all. A person may be damned for taking God's name in vain. He may also be damned for never naming the name of God.

The third commandment, as all the ten commandments, not only forbids something; it also requires something. It requires the holy, reverent, God-glorifying use of his names. We must learn to use the names of God, not randomly, but because of what they tell us about God.

In prayer we often use the names of God at random, addressing him by whatever name happens to pop into our heads as we pray. That is not the way the Bible teaches us to pray. There the names of God are used with care, and a particular name is used to emphasize some important truth about God that is connected with the request a person is making or the praise and thanks he is bringing.

We might, for example, use the name *Jehovah* in addressing God if we are pleading the promises of his covenant on behalf of our children. What better name to use at such a time! Or we might use the name *Holy One* if we are confessing our sins and truly desire to humble ourselves before God in repentance for them.

The Jews were wrong when they would not use the name *Jehovah* out of fear of its holiness and perfection. God has given us his names so that we may use them in speaking to him and about him. Not to speak to him and about him is to live as though there is no God—to deny him and reject him. That we may not do.

Our calling is to use the names of God, to use them with reverence and holy fear, and to use them in praising him, praying to him, speaking of him, and honoring him. Then, and then only, are we living in obedience to him and using his names aright.

Do you know his names? Do you use them?

The Name *Jehovah*

The name *Jehovah* is one of the most important names of God. It is this name that is translated LORD in the KJV. It is also part of the name *Jesus*. The Je- of Jesus is an abbreviation of the name *Jehovah,* as are similar abbreviations in many other Old Testament names (Eli-JAH, Jo-shua, JEHO-shaphat, and JE-dediah).

God revealed the name *Jehovah* to Moses and Israel as the proof that he remembered his covenant and would deliver his people from bondage in Egypt (Ex. 3:11–15). At that time he also revealed the meaning of his name *Jehovah:* "And God said unto Moses, I AM THAT I AM: and he said, Thus shalt thou say unto the children of Israel, I AM hath sent me unto you" (Ex. 3:14).

The name *Jehovah,* therefore, reveals God's immutability or unchangeableness. Created things not only *are,* but also *have been* and *will be.* They change, but with God there is no past, present, or future. He *is.* What for us is past or future is not past or future for him, as difficult as that may be for us to understand. All things are eternally before him, and with him the passing of years and millennia has no meaning and brings no change. It is difficult for us even to conceive of this, for we are constantly changing and live in the midst of change: "Change and decay in all around I see."[7] Yet this is to us another indication that he is God, for if we could comprehend him or understand him fully, he would be no greater than our own puny minds.

As Exodus 3 shows, the name *Jehovah* reveals God especially as the unchangeable one in relation to his people. It speaks of his unchangeableness not as an abstract idea, but of the unchangeableness of his love, his mercy, his promises, his grace, and his desire to save and bless those who are his own.

The name reminds us that God's people belong to him unchangeably and from eternity. They do not *come* to belong to him, but have belonged to him from before the mountains had their birth or ever he had formed the earth and the world (Ps. 90:2). Through all time and into eternity, therefore, he will be their dwelling place.

The name *Jehovah* is, above all other names, the name by which God reveals himself as the God of the covenant. This, too, is evident in Exodus 3, for it is in remembering and keeping his covenant that God reveals both the name *Jehovah* and its meaning.

Insofar, therefore, as the name *Jehovah* speaks of God's unchangeableness, it shows us that he is *faithful.* God's faithfulness is his unchangeableness in relation to his own covenant people whom he loves and whom he has chosen. Never does he forsake or forget them, but he loves them with an everlasting love. In that love he takes them to himself.

Let those who know his faithfulness use the name *Jehovah* often and with joy. There is indeed no greater name.

---

7. Stanza 2 of hymn number 335, "Abide with Me," in the *Trinity Hymnal* (Philadelphia: Great Commission Publications, 1974).

The Name *God*

The name *God* is the most commonly used name of the Almighty in Scripture. It is a name that speaks of his sovereignty, of his triunity, and of his infinite perfections.

It is also a part of many Old Testament names, such as E<small>L</small>-ijah, E<small>L</small>-isha, Dani-<small>EL</small>, Nathana-<small>EL</small>, E<small>L</small>-i, in each of which *El-* or *-el* is a shortened form of the name *God* (*Elohim* in Hebrew). It is part of those names because many of the people whose name included the name of God were used in some way to show something of his glory as God.

The name *Elohim* in Hebrew is actually a plural (literally "Gods"). This does not mean that there is more than one God, nor does it indicate that the religion of God's people was originally polytheism, the worship of many gods. Rather, it refers to the fact that God is more than one person (see Gen. 1:26, where God speaks of himself as "us") and to his manifold and infinite perfections and glories (he is many in glory and power and majesty, though only one in being).

The name *God*, therefore, is what is called in theology "a plural of excellency" or "a plural of majesty." It teaches us that he is God, that there is none like him nor any besides him, and that he alone is worthy of worship, praise, and obedience. It is no wonder that this name is the most commonly used in Scripture.

It is this name also that distinguishes him from the idols of the heathen. He is God over against the heathen and their idols, and that these idols are called "gods" only serves in the end to make clear that they are nothing and that he is truly God, for they cannot see, hear, speak, act, or save (Ps. 115:4–8). Those who make such gods are like the gods they make.

God is God also in relation to his people. To them especially he reveals the excellency of his sovereign grace and mercy and the majesty of his power and love. The plural form of the Hebrew name ought to remind every believer of the endless reasons he has to praise and worship this great God. We ought to use the name *God* to speak to him and about him whenever we want to emphasize these things. When we are troubled by the ungodly or discouraged because of persecution and other suffering, we need to remember that he is God. When we are worshipping him, that name is most appropriate. When we wish to remind ourselves of the three persons who are part of the Godhead, we use this name. On any occasion that we need to know his majesty, power, and infinite glory, this name should be on our lips and in our minds.

Let us, then, not abuse, but rightly use this great name.

The Name LORD of Hosts

The name LORD of hosts (1 Sam. 1:3; Ps. 24:10; Isa. 1:9; Hag. 1:2) or *God of hosts* (Ps. 80:7), or even LORD *God of hosts* (Ps. 59:5; Ps. 80:4; Jer. 5:14; Jer. 15:16) is a combination of various names of God with an added reference to "hosts." It is a name that speaks of God's sovereignty in relation to all his creatures, including men and angels.

The hosts referred to are the multitudes of created things, including the brute creation: the sun, moon, and stars, and the earth itself and its fullness (Gen. 2:1; Deut. 4:19; Neh. 9:6; Ps. 33:6). These hosts also include all the ranks and myriads of angels (Gen. 32:2; 1 Kings 22:19; Luke 2:13) as well as the hosts of darkness and hell. They also include the billions of men who live on the earth and all their works and might (Dan. 8:10–11; Eph. 6:12).

That God is the LORD of hosts means that all creatures are his servants and must, willingly or unwillingly, do his will in heaven, in earth, and in hell. The name LORD *of hosts,* therefore, is a name that speaks of God's sovereignty and purpose as he accomplishes that purpose through his creatures. He is not only above them all, but he also uses them all to perform his will and to bring to pass his eternal purpose. None can resist or question him (Dan. 4:35).

That all creatures are described as the hosts of the Lord means that they march in harmony, like a great army, to accomplish his will. Each creature must serve him individually, willingly or unwillingly, and they all *work together* like a vast and mighty army to do what he has purposed and planned.

The name LORD *of hosts* also reveals the wrath and justice of God, for it speaks of him as a God of war and battle (2 Chron. 20:15; Ps. 24:8; Isa. 13:4). By his mighty armies he executes judgment and justice and righteousness, destroying his enemies and saving his people.

What is so remarkable about the name LORD *of hosts* is that Satan and his hosts and the ungodly are all part of this mighty army of God. They do not act independently of him. Most remarkable of all, they themselves are the means in his almighty hand by which he accomplishes their judgment and eternal destruction. Even when they rebel against him, they can do only what he has purposed (Acts 4:28). That is the reason he laughs them to scorn when they rebel (Ps. 2:4). What a great God he is!

The many passages of Scripture that use this name, therefore, emphasize these truths and do so in the particular circumstances in which God's people found themselves and needed to be reminded of these truths. In Haggai, for example, God used the name LORD *of hosts* over and over to remind them that he was sovereign in relation to the enemies who tried to prevent them from rebuilding the temple. He was sovereign, too, in relation to the things of creation, particularly the silver and gold they lacked in order to make the temple as beautiful as Solomon's (Hag. 2:1–9). He reminds us of the same.

Let us remember, then, that this sovereign LORD of hosts is our gracious Lord, and so let us willingly march in his service.

The Name *Father*

The name *Father* is for God's people one of his most precious names, for it speaks to them of his eternal love for them. It is a name that emphasizes God's covenant relation to his people through Jesus Christ. It is the name, therefore, that they are taught, above all other names, to use in fellowship with him (Matt. 6:9).

The name *Father* is his name not only in relation to his people, but his name also in the Trinity. He does not *become* a Father when he adopts us. That would be a denial of his unchangeableness. He is *eternally* a Father as First Person of the Trinity.

That eternal fatherhood of God in the Trinity has its counterpart in his eternal love for us, his children. In eternity he chose us and set his fatherly love on us. From eternity he is the Father of his people. Amazing, is it not?

The name *Father* was rarely used by God's people in the Old Testament, however (Ps. 68:5; Ps. 103:13; Isa. 9:6; Isa. 63:16). Why was that?

The reason God's people so rarely spoke of him and to him as Father lies at the root of the difference between the Old and New Testaments. The difference between the two is not, of course, a matter of principle, but has to do with the fact that the Old Testament was the time of promise and the New Testament the time of fulfillment.

It is Christ's coming in the flesh that makes all the difference with respect to the name *Father*. Through Christ, God draws near to us and dwells with us in the holy temple that is the body of Christ (John 2:19–21). Through Christ he reveals to us the wonder of his love and brings us the fullness of salvation.

Perhaps we can understand this best if we think in terms of God's adopting us to be his children. In the Old Testament, too, believers were the children of God, but by promise. They had been chosen to be God's children and had even been told of his love for them. They had been separated from the nations and formed as his own family, but God still lived behind the veil and revealed himself to them only by types and shadows.

Only in the New Testament is the veil removed and are we given free access to the throne and presence of God (Heb. 10:19–22). Only in the New Testament does God draw so near to us as to be one bone and one flesh in Christ (Eph. 5:29–30). Only in the New Testament are we as children delivered from the bondage of the elements of this world and no longer treated as servants (Gal. 4:1–5). Only in the New Testament, therefore, do we have, by the Spirit of the risen and exalted Jesus, the boldness to cry unceasingly in every language and in every land, "Abba, Father" (Gal. 4:6–7).

That is not to say that believers in the Old Testament had nothing, but only to say that what we have in New Testament times is better. What was promised to the Old Testament saints is fulfilled in the New to us. Let us never forget it.

The Sovereignty of God

Almost all Christians claim to believe in the sovereignty of God. In many cases, however, this is but lip service.

That God is sovereign means very simply that he is *God*. It means, as A. W. Pink pointed out in his wonderful book *The Sovereignty of God*,[8] that God, as God, does as he pleases, when he pleases. It means that he is in complete control of *all* things that are and that happen.

God is sovereign in the creation. He is the sovereign Creator of all things in heaven and on earth. They have no existence apart from him and exist only for his sake. Evolutionism is a denial of God's sovereignty inasmuch as it puts God out of his creation and sets up blind chance and purposelessness in his place.

God is sovereign also as the God of providence. He brings to pass all that happens in the creation and controls and directs all to his own sovereign ends. Not only the good things, but the evil things—sickness, pain, death, war, hurricanes, famines, earthquakes, and other so-called natural disasters—come from him and are used by him.

This is denied by those who speak of these things as the work of "Mother Nature," by those who think that evil things come from the devil and not from God, and by those who think that *they* can change things by their praying. God is *God*. He alone is in control, and nothing happens apart from him.

God is sovereign as well over angels and devils. Of this Scripture clearly testifies. Satan could do nothing against Job without God's permission (Job 1:12; Job 2:6). It is God who binds and looses Satan (Rev. 20:1–2, 7), and Satan is accountable to God for all his wickedness and will be judged by God (vv. 14–15).

God is sovereign, too, in salvation and damnation. As we shall see, it is he who chooses some for salvation and not others (Rom. 9:21; Eph. 1:4). It is he who sent his Son to die for some and not for others (John 10:15, 26; John 17:2). He gives faith to some and not to others (Eph. 2:8–10). He is the one who opens hearts (Acts 16:14), who works in us both to will and to do of his good pleasure (Phil. 2:12–13). Even our good works are foreordained by him (Eph. 2:10).

God is sovereign also over sin. Not only does he eternally decree sin (Acts 2:23; Acts 4:27–28), but he also rules, governs, and uses sin for his own purpose. God's sovereignty means that *of* him, *through* him, and *to*

---

8. Arthur W. Pink, *The Sovereignty of God* (Grand Rapids, MI: Baker Book House, 1970).

him are all things (Rom. 11:36). It must be so, or he is not God. It must be so, that he alone may receive honor and glory and power and dominion now and forever.

Only faith can receive this truth. Even the hearts of believers sometimes balk at it, for it is the end of all pride, all self-sufficiency, all dependence on self, on other creatures, and on all human help and wisdom. But faith, having believed, finds comfort in this truth, for faith says, "This God is our God for ever and ever: he will be our guide even unto death" (Ps. 48:14).

Human Responsibility

Some think that there is a conflict between God's sovereignty and human responsibility. If God controls and directs all things, if he has eternally decreed all things including sin and brings all things to pass, then man cannot be responsible for what he does. He can say, "God caused it. He decreed it. It could not be otherwise. I am not at fault."

We believe in the absolute sovereignty of God, yet believe at the same time that man is responsible for his actions, his thoughts, and his motives. Indeed, all the objections that men raise against the sovereignty of God really are useless, for Scripture testifies that God *is* sovereign and that he *will* judge men for their wickedness and will not listen to their complaints. He will count even their complaints as sin (Rom. 9:20).

It may be true in human relations that a person causes something to happen and is therefore responsible. He may bring something to pass through the agency of others and yet bear the primary responsibility. I may not have actually pulled the trigger but be responsible, nevertheless, for a murder because I planned it and engineered it.

It is not so with God. Though we may not be able to explain the exact relationship between God's sovereignty and man's responsibility, it is nevertheless the case that God is sovereign and man is responsible. God is so great that he alone is able to decree and control all things without being responsible for the evil actions of men and devils.

One of the best examples of this is found in 2 Samuel 24:1 and

1 Chronicles 21:1. The second passage ascribes David's sin of numbering the people to Satan. Satan moved David to number the people. Nevertheless, as 2 Samuel 24:1 shows, God was also behind that sin. *He* moved David to commit it. This is a reminder that God not only permits sin, but sovereignly brings it to pass, and that God uses and controls even Satan in doing this. Yet when confronted with the sin, David does not say, "God made me do it," or "The devil made me do it," but he takes the full responsibility and says, "I have sinned" (2 Sam. 24:17; 1 Chron. 21:17).

The supreme example is the crucifixion of Christ. Acts 2:23 tells us that Christ was delivered to death by the determinate counsel and foreknowledge of God. God's decree and foreknowledge of all things brought Christ to the cross. Acts 4:26–28 tells us that those who crucified Christ did only what God in his decree had before determined to be done. Were those who crucified Christ not then responsible? Could they say they had no fault in the matter? They could not. Acts 2:23 tells us that their hands were still wicked hands, and that it was they who crucified and murdered Christ. God's sovereignty did not destroy their responsibility.

Do you take the responsibility for your sins? Whether or not you do now, you *will* in the judgment day. God's sovereignty will not excuse you. Only Christ can save you from the wrath of God.

God's Attributes

The greatest weakness in the church today is a lack of the knowledge of God. Many are like the Samaritans of whom Jesus said, "Ye worship ye know not what" (John 4:22).

John 17:3 shows the importance of *knowing* God: "This is life eternal, that they might *know* thee the only true God, and Jesus Christ, whom thou hast sent." What could be more important than that?

Yet the word of prophecy is true today: "My people are destroyed for lack of knowledge" (Hos. 4:6). It was the knowledge *of God* that God's people lacked in the days of that prophecy. Verse 1 makes that clear: "There is no truth, nor mercy, nor knowledge of God in the land." How true again today!

In the days of Hosea, the church had rejected knowledge. Especially its spiritual leaders, the priests, had rejected it and forgotten God's law. So God threatened that he would forget their children and turn their glory into shame (vv. 6–7). If only the church today would hear that Word of God and see that God is bringing these judgments upon it also! If only the church would return to the Lord and be healed!

Thinking of these things, we now begin to write of the attributes of God. By them especially we know him, whom to know is life eternal.

Attributes are personal characteristics—such things as eye color, type of personality, and the like. God's attributes are his oneness, his spirituality, his sovereignty, his grace, his goodness, and all the other words that are used in Scripture to tell us who he is. When we speak of God's attributes, therefore, we are describing him and his glory and the things he reveals of himself in his Word. Through these attributes we know who and what he is.

We must never think that God's attributes are just a matter of theological debate and discussion. They are vitally important for us. Scripture shows this by the different words it uses to describe God's attributes.

In Psalm 89:5 Scripture speaks of God's attributes as his *wonders*. His attributes, in other words, reveal to us how great and wonderful God is and make us stand before him in awe and amazement.

Psalm 78:4 calls the attributes of God his *praises*. From this word we learn the reason for the revelation of his attributes: that we might worship and adore him forever. If the church today does not honor God as it should, this is only because it does not know him as it should.

Psalm 78 also says that it is through this knowledge of God's attributes that the generations to come will set their hope in God and not forget his works, but keep his commandments (vv. 4–8). May God grant such generations to the church by restoring in the churches the knowledge of God and especially of his attributes.

God's Holiness

One of the most important of God's attributes is his holiness. Often he is called in Scripture the Holy One, especially in the prophecy of Isaiah.

His holiness is very important for us. Without it, no one can see God

(Heb. 12:14). We must be like him if ever we are to see him. We must be like him especially in holiness.

What is God's holiness?

The basic idea of holiness is separation—being set apart. The Old Testament priests were holy—*separated* in life and calling from all the other Israelites. Jerusalem was a holy city because it was *set apart* from all other cities in the world. Our calling to be holy includes *separation* from the wicked and their deeds (2 Cor. 6:14–18).

Jesus, too, is holy. According to Hebrews 7:26, this means that he is "separate from sinners." There is in him no sin, nor any possibility of sin. To deny his holiness is to deny that upon which all our salvation rests.

God's holiness means that he is "the high and lofty One that inhabiteth eternity" (Isa. 57:15). He is *separate* in glory from all others, "dwelling in the light which no man can approach unto" (1 Tim. 6:16). We may never forget this.

That holiness he has revealed in his holy name (Ps. 111:9). It is separate from all other names. We must keep it separate by not using it blasphemously or irreverently. How often that is forgotten today, not only in everyday speech, but even in prayer.

God's Word is also holy (Rom. 1:2) just because it is *his* Word. It must be set apart in our thoughts and our use of it from all words and wisdom of men.

The Lord's day is a holy day. That means that it is separate from all other days. It, too, must be kept holy for the glory of God and for the glory of the Lord Jesus Christ, to whom it now belongs by right of resurrection.

There are two sides to this separation: separation *from* something and separation *unto* something.

God's holiness means that he is separate *from* all sin, too pure of eyes to behold evil (Hab. 1:13). God has no pleasure in wickedness, nor can evil dwell with him (Ps. 5:4). Thus he not only separates himself from all evil, but also resists and destroys it, revealing his glory everywhere. His holiness also means that he is consecrated and dedicated *to* himself and *to* his own glory (Isa. 42:8).

If we are to be holy, we must not only be separated *from* sin, but also be separated *unto* God. Just to separate a drunkard from his drunkenness is not to make him holy. He must also be separated or consecrated to God. So must we be consecrated to God in everything. Only then will we be holy as he is holy (1 Pet. 1:16). Only then shall we see him and dwell with him.

God's Oneness

"Hear, O Israel: The LORD our God is one LORD." In their context, these words from Deuteronomy 6:4 show the fundamental importance of God's oneness.

This text shows that the oneness of God is at the heart of everything God commands in his law, and on it depend all that is written in the law and the prophets (Matt. 22:35–40; Luke 10:25–28). There really is no other law but this: God is one.

That God is one is the foundation for our whole calling as God's people (Deut. 6:5). It is the truth that must be hung at the entrances to our houses so that it may be always at hand and always before our eyes (vv. 8–9). It must be the heart of what we teach our children, the gist of all our speech, our guiding principle, the theme of our meditations, and the foundation of our prayers (v. 7). It is the source of every blessing (vv. 10–11) and the cornerstone of our righteousness before God (v. 25). To forget God's oneness is to forget and forsake the Lord who brought us out of bondage (v. 12).

Why is God's oneness so important?

First, it is part of the truth of the Trinity, and therefore part of the truth that this God is the *true* God. He is three persons, yet one. To worship and serve any other besides this God, who is three-in-one, is to turn from the true God to idols. All our hope and salvation depend on that. Listen to 1 Corinthians 8:5–6: "For though there be that are called gods, whether in heaven or in earth, (as there be gods many, and lords many), but to us there is but one God, the Father, of whom are all things, and we in him; and one Lord Jesus Christ, by whom are all things, and we by him."

Second, God's oneness also means that he is the *only* God. There is no other. Nothing, no one, can even be compared with him (Isa. 40:18).

This is the reason God's oneness is a truth that governs the whole of our life. Because he alone is God, there is no other for us to love, worship, serve, and obey. Him only may we know, honor, and fear. To him alone do we submit. In him alone do we trust. From him, and from no other, do we seek all things, and to him only do we pray.

That is what the Word of God means in 1 Corinthians 8:5–6. We are in him and by him *only*. At work, at play, at home, at school, at church, awake and asleep, eating, thinking, speaking, praying, walking—for all time and for all eternity there is for us but one God. Anything else is idolatry.

It *ought* to be so for all men, for this one God created them and gives them life and breath and all things (Acts 17:25). It *is* so, by grace, for believers, for this incomparable God has made himself their one and only Savior, delivering them from pride and sin, and opening their eyes to see that he alone is God.

Thinking of God's oneness, Moses says, "Thou shalt love the LORD thy God with *all* thine heart, and with *all* thy soul, and with *all* thy might" (Deut. 6:5). Do you?

God's Immutability

We often think of the immutability or changelessness of God at the end of one year and the beginning of another. Many things happen in the world every year, and all bring change to our lives. There is constant economic, social, and political change. Every day brings news of great changes that affect all of our lives. The world in which we live is hardly recognizable as the same world into which our grandparents were born.

Political changes and war have redrawn the boundaries of nations, destroyed nations, and created nations. We have moved from the dark ages to the space age, though it is doubtful that the space age is, in fact, any less dark than the ages that preceded it. Perhaps it is even darker because we live much closer to the end of all things.

Even in the church there have been changes. The passing years have not only brought the great Reformation of the church, but the loss again of almost everything the Reformation won. The love of many has waxed cold; iniquity abounds (Matt. 24:10–12). More and more the faithful church appears to be "a besieged city" (Isa. 1:8). Things, at least for the present, do not bode well for the church of Jesus Christ.

In our families, too, many of us experience great changes, not all of them pleasant. For some, a new year brings happiness and health, marriage and children, success and well-being. But for others it brings only loss and trouble, suffering and pain. Some of us still mourn loved ones who have died in past years. Some have endured grievous trials.

What will another year bring? Another decade? Another century?

No one knows, though many think themselves prophets. Only of this can we be certain: that as long as the world lasts, the changing years bring even more change and decay, for the world in which we live is still the same old world of sin, darkness, and death.

But God does not change. That is what his immutability means. He *cannot* change. He is Jehovah who changes not (Mal. 3:6), "the Father of lights, with whom is no variableness, neither shadow of turning" (James 1:17). We confess this, saying, "From everlasting to everlasting, thou art God" (Ps. 90:2).

God has not changed his purpose and plan for all things. He still unchangeably wills the salvation of his people. Nor has he changed in power so that he is no longer the Almighty, the sovereign God of heaven and earth. He still controls and directs all things (Ps. 115:3), including everything that happens to us. Above all, he has never changed in his love and grace. He has not forgotten or forsaken us, even when it seems so to us. Especially of that we can be sure, because our Lord Jesus, the one through whom our immutable God reveals himself, is "the same yesterday, and today, and for ever" (Heb. 13:8). In him, the immutability of God is the assurance that all things will work for our good (Rom. 8:28) and that the good work of grace will in due time be finished (Phil. 1:6).

Is it not wonderfully comforting to know that our God does not change? In him, through the unchangeable Jesus, we rest.

God's Spirituality

Everything the New Testament teaches about the worship of God is founded on the truth that God is a *Spirit.* In John 4:24 Jesus says, "God is a Spirit: and they that worship him must worship him in spirit and in truth." What does that mean, and why is it so important? Why is God's spirituality foundational for our worship as individuals and as churches?

In the worship of God, God's spirituality means especially that he is *invisible.* Not only is he not seen, but he is so great and so glorious that he *cannot* be seen. Just as our mortal eyes cannot look at the sun, so no man can behold the glory of God and live (1 Tim. 6:16; note the words "nor *can* see").

All we shall ever *see* of God is his glory in the face of Jesus Christ, in whom dwells all the glory of the Godhead bodily (2 Cor. 4:6; Col. 2:9). "He that hath seen me hath seen the Father," Jesus says in John 14:9.

This is crucial for the worship of God.

First, because God is a Spirit, he cannot be worshipped with images of any kind, either graven by hand or conceived in the heart and mind of man. Who can make an image of the unseen God? And how, if such an image is made, will it be anything but a lie?

If this is true, every false doctrine, every ill-spoken word about God, is also a "graven image" that falls short of his glory. Let us be careful, then, what we say and think of God in our worship!

Second, because God is a Spirit, he must be worshipped only in and through the Word, for that is where he reveals himself and his glory. This is what Jesus means when he says, "They that worship him must worship him . . . in *truth*" (John 4:24).

The truth must be the content of our worship, but it must also be the *rule* for our worship. The truth of Scripture regulates both *what* we do in worship and *how* we do it. It must be so. How can man decide the content and way of worshipping a God whom he has never seen? How can he know what is fitting?

Third, because God is a Spirit, he must be worshipped from the heart and not by mere outward rites. "Worship *in spirit*" in John 4:24 does not mean "through the Holy Spirit," but "with our spirits." It is the opposite of all that is outward, fleshly, and carnal.

How often all this is forgotten today! All sorts of things are substituted for truth in worship. In place of spiritual worship is found mere outward formality or a nauseating display of fleshly and carnal things that is little more than worldly entertainment. Such cannot be pleasing to God.

An example of worship displeasing to God is worship through images and pictures. These God abhors. They do not—cannot—represent him whom no man hath seen, and the use of them produces a worship based on sight and touch, a worship that does not match the spirituality of God, who is unseen and untouchable.

Pray, then, that the Father, by the power of his sovereign grace, may teach many that he is Spirit and may find many true worshippers to worship him in spirit and truth in these days of idolatry and neglect.

God's Self-sufficiency

One of the most humbling truths the Bible teaches us is that God is *independent* and *self-sufficient*. He does not need anything outside himself. Not only are all things his—the cattle on a thousand hills and all else—but they add nothing to him. If he had never created anything, he would still be complete and all-glorious.

That is what the Word of God means in Romans 11:34–36: "For who hath known the mind of the Lord? or who hath been his counsellor? Or who hath first given to him, and it shall be recompensed unto him again? For of him, and through him, and to him, are all things: to whom be glory for ever. Amen."

No man can know all that is in the all-knowing mind of God, and because God is all-knowing, no one can tell him anything he does not already know perfectly and eternally. He does not need us to inform him, not in prayer either.

Nor can anyone give anything to God. Even when we "give" thanks, praise, and glory to him, we add nothing to his glory. The salvation of the whole church adds nothing to his glory, but is only a revelation of the glory he already has in himself. He is the source, the means, and the end of all things.

More than anything else, the great name *Jehovah* reveals God's self-sufficiency. According to that name, he is the I AM, the all in all.

This truth is especially important in our salvation. Many have the idea that God cannot be a merciful God, a God of love and grace, without us. He needs us, so they think, to be a God of love and mercy. Some would even say that he cannot be a God of love unless he loves all men and shows grace to all. That is a denial of God's self-sufficiency. If we had never been created, he would still be the God of all grace, a God of perfect love. Having created us and seen us fall into sin, his glory as a gracious, loving, merciful God would be no less if he saved no one at all.

What a humbling truth that is. How it magnifies the grace and mercy God does show, though it be only to some. What a great God he is!

But there is more. The other side of God's independency is our dependency—that we have nothing of ourselves, can do nothing of ourselves, and are nothing apart from him. How foolish we are when we seek to live apart from him! How foolish we are when we do not look to him and pray to him for everything necessary for body and soul.

Let us confess not only in word, but also in deed, God's self-sufficiency and our dependency by trusting in him for all things and by extolling the wonder of his grace and mercy shown to such as we are.

God's Omnipresence

Knowing God is life eternal. It is also the great difference between a life of holiness and a life of sin, between a life filled with spiritual peace and a life like the troubled waves of the sea that cannot rest (Isa. 57:20–21).

An important part of the life-giving knowledge of God is the knowledge of his omnipresence. As the omnipresent one, God transcends all limitations of place and space. Distance and place have no meaning for him. He is everywhere, the God who fills all things and yet is not contained by them. He speaks of this in Jeremiah 23:23–24: "Am I a God at hand, saith the LORD, and not a God afar off? Can any hide himself in secret places that I shall not see him? saith the LORD. Do not I fill heaven and earth? saith the LORD."

What a truth for our lives! What could have greater power for holiness, humility, and godly fear than the knowledge that God is present wherever we go and whatever we do?

Many think that they can hide their wicked deeds. And indeed they do hide them from other men behind closed doors, under darkness, and by secrecy. But God knows what they do. He is there even as they do their wickedness: "The eyes of the LORD are in every place, beholding the evil and the good" (Prov. 15:3).

How foolish, then, for anyone to think he has escaped detection in sin because there were no witnesses. How foolish we are when, like Israel at Mt. Sinai, we sin in the very presence of God. He is always present, a witness to every deed, word, and thought. He is the omnipresent Judge.

Yet it is a comfort, too—for those who repent and believe—to know that God is everywhere. He is present for them in a very special sense. He is *nigh* unto those who are of a broken heart and a contrite spirit, to those who call upon him in truth (Ps. 34:18; Ps. 145:18). He is present as their Father and Savior. He hears their cries, sees their broken hearts, and heals and saves them.

God is near his people, too, in their trials and temptations: "In all their affliction he was afflicted, and the angel of his presence saved them: in his love and in his pity he redeemed them; and he bare them, and carried them all the days of old" (Isa. 63:9). It is no different today.

In Christ, God is near to his people. Christ is Immanuel, God with us, a saving revelation of God's omnipresence. In Christ and through him, God is forever with us as our God, Savior, and Father.

Are you aware of God's omnipresence? Does the knowledge of his presence turn you from sin and produce in you sanctification of heart and life? Do you say, "No matter where my way leads, 'even there shall thy hand lead me, and thy right hand shall hold me'" (Ps. 139:10)?

God's Love

The love of God, sadly enough, is the subject of much debate among Christians. Questions about whether God loves everyone and wants to save everyone are answered very differently. These questions are important. They have to do with predestination, the eternal love of God for some, and with the death of Christ, the great revelation of God's love.

It is not our purpose here to deal with such passages as John 3:16 and the meaning in that verse of the word *world*. If anyone is interested in an explanation of this passage, we suggest he read the pamphlet "God So Loved the World..." by Homer C. Hoeksema,[9] or the explanation given in the appendix to Pink's *The Sovereignty of God*.[10] Here we want to show that the answer to all questions about the love of God can be found by understanding what the love of God is.

God's love, above all, is his love for himself, his own glory, and his own holiness. First John 4:16 indicates this when it tells us that God *is* love. In himself as Father, Son, and Holy Spirit, God is the epitome of all love. To be a God of love, he does not need us, nor is his glory as the God

---

9. Homer C. Hoeksema, "God So Loved the World..." This pamphlet is available from its publisher, the Evangelism Committee, Crete Protestant Reformed Church, 1777 E. Richton Rd., Crete, IL 60417, www.prccrete.org.

10. Appendix III, "The Meaning of the 'Kosmos' in John 3:16," in Pink's *Sovereignty of God* (Baker Book House edition).

of love incomplete without us. From eternity to eternity he *is* love, in and of himself, in the Trinity.

Scripture defines this love as "the bond of perfectness" (Col. 3:14). It is more than mere sentiment or an emotion or feeling. It is the bond that exists between the three perfect persons of the holy Trinity.

Because God loves his own glory (Isa. 42:8; Ezek. 39:25), and because love is the bond of *perfectness,* God cannot love men except in and through Jesus Christ. That is the reason election, the eternal love of God for some, is "in Christ." Only in him are we perfect. That is also why the word *world* in John 3:16 cannot refer to every person (see John 17:9; 1 John 4:7–9, and the word *us* in the latter passage). God cannot establish a bond of perfectness with those who are outside of Christ.

Psalm 5:4 is further proof that God cannot love us apart from Christ: "Thou art not a God that hath pleasure in wickedness: neither shall evil dwell with thee." There is no bond of perfectness possible between God and evil. Those he loves must be chosen and redeemed in Christ to be the objects of God's love.

The other side of this is that God hates evil and the evildoer (Ps. 5:5–6). That is a hard saying, but the alternative is blasphemy. To say that God loves men without saving them from their wickedness and sin is to say that the holy and righteous God loves evil. Who dares think such a thing?

Let us not forget, either, that this understanding of the love of God is where the delight and joy of believers rests. It means that God will save his people from all their sins and make them perfect. His love is the bond of perfectness. It means that he will take them into his fellowship and make them partakers of the divine nature. His love will make them perfect. "God is love; and he that dwelleth in love dwelleth in God, and God in him" (1 John 4:16). What blessedness and bliss!

God's Grace

What is grace? We speak often of sovereign grace or of saving grace, but do we really know what grace is?

It is evident that some do not know. They speak of "common grace," suggesting that God is gracious to all. If they really knew what grace is, they would not think that grace is common. Others complain that God cannot really be gracious if he does not save everyone or at least give everyone a chance. If they knew what grace is, they would not think such thoughts.

We may not know as well as we think we do what grace is. Do we know that grace is an *attribute* of God? Do we know that God is gracious in himself and would be gracious even if we had never been created, even if no one had ever been saved? Even then, grace would be an attribute of God, one of his beauties. He would still be gracious even if we were not the objects and recipients of his grace.

That is what we mean when we say that grace is an attribute of God. Grace does not only characterize God's dealings with us. It belongs to what he is, and he can no more be without grace than he can cease to be God Almighty.

We often define grace as "undeserved favor." Although that is not incorrect, it is not a complete definition of grace. That definition describes only what God's grace is *to us* and emphasizes that his saving grace is sovereign and free—that he owes it to no one. It does not tell us what grace is as an attribute of God.

As the usual definition of grace suggests, it is God's favor; therefore, when we say that grace is an attribute of God, we mean that God is favorable *to himself.* That is, of course, simply to say that God loves himself first and desires his own glory above all things, something Scripture plainly teaches.

The word *grace* also has the meaning of loveliness or beauty, especially an inner loveliness or beauty that is evident in all of a person's conduct and speech. Thus we speak of persons being gracious, or of their speech or conduct being gracious (Prov. 11:16; Col. 4:6). Scripture itself speaks of certain persons finding grace or favor (being beautiful) in the eyes of God (Gen. 6:8; Luke 1:30).

When we say that God is gracious, we mean that in all of his glory, he is beautiful and lovely beyond all else, and that the beauty of his own inner purity and glory shines out in all his actions and speech. Thus he finds favor in his own eyes. As three persons in one God, he loves himself and his own works above all and considers his own work incomparably lovely. This is what grace is as an attribute of God.

Humbling, is it not, to think that God does not need us to be gracious? He is forever gracious in himself, and he would be so even if he had saved no one. That he does save is, therefore, a very great wonder and something for which we may never cease to give him thanks.

Grace and Salvation

We have seen what grace is as an attribute of God. We must also say something about the grace God shows in saving us.

Following on from the idea that grace is an inner beauty or loveliness that shines out in all a person is and does and that causes others to look upon him with favor, we may say that God's grace as it is revealed in our salvation is the gift of his own beauty to us, so that we become like him and thus find favor in his sight. That loveliness of God, which he grants to his people when he saves them, becomes evident in all their conduct and speech. It is impossible for one who has received grace not to reflect something of the loveliness of God.

This is one of the reasons that the teaching of common grace should be rejected. It is a repulsive thought that the wicked and unbelieving should find favor in God's sight or have anything of his own loveliness. Nor could it ever be, then, that God would judge them and send them to hell, for he would be sending someone who had received something of his own beauty to the place of eternal darkness.

There are several other characteristics of God's saving grace that need to be mentioned. They, too, show why grace cannot be common.

First, grace is not only an attitude of God, but a *gift*. This is implied in what we have already said, but it needs emphasis. Scripture speaks often of God giving grace (Ps. 84:11; Prov. 3:34; James 4:6; 1 Pet. 5:5). We speak of grace as a gift of God when we want to emphasize the freeness and undeserved character of grace, but we must not forget that it is something actually given when God shows it to us, and not only an attitude on his part.

Second, grace is a *power*. That is really the same thing as saying that it is the grace of *God*. God's thoughts, God's attributes, and God's Words are not like ours—powerless—but always full of the power of the Almighty. That is another reason God cannot possibly be gracious to all.

His grace cannot be in vain, cannot be without power to save and deliver, cannot fail. To suggest that it can is to deny that God is God.

Third, grace is *saving*. Never once does Scripture speak of any other kind of grace to men. Just as election is particular and atonement is particular, so the grace predetermined and purchased by Christ must also be particular, shown savingly only to some.

That we should find grace in the sight of God is amazing, especially when we take this to mean that he finds us lovely and beautiful. This can only happen because he sees us in Christ, and through the work of Christ. Christ is beautiful as God's own only begotten Son, the fairest of ten thousand in his perfect obedience and devotion to God, and in him alone do we find favor with God.

God's Mercy

We usually think of God's mercy in relation to ourselves since we need that mercy. We think of it especially in terms of pity. God is merciful to us when he takes pity on us and delivers us from the misery and wretchedness of our sins (Prov. 16:6).

There is more to mercy, however. We may never forget that mercy is an *attribute* of God, something that characterizes his very being and that he is never without. That implies that God would be merciful even if we never existed as the objects of his mercy. He would be merciful if all men went eternally lost and none were saved. He would be merciful if he never showed mercy to anyone. He is merciful in himself (Luke 6:36).

That reminds us, too, how very wrong it is for men to say that God cannot be merciful, loving, kind, and gracious if he does not save all. He does not need to save anyone at all to be merciful. He needs no creature to be a God of mercy (Eph. 2:4). He is independent, self-sufficient, and in need of nothing. He is *God*.

What is mercy as an attribute of God? There are several things we must notice in answering this question.

We should realize that even in relation to ourselves, mercy is much more than the desire to deliver someone. It is, above all, the desire to see someone happy and blessed. The pity one feels for those who are perishing and the desire to deliver them are very much secondary to this. That helps us to see that God's mercy is, first, the desire that he himself be blessed above all and forevermore. He is not perishing or in need, and he is never the object of pity; nevertheless, he desires his own eternal blessedness and glory. That is his mercy as an attribute of his own being (Ex. 34:6).

It is only when God determines to show us mercy that his desire to bless includes pity, compassion, and the desire to save, for we are lost and perishing and the proper objects of his pity (James 5:11). Even in showing such pity to us, however, his ultimate desire is the glory and blessedness of his own name and being. Therefore, he not only saves us in his mercy, but he also lifts us up to be with him and to enjoy him forever.

As an attribute, God's mercy is also powerful. It is not, as some suggest, a mere helpless feeling of pity on the part of God, one which he feels toward all but is unable or unwilling in every case to fulfill. Like the other attributes of God, mercy is sovereign, almighty, unchanging, and eternal, and therefore never fails when God shows it, as he does, to some of mankind (Eph. 2:4–5; Titus 3:5; 1 Pet. 1:3). God's mercy cannot be an empty and unfulfilled feeling. It does not leave the objects of his mercy to go to hell after all. Because mercy is *God's* mercy and an almighty attribute of his own divine being, we do not believe that God's mercy is "common" in the sense that God is merciful to all.

We are thankful, however, beyond anything we can say, for the mercy God shows to us, especially since we know it is wholly undeserved and not shown to all. That God should pity and bless such as us is beyond belief, and yet fervently believed by all his own.

God's Righteousness

Like his grace, mercy, and love, God's righteousness is a "communicable" attribute, which means that he gives it to us as a gift, so that we, too, are righteous. That God should give us his own attributes and so make us like himself is a great wonder. Even more wonderful is that he gives these gifts to us who are sinners (Rom. 4:5).

Among all God's gifts, there is none so important as his righteousness. When he gives us this gift, he gives it because we have no righteousness at all of our own, and without righteousness we stand to be condemned by him. When he gives us the gift of his own righteousness, we stand before him justified, innocent, and without any possibility of condemnation.

Do you know that justification is the gift of God's own righteousness? It is the gift of a righteousness that is not to be found in this world, that comes instead from heaven, and is therefore, as Luther often said, an *alien* righteousness (Rom. 3:21). This righteousness God obtains for us through the suffering and death of his own Son, and he gives it to us through the work of the Holy Spirit and by faith (Hab. 2:4; Rom. 1:17; Rom. 3:22–26).

The wonder is that this righteousness is all of God. That needs emphasis since so many evangelicals today are abandoning the Reformed doctrine of free and gracious justification and teaching a justification by faith *and* works, a doctrine that is not much different from the teaching of Roman Catholicism. The truth is that God not only provides the righteousness—his own—but he also earns and obtains it in the person of his Son. We do nothing to earn it or obtain it (Rom. 3:24). Even the faith through which that righteousness is given to us, so that it becomes our righteousness, is not a work of our own, but a gift of God (Eph. 2:8–10). There are no works in justification but God's own works in eternity, in Christ, and in the Spirit (Rom. 11:6).

Nevertheless, God is not righteous in order that he may have something to give us. He has no need of us to be righteous. He is righteous in himself (Ps. 11:7; Ps. 116:5; Dan. 9:7; John 17:25; Rev. 16:5).

What does it mean that God is righteous? Righteousness is conformity to the law, but to what law does God conform? To what standard does he measure? The answer is that he is himself the standard of what is good and evil (Ps. 35:24). His perfection is the standard to which all his creatures must conform and to which he also conforms in all his words and works. Never can he be accused of injustice (Rom. 9:14). Never can any fault be found with a single word or a single action of God (Ps. 19:9; Rom. 9:20). What he does is right, because he does it. That is his righteousness.

That God makes us righteous means that he causes us by a wonder of pure grace to conform to the standard of his own perfection. He did that by sending his Son to suffer for our sins and to earn for us his own favor. Thanks be to him.

God's Wisdom

God is wise. We believe that, and yet how often we lose sight of it. It is worth reminding ourselves, therefore, of what Scripture teaches concerning the wisdom of God.

Wisdom for us is knowing how to do everything for the glory of God. Most people know how to do things for themselves or for their own profit, but they do not know how to do them for the glory of God. They have knowledge, but they do not have wisdom. They are the fools who have said in their hearts that there is no God (Ps. 14:1).

Wisdom is a gift of God. Only he can teach us how to do all things for his glory. His Word is the source of all wisdom, and his Spirit the teacher, for we cannot learn anything until the Spirit changes our hearts.

God promises wisdom to all who ask. He says that he will not withhold his wisdom from anyone who asks in faith (James 1:5–6). There is, then, no excuse for foolishness. We may lack knowledge because of youth or little education, but if we lack wisdom we have no excuse. Lack of wisdom comes from our not seeking God.

There is no excuse, either, for complaining about God's dealings with us. Not only does he tell us in his Word that he is all wise, but he also promises us the wisdom to understand and use that knowledge for his glory, submitting to him in our afflictions, praising him for his goodness, and trusting in his mercy.

We show that wisdom God has given us, too, in living for his glory and not for ourselves. By grace we show that we are no longer foolish but wise, discerning the will of God and seeking his honor in all we do. Even when we find in ourselves the foolishness of sin and a lack of true wisdom, we show that he has given us wisdom by seeking him as the source of the wisdom we need and by trusting that he will give liberally and withhold not.

Wisdom is not only a gift, but also an attribute of God. As an attribute, wisdom is God's knowledge of all things and his wonderful ability to do all things for his own glory. He does not only know things as they come to pass and then determine how to use them, but he knows all things eternally and has therefore in wisdom decreed and foreordained all things so that they may show forth the glory of his justice and of his grace.

Because God does all things in wisdom for his own glory, we may be sure that even the "bad" things that happen to us will not separate us from his love but will be good for us. In wisdom God knows eternally how all things serve his glory, including our troubles. In wisdom he sends us all things for our good and for his glory. His wisdom gives us reason to trust him and to believe that he is our Father.

What an attribute for our lives! It is when we forget the wisdom of God that we begin to question his dealings with us. When we do not remember that he is wise, we grumble and complain about his ways with us, especially when those ways are hard. His wisdom is our assurance that all things must work together for our good and that we have nothing to fear and nothing of which to complain.

God's Transcendence

Another attribute of God is his transcendence. This attribute, like many others, reminds us that he is God and he alone. His transcendence means that he is above everything, and that there is nothing and no one besides him or equal to him.

God is *above* the creation. He must be, because he is the Creator. As an artist is greater than any of his own works, so God is greater than his works. God's transcendence, therefore, is the answer to pantheism, which identifies God with the creation. It is this evil teaching that lies at the root of much modern thinking, especially the thinking of the New Age movement and of various environmental groups, to whom the things of creation are everything.

God is also above time and space. His eternity is his transcendence in relation to time, and his omnipresence is his transcendence in relation to space. Time is something he made, not something by which he himself is bound. That is difficult for us to grasp, since we are forced to speak of him in the past, present, and future, but in reality he is eternally the I AM — in relation to the past as well as to the present and future. There is no time with him. Nor is he contained by the universe. All its vast extent and myriads of creatures are the work of his hands. He is present in it and with it, but remains always above it.

He is transcendent also in relation to us. It is for this reason that we can never fully comprehend his works or ways. Always his ways and his thoughts are higher than ours, and we must believe in him without fully understanding him (Isa. 55:8–9). His works are greater than we can search out. His ways are past knowledge. His glory is unsearchable. His attributes are uncounted, his praises without end, his honor from everlasting to everlasting.

Yet the believer is not troubled by the transcendence of God, for even in his transcendence God is not afar off (Jer. 23:23) but draws near, making himself known to the faith of his people and revealing all his loveliness and goodness. His people love his transcendence, for it reminds them that the one from whose hands they receive all things is the living and true God to whom nothing can compare. They find in his transcendence a reason to depend on him and to trust in him and to build their faith and hope upon him. Even when he sends them things that are unpleasant and that bring them suffering and trouble, they still say, "My flesh and my heart faileth: but God is the strength of my heart, and my portion for ever" (Ps. 73:26).

Only God is able. Only God is great. Only he transcends our thoughts and words and works. He alone, therefore, is worthy of our trust.

God's Simplicity or Perfection

In books of theology, you will sometimes read of an attribute called God's simplicity. The word is confusing, and since it is not found in Scripture, it might be better to use a different word—perhaps perfection. God's simplicity is part of his oneness; he is *one* in all of his attributes and works. There is no disharmony, no conflict, no contradiction among his works or attributes. They are all one. God is perfect and without weakness or flaw in any way.

God's perfection is taught especially in those passages that say God *is* love, *is* truth, *is* light (1 John 1:5; 1 John 4:8; 1 John 5:6). That he *is* light means that there is no room in him for darkness. That he *is* love means that there is no possibility of anything in him that would compromise his love. This also means that his attributes are not really separate characteristics. They are like the facets of a diamond that cannot be separated from each other. Each sparkles and shines with its own glory, yet all together they make up one precious jewel. To separate them is to destroy them.

Consider God's mercy. It is not only the pity he feels for us in the misery and bondage of our sins, but also the power by which he delivers us from that misery. It is not a mere desire to help us, but the help he actually gives. His mercy and omnipotence are perfectly one, never separated, never in conflict.

Think, too, of God's love. God's perfection or simplicity means that his love cannot be separated from his justice, his eternity, his omnipotence, or any of his other attributes.

God's love is always just, never revealed except in the way of perfect justice. In other words, he never loves anyone except in the way of fulfilling the demands of his own justice by sending Christ to die in their place.

God's love is always eternal. There is no such thing as a love of God that is only for the present but not from eternity to eternity. Those he loves he has always loved and will always love. So, too, is his love omnipotent (almighty). It is never an empty sentiment, but it is a power that makes us the proper objects of his love.

God's perfection is one of the reasons we believe that God does not love everyone or show grace to everyone. That would be saying that there is a love or grace of God that is separated from his almighty power. It would be to say that there is a love and grace of God in conflict with his justice, holiness, and righteousness, for he would be showing love to those who are not and never will be righteous and holy in Christ.

What a blessing for believers to know the truth about God's perfection! To know it is to realize that his mercy is never in vain, his grace never unrequited, and his love never wasted.

The Trinity

The biblical doctrine of the Trinity is the most important and also one of the least appreciated of all the doctrines of the Bible. Though most believers understand that this doctrine separates Christianity from all heathen religions and from the sects, they do not see its value. It seems to them to have little connection with their life or their assurance.

We wish especially to show that the doctrine of the Trinity is of the greatest possible value to believers. To know the Father, the Son, and the Holy Spirit is to know God. To know God is life eternal (John 17:3).

Belief in the Trinity is not tritheism, belief in three gods. Sects like the Jehovah's Witnesses and false religions like Islam say that Christians believe in three gods. They are wrong. We believe that the Lord our God is *one* Lord (Deut. 6:4). The word *Trinity* emphasizes this. It means "tri-unity."

Following the teaching of Scripture, we also believe that in God there are three persons: the Father, the Son, and the Holy Spirit. Moreover, they are real *persons*—distinct and individual personalities with different names, Father, Son, and Holy Spirit—names that reflect their personal characteristics.

Many who claim to believe in the Trinity actually deny that the Father, the Son, and the Holy Spirit are real persons. Some, for example, speak of the Holy Spirit not as a person, but merely as a power that can be manipulated and used. Others teach a "oneness" doctrine that sounds very biblical, but is really a denial of the Trinity. According to this false teaching, Father, Son, and Holy Spirit are only different *offices, names,* or *ways* in which the one God reveals himself. This teaching was condemned in the early history of the New Testament church. Then it was called monarchianism or Sabellianism.

In contrast, the Bible ascribes to the Son, to the Holy Spirit, and to the Father all the characteristics of real persons, while emphasizing that they are all one God. They are not mere names or powers or works of God. If they are not real persons, all that we believe about Jesus Christ is worthless, and we have no person in the Trinity to come in the likeness of our sinful flesh, to stand in our place, to take our sins as his own, to die for us and make redemption for us, and to represent us before the Father. Nor do we have the person of the Holy Spirit to live in our hearts and to bring us into a close, *personal* relationship with God. Our confession of the Trinity, therefore, is the confession of Psalm 48:14: "This God is our GOD . . . he will be our guide even unto death."

The Importance of the Trinity

Often the important biblical doctrine of the Trinity is little appreciated by those who believe it. They know that this doctrine, more than any other, separates Christianity from all heathen religions and from the sects, but do not see that it is important to them personally. It seems abstract and a doctrine that has little to do with life or assurance. Nevertheless, this doctrine is very important, even for such practical matters as family living.

Consider, first, that the doctrine of the Trinity teaches us that this triune God is the only true God. It does this by showing us that he is beyond our understanding. It makes us ask with Job, "Canst thou by searching find out God? canst thou find out the Almighty unto perfection?" (Job 11:7). God is God; if we could fully understand him, he would be no greater than our finite minds. He would not be God at all, but an idol fashioned by our minds and hearts!

In this way the doctrine of the Trinity is the source of all true repentance, humility, reverence, and worship. Reminding us that God is God, it brings us to our knees before him so that we say with Job, "I have heard of thee by the hearing of the ear: but now mine eye seeth thee. Wherefore I abhor myself, and repent in dust and ashes" (Job 42:5–6).

Second, the doctrine of the Trinity teaches us that God is all our salvation and all our hope. Everything we need is in him. He is the Father, our Father for Christ's sake. He is the only begotten Son, our Elder Brother. He is the Holy Spirit, who comes and goes like the wind, and who can be in our hearts and work there with irresistible power even before we know of his presence.

When we need to know the love of God, we think of him and pray to him as children to a Father. When we think that there is no one who knows our needs and understands our trials, he reminds us that his Son has come in the flesh and has been touched with the feeling of our infirmities (Heb. 4:15)—that his Son is indeed our Elder Brother. When we feel far from God and from all peace, his Spirit testifies with our spirits that we are children of God.

In trouble and distress, in loneliness and sorrow, in joy and obedience, we find him to be our God, not a god who is far off like the god of Islam, but a God who is near, a Father, a Son, and a Holy Spirit.

He is our God whom we love and in whom we may safely put our trust.

There is no God besides him, and no other worthy of our reverence and praise.

The Trinity and the Family

Nothing shows the importance of the biblical doctrine of the Trinity so much as its connection to family life. It is the foundation of the family and of our various callings in the family.

Understand! The confession that God is a triune God is the confession that he is a *family* God. In the Trinity God reveals himself as a Father, a Son, and a Holy Spirit. In the Trinity, therefore, God is a family. In that family he lives one life of perfect fellowship, in perfect harmony and love.

This is why God's Word speaks so often of families (Ps. 68:6; Ps. 107:41). This is why God saves families (Jer. 31:1; Amos 3:2; Acts 16: 31–34). The family is always a reflection of his own glory as the triune God.

This has many practical implications. For one thing, it explains the deterioration of the family and of family values today. Created to be a reflection of God's own trinitarian family life, the family cannot prosper apart from him.

Moreover, the Trinity is where we learn how to live as families. That we go to God to learn about family life does not only mean that we go to his Word in the Bible. It also means that we go to him as Father to learn about being fathers (and mothers) to our children. It means that we bring our children to his holy child Jesus to learn about their calling as children. It means that we go to him as Holy Spirit to learn about peace, unity, love, fellowship, and all the other blessings of family life. Only the Spirit can teach us these things. He is the source of these blessings in the Godhead and in our families.

The Bible itself draws this parallel in Psalm 103:13: "Like as a father pitieth his children, so the LORD pitieth them that fear him." The same parallel is drawn in Ephesians 6:1–4 and Colossians 3:18–21. The obedience of children, the submission of wives, the love of husbands, and the mercy of fathers is not "right" and "fit" and "well-pleasing" just because it is what God commands, but because he is the Father of our Lord Jesus Christ (Eph. 1:5), the dear Son and firstborn of every creature (Col. 1:13, 15), and because he is the one Spirit (Eph. 4:4).

What is true for the family is true for the church. The church is called a *family* or *household* (Gal. 6:10; Eph. 2:19; Eph. 3:15). The church is built up of families (Acts 5:42; Acts 20:20) and, with its officebearers, takes the form of a family (1 Cor. 4:15; Gal. 4:19; 1 Tim. 5:1–2). In fact, the church *is* the family of God, acknowledging God as Father and submitting to the rule of Christ, the Elder Brother, and living in the house of God (2 Cor. 6:18; Heb. 2:13). Therefore, the church also must learn about its family life from its family God: Father, Son, and Holy Spirit.

The most important thing for our families, therefore, and for the larger family of the church, is to know God and to know him as he reveals himself in the Trinity. May God grant us this knowledge!

The Covenant

God's covenant is something Scripture speaks about often. What is that covenant? Why does Scripture refer to it so often? These questions require an answer.

We should remember that the covenant is *God's* covenant, first of all. That means it is a covenant that God has in himself and with himself. When he makes a covenant with us, therefore, it is only a revelation of something that he has even without us.

This, of course, is true of all that God reveals. Whatever he reveals to us is a revelation of himself: his being, his glory, his power, and his works. That is a very humbling thought. In reference to the covenant, it means that God does not need us in order to be a covenant God. He is a covenant God in himself.

We believe that God's covenant is the relationship between the three persons of the Holy Trinity: the Father, the Son, and the Holy Spirit. We will be showing that the covenant is a relationship or bond. If that is true, it is, from the start, the bond that makes the three persons of the Trinity one God.

There are Scripture passages that describe the relationship between the three persons of the Godhead in the Trinity. Proverbs 8:22–31 is one such passage. "I" in these verses, identified as "wisdom" in verse 12, is the Son (compare with 1 Cor. 1:24). He is described in verse 30 in relation to the Father as being "by him, as one brought up with him . . . daily his delight, rejoicing always before him." That is God's covenant as it exists eternally in God himself between the Father, the Son, and the Holy Spirit.

Other passages that describe this relationship are John 10:15: "As the Father knoweth me, even so know I the Father"; and 1 Corinthians 2:10: "The Spirit searcheth all things, yea, the deep things of God." What a blessed life God lives within himself!

When God establishes his covenant with us, he takes us into that relationship and makes us part of it. He takes us into his own family and becomes our Father through Jesus Christ and the Holy Spirit. What a wonder!

The Bible talks about this in 2 Peter 1:4, which says that we are made partakers of the divine nature. That is the realization of God's covenant with us, something so wonderful that we would not even dare think it if the Bible did not say it. Jesus speaks of it also in John 17:23: "I in them, and thou in me, that they may be made perfect in one; and that the world may know that thou hast sent me, and hast loved them, as thou hast loved me."

Into that blessed relationship we are taken when God establishes his covenant with us. In that relationship we receive of his fullness and grace for grace (John 1:16). Thus he dwells in us and walks in us and is our God forevermore (2 Cor. 6:16). To live apart from him, therefore, really is death (Ps. 73:27). To know him is life eternal (John 17:3).

But we may never forget that he does not need us to be a covenant God. His covenant with us is always a covenant of grace—pure and undeserved favor.

The Everlasting Covenant

Scripture speaks often of the fact that God's covenant is everlasting. It is *from* eternity because it is the relationship between the three persons of the holy Trinity. But it is also *to* eternity because God takes us into that blessed trinitarian relationship and makes us partakers of the divine nature (2 Pet. 1:4). That relationship of fellowship and love will never end. God will be our God forever and ever, and we shall always be his people (Rev. 21:3).

Believing this, we do *not* see God's covenant as an agreement or contract, as is so often taught. It is not an agreement among the three persons of the Trinity to bring salvation to God's people, nor is it an agreement between God and his people in Adam, or in Christ.

The covenant cannot be an "agreement."

An agreement or contract is not lasting. When its terms—whatever they may be—have been fulfilled, the agreement itself is finished and can be discarded. It may be a matter of historical curiosity, but it does not continue in force.

To put it a little differently, an agreement or contract is only *the means to an end*. A bottle of medicine is also a means (a way) to renewed health. When we are healthy again, we no longer need the medicine and can discard it. If the covenant is only a *means* to salvation, that is, an agreement to provide salvation, we would not need the covenant any longer once we had received our salvation.

But since Scripture tells us the covenant is everlasting, it cannot end or become unnecessary. It is not the *means* but the *end* (goal) itself. It is not the *way* of salvation but *salvation itself*. It is not a contract that when fulfilled will fall away, but a blessed relationship that will continue for-ever—a relationship between God and his people in Christ.

Is not the essence of salvation the relationship that God establishes with his people in Christ? Is not Revelation 21:3 talking about the high-est glory of salvation when it promises a day in which God will be our God and we his people? That, we believe, is God's covenant. And that covenant is everlasting.

Eternal life, Jesus says in John 17:3, is to know God and Jesus Christ whom he has sent. That, too, is God's everlasting covenant with his peo-ple. Truly there can be nothing more wonderful. Even streets of gold cannot compare with that. The everlasting covenant, and it alone, is the true glory of salvation, of heaven, and of eternal life.

Not all shall enjoy it, however. Only they shall see God and know him who have believed in Jesus Christ, for he is the way into the pres-ence of the Father. That is why John 17:3 speaks not only of knowing God, but also of knowing Jesus Christ.

One Covenant

If God's covenant is everlasting, and Scripture often says that it is, then there can be only one covenant. A temporary covenant can be replaced, but God's covenant is not temporary.

Also, if the covenant is unbreakable, there can be but one covenant. That it *is* unbreakable, Scripture testifies in Judges 2:1, Psalm 89:34, Jeremiah 33:20–21, and many other passages. It is therefore also the only covenant.

If the covenant is God's covenant, and if God's covenant is the relationship between the three persons of the Trinity, then, too, the covenant must be one, because God is one.

We hold to *one* covenant over against dispensationalism, with its many covenants. And we teach one covenant over against the Baptist position, which distinguishes between the old covenant and the new, at least as far as the sign of the covenant is concerned. We also reject the older teaching that there is a separate and distinct "covenant of works" with Adam.

The many Scripture passages that speak of an everlasting covenant (singular) prove this. We refer our readers to such Scriptures as Genesis 17:7, 2 Samuel 23:5, Psalm 105:8–10, Isaiah 55:3, Ezekiel 16:60–62, and Hebrews 13:20.

But what about all the passages that speak of covenants in the plural (Rom. 9:4; Gal. 4:24; and others)? And what about the passages that speak of an old and a new covenant (Jer. 31:31–33; Heb. 8:6–13)?

Unless we are willing to accept the idea that the Bible can contradict itself (and that therefore God can contradict himself), we must reconcile these passages with those that teach one covenant. Scripture helps us do that by some of the language it uses.

Scripture speaks of God's *remembering* his covenant (Lev. 26:42; Luke 1:72), *giving* his covenant (Num. 25:12; Acts 7:8), *declaring* it (Deut. 4:13), and *keeping* it (1 Kings 8:23). These expressions help us see that when God establishes his covenant or makes a covenant, he is not discarding the old and bringing in an entirely new covenant, but only giving a *new revelation* of his *one covenant of grace*. In that sense only are there old and new covenants, or more than one covenant.

This one covenant can never be anything but a covenant of grace.

There is no other basis on which we can live in a relationship with God except his undeserved favor toward us. Even Adam, though he by his obedience could continue to enjoy a covenant relationship with God, was not in that relationship by merit.

We reject, therefore, the teaching that the covenant with Adam was a covenant of works based on merit, and not on grace. Especially we reject the idea that in that covenant Adam could have merited eternal life by his obedience.

Luke 17:10 destroys every possibility of merit when it says, "So likewise ye, when ye shall have done all those things which are commanded you, say, We are unprofitable [unmeriting] servants: we have done that which was our duty to do." The everlasting covenant of God is all of grace.

The Covenant of Grace

If God's covenant is a relationship or bond between God and his people, it can only be a covenant of *grace.*

That we should live in a relationship of friendship, fellowship, and love with the living God must be *undeserved favor* toward us on God's part. It is almost unthinkable that God should dwell with *us* and be our God, but he promises, nevertheless, to us as sinners, "I will dwell in them, and walk in them; and I will be their God, and they shall be my people" (2 Cor. 6:16). How wonderful!

What is true for us was also true of Adam. Who would dare say that Adam's creation as one who knew and loved God was anything but undeserved favor? Certainly it was not based on merit, for until he was created in such a high position, he had no opportunity to merit with God. Nor can *anyone* ever merit with God, as we learn from Luke 17:10: "So likewise ye, when ye shall have done all those things which are commanded you, say, We are unprofitable servants: we have done that which was our duty to do."

We reject, therefore, any talk of a covenant of works based on merit. We are not unwilling to speak of the covenant of works as a description of God's covenant with Adam, though we would very carefully qualify any such talk. It should be clearly understood, if we are to speak of a covenant of works, that this is not *another* covenant, but a revelation of the *one* covenant of God; also Adam's obedience and good works were not the basis or reason for the covenant, but only the way in which Adam continued to enjoy that covenant.

This is just another way of saying that the covenant is made and kept by God alone without man's help or cooperation. It is to say that the covenant never depends on man, even though he has duties and responsibilities in the covenant.

Perhaps an analogy will help. We know that we must eat to live, but we recognize that our life does not *depend* on food and drink. Nor do we receive our *life* from food and drink. Our life depends on God, from whom we receive it every moment. Food and drink are only the *means,* not the *reason* for life. So it is in the covenant. Obedience is only the means by which we enjoy the blessings and privileges of God's covenant, but never the reason for the covenant.

Because the covenant is of grace, it is a sure and everlasting covenant that cannot be broken. Though Adam was unfaithful, and we with him, God remains faithful, never breaking his covenant or altering the thing that has gone out of his lips (Ps. 89:34). Great is his faithfulness. To him alone be glory as the God of the covenant.

The Covenant Promise

One of the most precious aspects of God's covenant is the promise by which he makes his covenant known to us. In that promise he shows that his covenant really is a covenant of grace. By that promise he multiplies mercy and adds grace to grace.

That promise is found repeatedly in Scripture and is a kind of covenant formula. With minor word changes, it is this Word of God: "I will be your God and ye shall be my people" (Gen. 17:7–8; Deut. 7:6; 2 Cor. 6:16; Rev. 21:3).

One could not imagine a greater promise than that or anything better than having God as our God, knowing him, loving him, and having fellowship with him. Yet God adds grace to grace and blessing to blessing, for that is not the whole promise of the covenant.

In mercy God adds to this the promise that he will also be the God of our *children*. Although we ourselves do not deserve anything from him, he not only promises us salvation, but he promises it as well to our children. What unspeakable grace!

That Word of God regarding the children of believers is part of the covenant promise, in both the Old and the New Testaments. It is found first in Genesis 17:7–8 at the beginning of God's dealings with Abraham. It is found again at the beginning of the history of the New Testament church in Acts 2:39.

We must understand that this promise never was, and never will be, a guarantee that God will save every one of our children. There are always Esaus and Cains in the families of God's people, to their great grief. God's promise is that he will continue his covenant with his people and their families, and that they—with their families and in their generations—will not be cut off.

This is the promise that is commemorated and signified when the infants of believers are baptized. This is the promise that motivates all covenant instruction and discipline and gives assurance that these will be effective. It is the promise by which God shows us just how great his grace is.

We would emphasize, too, that it is a *promise*, an oath sworn by God who does not change and who does not lie. That is something for parents to hold on to through all the trials and tribulations of rearing a family. It is a reason for them to continue to pray when a son or daughter is wayward and disobedient.

May God by this most precious of all promises show to many the grace and faithfulness of his covenant (Ps. 25:14).

Predestination

A doctrine that often gives people difficulty is predestination. The difficulty is that there is no other doctrine of Scripture that so plainly proves that God is God and requires us to humble ourselves before him and to acknowledge his greatness. Such humility is very difficult for our proud and sinful hearts, for in our foolish pride we wish always to be the captains of our own fate.

Predestination, as the word suggests, means that God eternally determined the destiny of his rational, thinking, and willing creatures, including both men and angels, fallen and unfallen. He did this in his eternal counsel before the creation of the world (the prefix *pre-* of the word *predestination* means "before"). In eternity God chose some for heaven and rejected others. That sovereign and eternal choice of God, not man's own choices, determined man's everlasting destiny.

There are many objections against this doctrine. It is said that it makes men mere puppets in relation to God; that it is harsh and tyrannical of God, especially in determining eternally to send some to hell; that it makes God the author of sin; and so on. Nevertheless, Scripture clearly teaches predestination.

The English word *predestination* is used four times, in Romans 8:29 and 30 and Ephesians 1:5 and 11—just where we would expect to find mention of this doctrine. The Greek word translated as *predestinate* means "to mark off beforehand," and it is used in two other passages (Acts 4:28; 1 Cor. 2:7), but is translated differently. The idea of predestination is found in numerous other passages as well, perhaps nowhere so plainly as in Romans 9:11–13: "(For the children being not yet born, neither having done any good or evil, that the purpose of God according to election might stand, not of works, but of him that calleth;) It was said unto her, The elder shall serve the younger. As it is written, Jacob have I loved, but Esau have I hated."

Even the angels and devils are predestined by God. This is clear from 1 Timothy 5:21, which speaks of *elect angels,* and Jude 6, which speaks of the fallen angels who are "reserved in *everlasting* chains under darkness unto the judgment of the great day." As it is with the angels, so it is with men: some are chosen to eternal life and heaven, referred to in the Bible as *election,* and others are passed by or rejected, sometimes referred to as *reprobation.*

Many will accept that the Bible teaches election, but they do not like the doctrine of rejection, or reprobation. That election and reprobation go together is plain, however, for we cannot speak of some being chosen without at least implying that there are those who are *not* chosen by God to eternal life. Not to be chosen is the same as rejection or reprobation, even if those words themselves are not used. Scripture clearly teaches both election and reprobation.

Both are sovereign and eternal acts of God and prove that he "doeth according to his will in the army of heaven, and among the inhabitants of the earth: and none can stay his hand, or say unto him, What doest thou?" (Dan. 4:35).

Unconditional Election

Having written about predestination, we wish now to write more about the wonderful, biblical doctrine of election. Election is the beautiful side of the awe-inspiring doctrine of predestination.

It is impossible to deny that the Bible teaches election, so often does the Bible speak of it. The question, therefore, is not whether there *is* election, but what it is and when it happens.

We believe that election is God's sovereign choosing of some to salvation and eternal life, and we believe that God made this choice in eternity. He does not choose in time in response to what men do, but has chosen some from "before the foundations of the world" (Rom. 9:10– 13; Eph. 1:3–6).

To see that this doctrine of election is not something to be hated and denied, we must realize that election is not only a choice that God makes, but a revelation of his eternal and unchangeable *love*. The Bible not only tells us *that* God chose some, but it also tells us *why* he chose them. By doing so, Scripture gives us a glimpse, as it were, into the very heart of God. God chose some people simply because he *loved* them.

This love of God is eternal. He has always loved his people.

This love of God is unconditional. It is not a response to what men do. God does not love them because they first loved him. *He* was the first to love, and he loved from eternity (1 John 4:19).

This love of God is sovereign and powerful. It never goes unfulfilled, but by the death of Jesus Christ obtains complete salvation of all those for whom Christ died (John 3:16).

We believe that the word *foreknowledge* in Scripture refers to this love of God. It refers not to mere foresight, but to the love of God before time. The word *know,* which is part of the word *foreknowledge,* is used elsewhere in the Bible to describe intimate love, like the love of a husband for his wife and of a wife for her husband (Gen. 4:1, 25).

This is the way God "foreknows" his people (Gen. 18:19). He does not only know who they are, but he deeply, tenderly, intimately loves them through Jesus Christ, and that from eternity.

What a reason for thankfulness! God's love is amazing in the shadow of the cross of Jesus and in light of what he did there for lost sinners. But how much more amazing is the love of God when we remember that eternally, unchangeably, and unconditionally he loved his own. This is indeed a love that "passes knowledge," the height and length and breadth and depth of which cannot be measured (Eph. 3:17–19).

Reprobation

All Calvinists believe that God has graciously chosen some to salvation—*election*. Some also believe that God has eternally rejected others—*reprobation*. There is a difference of emphasis, though. Some use stronger language, saying that God destines some to destruction; others prefer more passive language, saying only that God eternally "passes some by" or "determines to leave some in their sins." In either case, the reference is to reprobation.

Election and reprobation together are called double predestination. The Reformed creeds clearly teach double predestination. The Canons of Dordt, which are the original Five Points of Calvinism, teach it,[11] as does the Westminster Confession of Faith.[12]

Does the *Bible* teach reprobation? Consider the following passages.

Romans 9:10–13 says that before Jacob and Esau were born, God revealed that he hated one of them. Romans 9:21–22 calls some persons vessels *made* unto dishonor and "vessels of wrath *fitted* to destruction." 1 Peter 2:6–8 says that some were *appointed* to stumble through dis-

---

11. Canons of Dordrecht (Dordt), First Head of Doctrine, Articles 15–18. Summed up in the acronym TULIP, the five points of Calvinism are total depravity, unconditional election, limited atonement, irresistible grace, and the perseverance of the saints.

12. Westminster Confession of Faith, Chapter 3, Article 7.

obedience. Jude 4 speaks of men *ordained* to condemnation. Jude 6 even teaches reprobation in reference to fallen angels (devils).

Note, too, in these passages the strong language that Scripture uses. If anything, the Bible supports the teaching that God does, indeed, determine and destine some to destruction, rather than only eternally passing them by or leaving them in their sins. In any case, however, the Bible clearly teaches a predestining to destruction.

We would emphasize two things in speaking of reprobation: first, it neither makes God the author of sin, nor absolves the wicked from accountability for their sins; and second, God has a purpose in reprobation.

The great difference between election and reprobation is this: God, because he has sovereignly chosen his people from eternity and determined all things necessary for their salvation, takes all the credit—all the glory of their salvation—for himself. Though he is equally sovereign in reprobation, he takes none of the discredit. In this respect, election and reprobation are not equal. God is the author of salvation because of election, but he is not the author of sin because of reprobation.

In Romans 9:17–20 even the suggestion that God is wrong to find fault with sinners is called "replying against God." It follows, too, that the wicked are held fully accountable for their sins. This is clear from Acts 2:23, which not only tells us that the sin of crucifying Christ was foreordained by God, but also that it was done with "wicked hands."

All this does not imply that reprobation is arbitrary. It is not true that God eternally rejects some for no reason. Romans 9:22–23 gives two reasons: that God might make his wrath and power known, and that he might make known the riches of his glory on the vessels of mercy. Even reprobation serves God's purpose of showing his mercy to his people, as is clear in the crucifixion of Christ (Acts 4:24–28).

Though we find reprobation a difficult doctrine for the flesh, we nevertheless believe that it must be taught so that men may tremble before God's wrath and power and be in awe of his great mercy (Isa. 43:4). Oh that many would tremble and be in awe today!

God's Decrees

Do you believe that God has predetermined *all* things? If he has not, why do things happen? We wish to consider these questions under the next few topics.

We want to show that the Bible teaches God's determination of all things. It does this by speaking of God's *decrees.*

God's decrees are his sovereign, eternal determinations concerning all things that are, that have been, and that will be—in creation, in history, and in salvation. The Bible uses the following words to tell us about these decrees.

His *counsel* (Ps. 73:24; Eph. 1:11), emphasizing that these are the deliberations and purposes of all three persons of the Trinity.

His *purpose* (Isa. 14:24–27; Eph. 3:11), showing that his decrees are not arbitrary, but all have his glory as their ultimate goal.

His *good pleasure* (Isa. 44:28; Luke 12:32), stressing that God's decrees do not depend on anyone or anything but himself, not even on the foreseen actions of men or other creatures. His decrees are free and independent. He decrees all things because it pleases him to do so.

His *will* (Rom. 1:10; Eph. 1:5), showing that his decrees are not mere fate, but the thoughts of the heart of the living God.

His *determination* (Isa. 19:17; Luke 22:22), emphasizing the important truth that his decrees are fixed and unchangeable.

His *decree* (Ps. 2:7), reminding us that he determines all things as the great King, the sovereign Creator and Lord of heaven and earth.

Just the number of words used to describe God's decrees shows how important they are. Knowing them is especially important if we are to have any hope or peace in this wicked, troubled world.

To believe that God has predetermined or foreordained all things is the greatest comfort anyone can have. Then we can know that things do not happen by mere chance or fate but by the determinations of one who is all-wise and good. Then we do not need to conclude that there is another power—an evil power—that determines much of what happens in our lives and in history. That would leave us without hope or peace.

To have comfort in the truth that God determines all things, however, a person must *be convinced* that God is wise and good, and he must know God's grace and mercy. This is possible only through faith in Jesus Christ. He is the power and wisdom of God (1 Cor. 1:24). To know God through him is to be sure that God is good.

God's All-comprehensive Decrees

Scripture often speaks of God's decrees, which are his sovereign, eternal determinations concerning the things that are, that have been, and that will be in creation, in history, and in salvation.

But do these decrees predetermine *everything*?

Scripture teaches very clearly that God has predetermined all things. He has decreed the following:

- The earth and its foundations (Prov. 8:29).
- The sea and its bounds (Job 38:8–11).
- The rain (Job 28:26).
- The sun, moon, and stars (Ps. 148:3–6).
- The times and eras of history (Isa. 46:9–10).
- The physical and ethnic boundaries of the nations (Acts 17:26).
- Our birth and character (Ps. 139:15–16).
- Our way of life (Jer. 10:23), even our thoughts and words (Prov. 16:1).
- The power and authority of men, also of ungodly men (Ex. 9:16).
- The wickedness of men (1 Pet. 2:8), including the wickedness of those who crucified Christ (Acts 4:24–28).
- The coming of the antichristian kingdom (Rev. 17:17).
- The damnation of wicked men (Matt. 26:24–25; Rom. 9:22).
- The judgment of the fallen angels (Jude 6).
- The end of all things (Isa. 46:10).
- The birth (Ps. 2:7–8), life (Luke 22:22), and death (Rev. 13:8) of Christ.
- Every part of salvation, including calling (Rom. 8:28), the faith of those who believe (Acts 13:48), justification (Rom. 8:30), adoption (Eph. 1:5), holiness and good works (Eph. 1:3–4; Eph. 2:10), and the inheritance in glory (Eph. 1:11).
- All things in heaven, on earth, and in hell (Ps. 135:6–12).

It should not be hard for a believer to accept this. Whatever it may mean to others, to the believer it means that not wicked men, not the devil, but *God* is in control of all things.

This means that nothing just happens—especially that nothing happens to God's people that is not already ordained by their heavenly Father. All things, therefore, must work together for good to those who love God, for their Father has decreed all things.

An ignorance of God's sovereign determination concerning all things is the reason we see "men's hearts failing them for fear, and for looking after those things which are coming on the earth" (Luke 21:26). Without a sovereign, decreeing God, they are without hope (Eph. 2:12).

Let us confess before the world that "our God is in the heavens: he hath done whatsoever he hath pleased" (Ps. 115:3).

God's Efficacious Decrees

God's decrees are not some plan on paper tucked away in a pigeon-hole somewhere in heaven, but the living and powerful will of God. His decrees are not something that God consults from time to time to see what it was he planned to do, but they are the thoughts of his own unchangeable mind, which is the source and cause of all that happens.

When God wills something—and he does will all things—then what he has willed must come to pass and does come to pass because he willed it. Scripture is very clear about this. In Isaiah 46:9–10 God says, "I am God, and there is none like me, Declaring the end from the beginning, and from ancient times the things that are not yet done, saying, My counsel shall stand, and I will do all my pleasure." In Psalm 73:23–28 Asaph speaks of being guided by the counsel of God, not because he knows what is in the will of God beforehand and then follows it, but because that counsel has determined his whole life and all its circumstances.

Acts 2:23 emphasizes this same truth in connection with the death of Christ. It says that he was *delivered* into the wicked hands of his enemies by "*the determinate counsel and foreknowledge of God.*" What was true of the death of Christ is also true of our obtaining an inheritance from God. We obtain it, "being predestinated according to the purpose of him who *worketh all things after the counsel of his own will*" (Eph. 1:11).

No one, therefore, can ever thwart or change God's will. There are those who think they can. Some think they can change God's mind and will through prayer, either by praying often or by getting sufficient people to pray. Others think they can manipulate God and get him to do their will by silly religious tricks, but it is not so. God's will is almighty and unchangeable.

Of this, too, Scripture clearly testifies. In Daniel 4:35 Nebuchadnezzar, an ungodly king, is forced to acknowledge that no one can say to God, "What doest thou?" Romans 9:19–20 tells us that nothing can resist his will.

God is sovereign even in the acts of his thinking and willing creatures — men and angels. Proverbs 16:9 tells us that although we plan our way, the Lord directs our steps. The preparations of the heart and the answer of the tongue are also from him (v. 1). Even the king's heart is in God's hand, and he turns it to his own purposes (Prov. 21:1).

That God's decree is all-powerful and unchangeable is of great comfort to those who believe. It is the reason, above all others, why their salvation is sure. Their will may change and their mind fail, but God's will and mind never change. This is the reason for their believing that all things must work together for their good (Rom. 8:28). God has sovereignly and unchangeably decreed all things, and in decreeing their salvation, he will not be thwarted or fail because of angels or principalities or powers or things present or things to come or life or death or any creature (Rom. 8:38–39).

Of him, through him, and to him are all things. What a great God and Savior he is!

God's Unconditional Decrees

When we speak of God's decrees, and especially of predestination, it is important to see that his decrees, including the decrees of election and reprobation, are unconditional. Indeed, the second of the Five Points of Calvinism is described as unconditional election.

What does this mean?

It means that God in his decrees does not depend upon any creature: his will — not man's — is supreme. God's decrees are his will, and his will is his decision concerning all things. That God's decrees are unconditional means that his decisions are before all other decisions of men and angels and that he does not wait on the decisions of men.

That God's decrees are unconditional means especially that in everything he has decreed, he does not wait for men to make their decisions because he cannot or will not interfere. Put very simply, man's decision is not the reason for God's decision, but God's decision is the reason for man's decision. If it were not so, man, not God, would be sovereign, and man's will, not God's will, would be supreme.

God's unconditional decreeing is denied by those who believe in the free will of man. They insist that in salvation, it is man's decision, not God's, that really matters. God can or will do nothing, they say, until men have made decisions for or against Christ and the gospel. This is a blatant denial of the sovereignty of God and can in no wise be reconciled with that doctrine. It makes God—the living God—dependent on his creatures.

Election, then, becomes God's reaction in time to men's decisions. This false teaching says that God chooses those who first choose him, and that he loves those who love him. This not only contradicts Scripture, which teaches that we love him because he first loved us, but it also denies that election is eternal and unconditional and that the God of election is sovereign. According to such teaching, God is little different from the gods of the heathen, who, like their makers, can only react to men and their doings.

Others, realizing that election is eternal, focus on God's foreknowledge and say that God looked ahead in time, foreknew and foresaw who would believe, and then chose them for what they would do. Such an election also makes God dependent on man, and little different from a fortune-teller.

Scripture teaches that God's decrees are unconditional. Romans 9:15–16 says that God has mercy on whom *he* wills, not on those who accept his mercy, and therefore salvation "is not of him that willeth [chooseth], nor of him that runneth [worketh]." Ephesians 1:5 teaches that God chose people only according to the good pleasure of his will—in plain English, simply because he wanted them, not because they wanted him.

How thankful we ought to be that God's decrees are sovereign and unconditional and not dependent on our frail and changing wills.

God's Wise Decrees

That God is wise is the clear teaching of Scripture, but God's people often forget this, especially when they are suffering or when things do not go well for them. Then it is difficult to see the wisdom of God, and one must at such times believe without seeing.

In wisdom God has decreed everything. That is the reason all things work together. They do not happen at random and independently of other things, but all the things fit together and work together like the parts of a well-oiled and well-running machine. They do so because God is wise. He knows how to make all things work in perfect harmony according to his own purpose. It must be so, for all things must serve the glory and honor of God, which is his own high purpose.

Included in his purpose is our salvation, for few things bring as much glory and honor to him as the revelation of his grace in the salvation of his people. Thus through God's wisdom all things work together for good to those who love him and who are the called according to his purpose (Rom. 8:28).

This is what we must believe in our afflictions and troubles. Not only must we see that there is a purpose in all things, a purpose we usually cannot discern, but also we must believe this purpose to be wise and good.

If we believe this, we will not complain or be afraid, troubled, or discouraged by what happens to us. Our God is wise and knows far better than we do what is best for us and what is necessary for our salvation. Indeed, if we know by faith the wisdom of God, we will in the end be thankful for everything that happened to us, even the troubles. We will find that the valley of Baca—what seemed to us a dry and desert valley—was, in fact, a well full of pools of living water and of grace (Ps. 84:6).

As a versification of Psalm 131 has it, knowledge of God's wisdom teaches peace.

> Not haughty is my heart,
> Not lofty is my pride;
> I do not seek to know the things
> God's wisdom hath denied.

With childlike trust, O Lord,
In Thee I calmly rest,
Contented as a little child
Upon its mother's breast.

Ye people of the Lord,
In Him alone confide;
From this time forth and evermore
His wisdom be your guide.[13]

The Will of God

Sometimes in Scripture God's decrees are described as his *will*. This Word tells us that God's decrees are not a dead plan that God has stored away somewhere in heaven, but are the very *mind* of God. When we talk about his decrees, we are talking about *him*.

This is extremely important. It means, for one thing, that God's decrees manifest all the attributes of God himself. His decrees, like him, are eternal, unchangeable, perfect, and sovereignly free.

This needs emphasis, because there are many who teach that God wants (wills) all men to be saved, but that their salvation now depends on their choice. God's will, in that case, would not be sovereign.

Others teach that God has two wills, the first of which is eternal, unchangeable, and sovereign (irresistible); the second of which is changeable, resistible, and temporary, contradicting the first will of God. They say that God does eternally choose *some* to salvation in Jesus Christ; that is, he *wills* their salvation. However, so it is said, God also *wills* the salvation of *all* men, because he expresses in the preaching of the gospel a desire (will) that all men be saved.

According to this teaching, God wills (in the gospel) and doesn't will (in predestination) the salvation of some. And insofar as he does will the salvation of all in the preaching, that will is never fulfilled, is

---

13. Psalter 366, in *The Psalter with Doctrinal Standards, Liturgy, Church Order, and Added Chorale Section* (Grand Rapids, MI: William B. Eerdmans Publishing Company, 1927; repr. 1998).

only for the here and now and not for eternity, and is incomplete and unfulfilled.

We object to this teaching, because it says that God's will, and therefore God himself, is incomplete, unfulfilled, changeable, resistible (not sovereign), and temporary. It says that there is contradiction (imperfection) in God. It even teaches that he is not one, but two, since he is of two minds about things. All of this denies that God is really God.

Scripture teaches that God has one will and that he accomplishes everything he wills. Psalm 115:3 and Psalm 135:5–6 plainly teach this in the context of some powerful statements about idolatry. To say that God does not do all his will—that his will can remain incomplete and unfulfilled—is to say that he is not God and thus to commit the sin of idolatry. This is what these psalms teach.

What do you believe? Do you say that God is of two minds about men and their salvation? Do you dare say that his will is no stronger than yours and that he can be frustrated in what he wills?

Is it not biblical and much more comforting to believe that "our God is in the heavens: he hath done whatsoever he hath pleased"? He is, after all, God.

God's Will of Command and Will of Decree

We have defended the truth that God has but one will concerning salvation and damnation. He cannot will (in the gospel) and not will (in predestination) the salvation of men.

There is, however, a legitimate distinction to be made in speaking of the will of God. Scripture uses the word *will* to refer not only to God's decrees, but also to his commands. His commands, too, are his will for our lives, though in a different sense.

In his decrees God wills certain things for our lives in the sense that he sovereignly *determines* them. In his law he also wills certain things for us, but in the sense that he *commands* them. Ephesians 1:5 speaks of his *will of decree*, Matthew 7:21 of his *will of command*. His decrees reveal what he intends to do, while his commands reveal what *man* ought to do. His will of decree includes everything that God has foreordained and that will ever come to pass. His will of command reveals everything that man ought to do and be.

This distinction is sometimes used in defense of the idea that God has two contradictory wills: that he commands (wills) all who hear the gospel to believe in Jesus Christ, while he has decreed (willed) that some will not believe. This, we believe, is playing with words, since command and decree are two different things, though the word *will* is used to refer to both. In the case of the decree, the word *will* refers to what God has eternally determined. In the case of his command, it refers to what is acceptable and pleasing to him. These two are not the same thing, yet there is no conflict between them. It may be true that God commands what he has not decreed, but even then there is no conflict. Why? Because the command is not an empty word, but something that God uses to fulfill his decree.

To put it more plainly, when God commands someone to believe, that command either draws him irresistibly to Christ in saving faith (John 6:44), or it hardens him in unbelief (Rom. 9:18; 2 Cor. 2:15–16), thus fulfilling what God has decreed. No conflict exists at all.

Nor is there any conflict in practice. When confronted by the demands of the gospel, we need only know that faith is what God requires of us. We must believe or perish. What he has decreed is not our concern and may not be our concern when faced with his righteous demands. We live by his commands, not by his decrees.

When seeking comfort and assurance, then we are concerned with God's decree. Then we must see that faith and obedience are the fruits of God's decree of election, seeing in faith, repentance, and holiness the proof of our election.

part 2

MAN AND HIS WORLD

Angels

The Bible says even less about angels than it does about heaven. This is not a fault in Scripture. All that we need to know for salvation *is* given. What would only satisfy our curiosity is not told us. In speaking of angels, therefore, we must avoid speculation and be content to learn that angels have a place in our lives and our salvation.

We know that angels are spirits and that heaven is their home. We also know from Scripture the names of two angels, Gabriel and Michael. There are different kinds of angels—archangels, cherubim, and seraphim, for example—and even different ranks of angels, as the word *archangel* (chief angel) suggests (see Col. 1:16). Scripture implies, too, that different angels have different tasks. Michael is a prince, captain, and warrior (Dan. 12:1; Jude 9; Rev. 12:7). Gabriel always appears as a messenger (Luke 1:19, 26), seraphim as angels who worship in God's presence (Isa. 6:1–4), and cherubim as guardians of God's glory and honor (Gen. 3:24; Ex. 25:18–22; Ezek. 10:1–20).

Scripture also informs us that there are many angels. Hebrews 12:22 talks of an innumerable company of angels. Some angels, however, fell with Satan (Rev. 12:4). The fall of some angels, as with men, is according to God's decree of election and reprobation. Thus we read not only of elect angels (1 Tim. 5:21), but of those, too, who are kept in everlasting chains until the judgment of the last day (Jude 6). The elect angels, as Hebrews 12:22 teaches, will also have a part in the glory of the new heavens and the new earth. The fallen angels, with wicked men, will be sent to hell (Jude 6; Rev. 20:10).

Beyond these things we know little. What we do know, however, is very comforting. All that the Bible says about angels can be summed up in the words of Hebrews 1:14: "Are they not all ministering spirits, sent forth to minister for them who shall be heirs of salvation?" What a wonderful truth!

The chief function of the angels, therefore, is to be God's servants in helping God's people and guarding their salvation (Dan. 10:13–14; Dan. 12:1; Rev. 12:7–10). That is why angels were present at all the great events of our redemption: Christ's birth (Luke 2:9–14), his temptations in the wilderness (Matt. 4:11), his agony in Gethsemane (Luke 22:43), his resurrection (Luke 24:4–7), and his ascension (Acts 1:10–11). They will be present, too, when he comes again to take his people to himself (2 Thess. 1:7).

The deep interest of angels in our salvation and final glory is also described in 1 Peter 1:12. There the Word says that they desire to look into the things that were spoken by the prophets concerning the sufferings of Christ and the glory that should follow. What a beautiful testimony to their concern for our salvation. What a comfort, then, to believe in angels.

We do not need our eyes opened like Elisha's servant to "see" these ministering spirits and their horses and chariots of fire all around us (2 Kings 6:17). Though we cannot see them, we know they are there. God tells us that in his Word.

Devils

There are as many questions about devils that cannot be answered from Scripture as there are such questions about angels. What we need to know *is* given in Scripture.

We know that the devils are all fallen angels. In many passages Satan and his demons are still called angels (2 Cor. 11:14; Jude 6; Rev. 12:7–9). Both 2 Peter 2:4 and Jude 6 say that through their sin they "kept not their first estate," a clear reference to their fall. Isaiah 14:4–23 suggests that Satan's sin was that of pride and rebellion against God.

The passage in Isaiah is a prophecy against the king of Babylon but is usually taken to refer also to Satan, since he was the power behind the king of Babylon, and since much of the prophecy in Isaiah 14 applies more clearly to him than to the king of Babylon. If this interpretation of the passage is correct, then Isaiah 14 also gives us the name Satan had before his fall: "Lucifer, son of the morning."

We know that Satan's fall took place before the fall of man, since Satan was the chief instrument of man's fall (John 8:44). Revelation 12:4, which is usually understood to refer to the fall of Satan and his angels, suggests that many angels fell with him. It is difficult to tell, however, whether the verse teaches that a literal third of the angels fell with Satan, because so many numbers in the book of Revelation are symbolic.

We know, too, that devils have great power. Satan himself is called both the *prince* and the *god* of this world (John 12:31; 2 Cor. 4:4). His power is so great that we cannot withstand him in our own strength (Eph. 6:11ff.). He is compared in 1 Peter 5:8 to a roaring lion who goes about seeking whom he may devour.

Satan's power is especially the power of lying, deceit, and temptation (John 8:44; Rev. 13:14; Matt. 4:1ff.). Through these means he holds in bondage the children of this world (2 Cor. 4:4) and is the great enemy of believers and of the church. His very names refer to this power. *Satan* means "adversary" or "accuser," and *devil* means "slanderer." Because of his lies and slanders he is also known as *Apollyon*, "destroyer" (Rev. 9:11). By his lies he murdered our first parents (John 8:44) and continues to murder men and women today.

It is important for Christians to realize that Satan, despite his power, can and must be resisted by grace, and that he will then flee. James 4:7 tells us this, and the temptations of Jesus give us much instruction about how we are to resist him: by knowing and confessing the Word of God, by prayer, and by fasting (see also v. 8).

We must know, too, that though Satan has great power, he is under the sovereign direction and control of God (Matt. 12:29; Rev. 20:2) and will be cast with all other workers of iniquity into the eternal fires of hell (Rev. 20:10). Thus, as Luther wrote in the hymn "A Mighty Fortress Is Our God," "The prince of darkness grim/We tremble not for him."[1]

What we know of devils is given to us so that clothed with the armor of God, we may stand fast against all their fiery darts. Let us do so and not tremble.

Creation in Six Days

Most people today do not believe that the creation story told in Genesis 1–3 is true. This is not surprising. What is surprising is that some *Christians* think it does not matter whether you believe the account of Genesis 1–3 or the theories of evolutionists. We believe it is essential to accept the biblical account of creation as literal history. The Bible shows why.

---

1. Third stanza of "A Mighty Fortress Is Our God," hymn 81 in the *Trinity Hymnal*.

For one thing, if you deny that Genesis 1–3 is true, you have really denied that the Bible is the inspired and infallible Word of God from beginning to end. You have denied 2 Timothy 3:16: "*All* Scripture is given by inspiration of God."

Not only that, but you have denied other parts of Scripture as well, and in doing so have made liars both of God and of our Lord Jesus Christ. Consider this. In the fourth commandment of the law, God says, "Six days shalt thou labour, and do all thy work: But the seventh day is the sabbath of the Lord thy God...For in six days the Lord made heaven and earth, the sea, and all that in them is, and rested the seventh day" (Ex. 20:9–11). Did God not know what he was talking about?

If you believe that man "evolved," then consider what Jesus says in Matthew 19:4–5: "Have ye not read [in Gen. 1:27 and Gen. 2:24], that he which made them at the beginning made them male and female, And said, For this cause shall a man leave father and mother, and shall cleave to his wife: and they twain shall be one flesh?" Jesus obviously believed the first two chapters of Genesis to be true. Should not we believe them also?

If you believe that man evolved and that there never was a real person named Adam, you will also be unable to believe in the fall and original sin as taught in passages like Romans 5, which say that it was a real man, the first man Adam, who fell, and through whom sin and death came on the whole human race. To deny the truth of Genesis 1–3 is to deny that there ever was such a man and to have no explanation for sin and death. Even more, if we do not believe that there ever was a real first Adam, how shall we believe in Christ as the "last Adam" (1 Cor. 15:45, 47) and in salvation through him?

It is impossible to deny the creation account of Genesis and still believe in Christ as Savior. Not only is Christ the last Adam, but the story of the creation and the fall is the reason we need him. No first man Adam means no fall into sin, no original sin deriving from Adam, and no need for Christ. Surely he did not come and die merely to set right the things that have gone wrong in man's evolutionary development.

The difference between creationism and evolutionism *does* matter. It matters even in believing unto salvation, though that is not to say that there are not Christians who have been misled and mistaught. Let us, then, make sure that we do believe in creation, in the Creator, in the Word that teaches creation, and in Christ, who is both Creator (John

1:3) and Savior of those who by God's grace know their great need and who know it from the creation story.

Evolutionism

It is often suggested that the theory of evolutionism, Darwinian or otherwise, is scientific and that when it conflicts with the biblical account of creation, it is the latter that must give way. Evolution is *fact,* so it is said, but the creation story is only a matter of religious belief. This is a lie.

The basic principles of evolutionism are not scientific facts at all, but matters of belief. Evolutionism is as much a religion as is belief in the Bible and what it teaches about the origins of this world. Indeed, evolutionism is the religion of those who want to explain this world without God, who wish to put him out of his world, both as Creator and as the God of providence.

Evolutionism, therefore, is really atheism—a religion that denies God and his place over the creation. It is an attempt of unbelieving man to explain all things without God. For this reason, too, there can be no compromise between Scripture and the teaching of evolutionary "science," falsely so called (1 Tim. 6:20).

An example of one of these "facts" of evolution, which is not a fact at all nor scientifically proven, is the principle of uniformitarianism: that all things take place according to fixed, never-changing, natural laws. If uniformitarianism is not true, then neither is evolutionism. Nor do scientists have any way of proving evolutionism to be true. Only one who has lived from the beginning until now, as God has, could prove that these so-called "natural laws" have not changed.

The Bible shows us that the principle of uniformitarianism is wrong. Uniformitarianism says that all things have continued the same since the beginning, whenever that was. It says that the rate of radioactive decay, the laying down of sediments, the formation of fossils, erosion, and such things have always proceeded according to fixed natural laws. The Bible shows clearly that this is not so in 2 Peter 3:3–7. Foreseeing the development of these unbelieving theories, the Holy Spirit wrote in those verses that all things have *not* been the same. Before the flood there was a different world altogether, a world that perished in the great flood and is no more. God himself intervened with a universal flood and changed the very nature of the world, as he will do once more when the end comes. Men's "scientific" theories, therefore, are of use only back to the time after the flood and can tell us nothing about the world before the flood.

We do not seek to prove creationism, however. The Bible's account of creation in six days is a matter not of proof, but of faith in God: "Through *faith* we understand that the worlds were framed by the Word of God, so that things which are seen were not made of things which do appear" (Heb. 11:3). Evolutionism is *unbelief.* Faith listens to and obeys God rather than man.

Theistic Evolutionism

Since Darwin, there have been many attempts by misguided Christians to bring evolutionism and the Bible together by finding some compromise between the two. These attempted compromises are all called "theistic evolutionism." Some examples of theistic evolutionism follow.

The *gap theory* inserts the billions of years required by evolution and its processes of development into a supposed "gap" between Genesis 1:1 and Genesis 1:2. The "evidences" of evolution, then, would be the remains of a first world that perished. There is not the slightest hint in Scripture of such a world, however.

The *day-age* or *period theory* rests on the notion that the days of Genesis 1 and 2 were actually long periods of time. This attempt, however, is easily answered by reference to Exodus 20:8–11, which makes it clear that the days of Genesis 1 and our 24-hour days were the same.

The *myth theory* claims that Genesis chapters 1–3 is not history, but poetry, myth, or some kind of teaching model from which truth can be learned, but which is not to be taken as factual. The difficulty with this theory is that Jesus and the apostles accepted the story as literal (Matt. 19:4; Rom. 5:12; 1 Cor. 15:45–47).

All these theories fail in light of Scripture's clear testimony to creation in six ordinary days and to the historicity of the first chapters of Genesis.

God himself speaks in Exodus 20:8–11 of creation in six ordinary days, days just like those in which we do our work. Jesus and Paul both believed in a real, historical Adam, the first man created by God and not the product of evolution (Matt. 19:4–6; 1 Cor. 15:45). Peter was a creationist (2 Pet. 3:5). So was John (1 John 3:12).

Dare we say that God did not know what he was talking about when he gave the law? Was Jesus talking nonsense when he used the creation of Adam and Eve as a model for marriage? Did Paul lie when he called Adam the "first man"?

The notion that our belief in the origin of the world does not matter is a lie, therefore. So is the idea that we can believe in evolutionism without that affecting the rest of our faith, especially our faith in Christ as Savior. The truthfulness of Jesus and of God himself is at stake.

At issue in the debate concerning evolutionism, however, are not only God's veracity and the veracity of the human writers of Scripture, but also the doctrine of Scripture itself. Scripture throughout testifies to the historical veracity of Genesis 1–11. Either Scripture is true and every man a liar, or men speak truth when they propound their theories, and Scripture is guilty of lies and deceit. Which do you think is most likely?

The Day-Age Theory of Creation

The *day-age theory,* sometimes called the *period theory*—that the days of Genesis 1 were actually long periods of time or ages—is only one attempt to reconcile evolutionism and Scripture. We deal with it to show how easily these attempts can be disproved. We want also to show that it is through careful study of Scripture that such ideas are disproved. Scripture, interpreting itself, is our sure and safe guide.

If anyone studies the use of the word *day* in Scripture, he will quickly discover two things. Such study will show that the word *day* in the Bible can indeed refer to a much longer period of time (2 Pet. 3:8–10). There can be no doubt about this.

However, further study will show that the word *day* never refers to a long period of time when used with the ordinal numbers (first, second, third, and so on). With ordinal numbers, the word *day* in Scripture always refers to an ordinary, 24-hour day. Since the word *day* is used with ordinal numbers in Genesis 1, it must refer to ordinary days. Thus Scripture interprets itself.

God himself establishes that these were ordinary days, first in Genesis 1 by speaking of morning and evening, and then in Exodus 20:11, where the days of creation are made the perpetual pattern for our use of the days of the week. The days of Genesis 1, God says, were days just like those in which we do our work. Further study will show that "evening and morning," when used together, *always* means one thing in Scripture: a day such as those we experience every day of our lives. Again, Scripture interprets itself.

There is a warning in this for every student of the Bible. That is, we must come to Scripture and hear what Scripture says. We must not bring our own interpretations to Scripture and force them upon the Word of God. Our duty is not to give our own interpretation of Scripture, but to study the Scriptures and compare them carefully in order that they may interpret themselves. Then we must believe and submit to their teaching.

Theistic evolutionism is a refusal to hear what the Scriptures say, not only in Genesis 1–3, but in all the other passages that interpret and shed light on these three chapters. Theistic evolutionism is a refusal to hear what the Spirit says, both as author of Genesis 1–3 and as sovereign interpreter of these chapters and of all Scripture.

The issue is not only creationism versus evolutionism, but the inspiration, authority, and sufficiency of Scripture. This is always so and is the reason why any attempt to combine evolutionism and Scripture results in loss of scriptural truth to the so-called scientific facts and theories of unbelieving evolutionism.

As someone once said, "If I had to choose between *God* saying that Jonah swallowed a whale, or a scientist saying that it is impossible for a fish to swallow a man, I would choose the former." God is true and every man a liar. What he says about creation cannot be wrong.

God's Providence

The word *providence* is not found in the Bible. It is used as a name for the biblical teaching that God is the everywhere-present Ruler of the whole creation.

As sovereign Ruler of the creation, God takes care of and provides for the needs of all his creatures. Note that the word *provide* is found in the word *providence*. Providence, however, does not only refer to this providing, but also to God's controlling, directing, and using all things for his own purposes. "He doeth according to his will in the army of heaven, and among the inhabitants of the earth: and none can stay his hand, or say unto him, What doest thou?" (Matt. 6:13b). This, too, is his providence.

Providence means that nothing just happens. There is no such thing as chance or luck (Matt. 10:29–30). All things are the work of God. Even the sinful deeds of wicked men and the activity of the devil are completely under God's control (Ex. 4:21; 1 Sam. 2:25; 2 Sam. 16:10; 2 Sam. 24:1; 1 Kings 22:19–22; Ps. 139:1–16; Prov. 16:1, 4, 9; Prov. 21:1; Isa. 10:15; Isa. 45:7; Isa. 63:17; Jer. 10:23; Dan. 4:17; Amos 3:6; Matt. 8:31; Acts 2:23; Acts 17:28; Rom. 9:18). Yet God is so great that he is not responsible for any of the wickedness that men do. Truly his ways are not our ways, nor are his thoughts our thoughts (Isa. 55:8).

When Scripture speaks of God's providence, it most often speaks of his "hand" (Ps. 109:27; 1 Pet. 5:6). It is by his hand that he provides for his creatures and gives them their life and breath. It is with his hand that he guides and directs the course of all things so that they serve his own wonderful purpose. His hand is his sovereign and almighty power.

Sometimes even men themselves are described as God's hand when he uses them to accomplish his purpose (Ps. 17:13–14) or when they are the instruments of his purpose (Gen. 49:24; Ps. 17:13; Isa. 10:15). And what is more, these men are unable to question God's dealings (Isa. 45:9), even when they are the instruments God uses.

There must be unspeakable terror in this thought for the ungodly, for no matter what they do or where they go, they are in God's hand and can do nothing apart from him who is their Judge and Executioner. By the same token there is endless comfort in God's providence for believers, because the hand that holds them is the hand of their Father (John 10:28–29), who has eternally loved them and who sovereignly and graciously cares for them. Scripture even speaks of them being *graven* into the hands of God (Isa. 49:16).

Knowing, then, that he is their heavenly Father, believers learn from this doctrine of providence that their Father is almighty. He is able to do all things necessary for their salvation. He controls all the circumstances of their life, including the things that seem to be against them. Sickness, death, poverty, affliction, and persecution do not come by chance, but all are under the sovereign control of the one who loves his people and gave his only begotten Son for them. Surely, then, all things must work together for good to those who love God (Rom. 8:28), and nothing can separate them from the love of God in Jesus Christ (v. 39).

Preservation and Providence

One aspect of God's providence is referred to as "preservation." By this we mean that it is God who gives life and existence to all his creatures and who "preserves" them and their lives. He does this not only for the brute creation—beasts and birds, planets and stars, grass and trees—but also for men, angels, and even devils (Ps. 104:10–24; Luke 8:26–33). In him all creatures live and move and have their being (Acts 17:28).

This is a great truth. It means that nothing exists except that God is constantly present with and in it by his almighty power, and that he is always upholding it. Things do not exist of themselves, but because of God. That is true of the chair on which I am sitting as I write this, as well as of the sun and moon in their courses.

This also means that the order and harmony in the creation are not the result of so-called natural laws, but are the result of God's omnipresence (his being everywhere) and his almighty power. Spring, summer, autumn, and winter do not come every year in the same order because of "natural laws," but because God faithfully sends them. The planets do not obey natural laws in keeping their courses, but they obey God, who guides and directs them.

This work of God in the creation is one of the means by which he gives witness of himself to every person (Acts 17:24–28; Rom. 1:18–20). There is no one who will be able to say of God in the judgment day, "I did not know you." Thus they will be without excuse, even though this testimony of God in the creation is not a *saving* revelation to men.

Living in the midst of such a testimony to the power and faithfulness of God, it is shameful that men do not praise him (Rom. 1:21). Especially this is true because God also preserves and provides for them. Instead of glorifying him and being thankful, they turn to idolatry and uncleanness, as Paul points out in Romans 1.

Idolatry, therefore, is not a seeking after God, but a turning away from him, and it is an evidence at the same time that even the heathen know something of the true God. In turning from him, they are given over by God to the grossest of sins, especially to the sin of homosexuality (vv. 24–27). But even this is evidence that they know him.

These vile sins are just punishment for the unthankfulness of such men. Acting like the beasts, who do not know God, they become worse than the beasts when God gives them over to sins that even the beasts do not commit.

God's presence and preserving power in the creation are a wonderful testimony to the believer of the God he knows and loves in Christ. One who knows that in God he lives and moves and has his being will never be afraid of anything, and he will be forever thankful, not only because God preserves and protects his spiritual life, but also because God gives him, day by day, life and breath and all things (Acts 17:25). He will die in peace in the confidence that the one who gives and preserves life also takes it away again, and that God is the faithful Father of his people, even in death.

Government and Providence

Another aspect of God's providence is *his government and rule over all things*. That God does rule is clear from Scripture (Ps. 2:2–4). As the Ruler of all things and as the God of providence, he is the "blessed and only Potentate, the King of kings, and Lord of lords" (1 Tim. 6:15).

That providential rule of God is:

All-encompassing. There is nothing, not even Satan or sin, that God does not sovereignly rule (Job 1:12; Job 2:6).

Sovereign. God not only rules all things, but he rules them in such a way that they must do his will and serve his purpose. In the case of men, angels, and devils, his rule is not compromised by, or dependent on, the will of his creatures (Job 9:12).

Righteous. God rules all things in such a way that the responsibility for the actions of men, angels, and devils remains their own. He cannot be charged with the evil they do, though he is completely in control of it and even brings it to pass (Rom. 9:17–20).

Purposeful. God not only rules, but does so according to a perfect plan to which everything must and does conform. Nothing happens by chance. Nothing surprises God or causes him to change his mind or will (Ps. 115:3; Ps. 135:6; Rom. 9:21–22).

Incomprehensible. So great is God as the Ruler over all that his ways are beyond our understanding (Job 9:10; Isa. 55:8). Though all things work together for the good of his people and for the damnation of the rest, it is not always possible for us to see that. We live by faith, not by sight (2 Cor. 5:7).

Gracious. God rules for the benefit of his people (Rom. 8:28). All things do not happen to work together for good to those who love God, but they do so because he controls and directs them through Jesus our Savior.

God's rule is not, however, gracious to all. His rule over the ungodly is the opposite of his rule over his people. It is a damning rule, not only because they reject his rule and despise his gifts, but also because he actively rules them for their own destruction and damnation. This is not to deny that he gives them good things—life and breath, food and shelter, fruitful years, and all the rest—but never out of love or in grace.

This providential rule by God must be believed, for what we see does not always appear to be under God's wise rule. Instead of order we see disorder in creation and society; instead of justice we see injustice, chaos, and apparent disarray in history and creation. Faith nevertheless believes and confesses that God is in control, that nothing happens by chance, and that by God's grace all is for good. Faith holds that all things *must* work for the good of God's people, and that they must work *together* for that good, to those who love God.

God's All-encompassing Providence

It must be emphasized as strongly as possible that God's providence is over all things in earth, heaven, and hell. That is simply another way of saying that God is sovereign. Scripture teaches that he sovereignly rules:

- Angels (Ps. 103:20–21).
- Devils (Job 1:12; Job 2:6).
- All men (Jer. 10:23; Acts 17:28).

- Men's hearts (Prov. 21:1).
- Men's actions (Prov. 16:9).
- Men's thoughts and words (Prov. 16:1).
- The sinful deeds of all men (Ps. 33:10; Prov. 16:4; Amos 3:6; Acts 2:23).
- The sins of his own people (Isa. 63:17).
- The hardening of men's hearts in sin (Ex. 4:21; Rom. 9:18).
- The weather and the seasons (Acts 14:17).
- The stars and planets (Ps. 104:19).
- The great things of the creation (Jer. 5:24; Dan. 4:35).
- The smallest and most insignificant things (Matt. 10:29–30).
- So-called natural disasters and unpleasant events (Ps. 105:29; Ps. 148:8).
- War and peace (Isa. 45:7).
- Life and death (Gen. 4:1; Ps. 31:15; Ps. 104:28–29).
- All things (Ps. 103:19).

God's providence is not only his rule, however. Let us not forget that he also brings all things to pass, directs and controls them, and uses them all to accomplish his own purpose and good pleasure (Ex. 3:19–20; Isa. 44:28; Isa. 46:9–10; Eph. 1:5; Phil. 2:13).

That is both the mystery and the miracle of providence. It is a mystery that God uses all things, including wickedness and those who do wickedly, without himself being responsible for wickedness. It is a miracle of grace that he sovereignly uses all things for the salvation of his own and for the good of those who love him and are the called according to his purpose. He does this for the sake of Christ, who suffered, died, and rose again for the sins of his people.

Providence and "Common Grace"

In his providence God provides for all his creatures (Acts 17:25). This means that God gives many good gifts to the wicked, including not only rain and sunshine, food and shelter, life and breath, but also a rational mind, a will, and a spirit.

Many conclude from this that God loves the wicked and is gracious to them. These things, they say, are God's "common grace," his grace for all, a grace that does not lead them to salvation but is nevertheless a testimony to them of God's favor and love to them. A common providence, however, is not the same thing as a common grace, and the two should not be confused. Nor does the Bible ever use the word *grace* to describe these common operations of God's providence.

This is not to deny that the gifts God gives the wicked are *good* gifts (James 1:17). But because God may give them good gifts does not mean that he loves them or is gracious to them. To say that God gives good gifts to the wicked still says nothing about *why* God gives those good gifts. The Bible teaches that he has other reasons than love or mercy for giving good gifts to the wicked. He gives them these good gifts in his wrath, as a snare to them (Ps. 11:5; Prov. 14:35; Rom. 11:9), for a curse (Prov. 3:33), and for their destruction (Ps. 92:7). By these gifts he sets them *in slippery places* and casts them *down to destruction* (Ps. 73:18 in the context of verses 3–7). This is clearly seen in the way the wicked use these gifts to sin against God and to make themselves worthy of condemnation.

This is so true that we are even commanded in Scripture to imitate God in our dealings toward our enemies—to do good to them, and to do it in the understanding that if they do not repent and believe, our good deeds will be for their destruction and condemnation (Rom. 12:20–21).

It should not surprise us that a gift that is in itself good can be given for such reasons. For a father to give to his infant son a razor-sharp butcher knife—something that is indispensable in the kitchen—would certainly lead us to question whether he was giving such a "good gift" in love and pity. The child will as certainly misuse it for his own destruction as the wicked do with every good gift God gives them.

Perhaps the greatest danger, though, in the teaching of common grace is that it destroys our comfort in God. If rain and sunshine, health and life, are in themselves grace, what are we to conclude when God sends us the opposite: sickness, poverty, drought, or death? Are these things his curse? Does he send them because he hates us? If grace is in "good things," have we no grace when God does not give us those good things? Are we not rather to conclude this: that all he sends us, his people, whether health or sickness, poverty or prosperity, life or death, he sends in his love and grace and for our good (Rom. 8:28), but that everything he sends the wicked, even though it be in itself "good," is nevertheless for their condemnation? How else shall we be comforted in all our sorrows and afflictions?

Providence and the Restraint of Sin

In his providence God controls and directs all things that happen. Even men's lives in every detail are under this sovereign control of God. "He doeth," as Nebuchadnezzar said, "according to his will in the army of heaven, and among the inhabitants of the earth" (Dan. 4:35). By his providence, therefore, God also controls and directs the sinful actions of men, as is evident from the example of Nebuchadnezzar and others (1 Sam. 2:25; 2 Sam. 16:10; 2 Sam. 24:1; 1 Kings 22:19–22; Acts 2:23; Rom. 9:18). Included in this sovereign and providential work of God is a restraining of sin. God, by providence, restrains in many different ways the wickedness of men.

Scripture gives us many examples of this restraint of sin. Genesis 6:3 is the first example in Scripture. There God restrained sin by shortening the length of man's life. He also restrained sin at the time of the tower of Babel by changing man's speech. Passages that speak of God's giving someone up to sin also imply a previous restraint of some kind (Ps. 81:11–12; Acts 7:42; Rom. 1:24–28).

Many cite these passages as examples of so-called common grace. That God restrains the sin of man, they say, is evidence of a gracious disposition of God toward all men. Some would even say that this common grace is the result of a non-saving work of God in the heart and mind and will of man, that it leaves man less than *totally* depraved, and that it prepares the way for the gospel by making it possible for a man to accept or reject the gospel as an offer of saving grace.

That there is such a restraint of sin does not, however, prove that it is a matter of grace. The question "How and why is sin restrained?" must still be asked.

Scripture clearly teaches that this restraint of sin is accomplished only by God's *power,* not by any *gracious* operation of the Spirit working some change in man's depraved nature. It is much the same, therefore, as putting a muzzle on a rabid dog. It prevents him from biting, but does nothing to recover him from his madness. In this way God uses many things, especially the fear of consequences, to restrain men's wickedness without changing their hearts. One of the best examples of a sovereign but non-gracious restraint of sin is found in Isaiah 37:29, where God says to the king of Assyria, "Therefore will I put my hook in thy nose, and my bridle in thy lips, and I will turn thee back by the way by which thou camest." There is nothing gracious about that.

This same passage from Isaiah reminds us of the purpose of this restraint. It has no other purpose than the protection and preservation of God's people in the world.

The common operations of God's providence are *not* a common grace. Grace is the power by which God saves his people (Eph. 2:8–10). There is no other kind of grace besides wonderful, amazing, saving grace. Praise God for it.

The Creation of Man

We believe that man was created by God. He did not evolve. Indeed, his creation was the crown of all God's works in the beginning and a powerful testimony to the greatness of God and to man's own unique place in God's world.

Scripture shows man's uniqueness in many different ways:

- God spoke with himself before creating man—something he did not do when creating other things (Gen. 1:26).
- God created man in his own image (Gen. 1:26–27).
- God created man by a twofold act of his own (Gen. 2:7) and did not simply call him into existence as he did with the beasts, birds, and fishes.
- God created man to live in fellowship with him (Gen. 2:15–17).
- God made a special home in which man could live (Gen. 2:8).
- Having created man, God spoke to him directly (Gen. 1:28).
- God gave man dominion over all the other earthly creatures (Gen. 1:28).

The scriptural account of man's creation differs radically from evolutionary theory, which views man as different from the beasts only in degree, not in nature and kind, and certainly not in his ability to know God and to live in relationship to him. Seeing no real distinction between man and beast, evolutionists begin to confuse the two in other ways as well, speaking of "animal rights," treating fetuses as something to be thrown away, and referring to heathen people as "primitive."

More importantly, however, the unique creation of man reminds us of what a high place man had in that first creation and how much he lost through the fall. Only the glory of his first estate can explain the misery of his present state. Only one created to live in fellowship with God can now live in Satan's fellowship. Only one created so high could fall so low. Only one created for everlasting life can, by his sin, bring upon himself everlasting death.

Evolutionists cannot understand man's present condition, and so they hope for remedies in education, social reform, politics, and other such human "solutions." An evolutionist does not, and cannot, believe that man is lost, his condition miserable, and his state helpless. He cannot see that earthly and temporal solutions to man's problems are hopeless. Only in Scripture do we have a correct understanding of man's original condition and great need.

Understanding what man was, and what he has become through sin, we see that it is impossible for him to lift himself up again by his own "bootstraps," or even to find the remedy he needs. We look not for any humanly conceived solution, but to Jesus, the one, divine solution and remedy for man's misery.

Man in the Image of God

One of the most wonderful things about man's creation is that he was originally created in the image of God. He was, then, *like God* in some ways. Nothing could possibly be more wonderful than that.

Man could not be like God physically, since God is a Spirit whom no man has seen or can see (John 4:24; 1 Tim. 6:16). The likeness, therefore, was a *spiritual* likeness. The Bible tells us in Ephesians 4:24 and Colossians 3:10 that there were three spiritual ways in which man was like God. He had righteousness, holiness, and true knowledge of God. That was what man was like before he fell into sin and condemnation.

He had the image of God in order that he might know God, love him, and live in happiness with him. This is impossible for the beasts and for the brute creation, which have nothing of the image of God.

The question is often asked, however, whether fallen, sinful man has anything left of the image of God. This is an important question. If man has anything at all of the image of God in his sinful condition, there must still be something good and worthwhile in him, for God is always good. If man has nothing left of the image of God, there cannot be anything good in him anymore, for God alone is good.

The Bible gives a very clear answer to this question, and the Bible's answer is that fallen man has *nothing* left of the image of God. It is impossible to believe that the totally depraved sinner might still be like God. Jesus says in John 8:44 to the unbelieving Pharisees and to all who do not believe in him, "Ye are of your father the devil, and the lusts of your father ye will do." In other words, the only spiritual likeness men now have is the likeness of Satan, and that shows in their deeds.

The Bible also answers the question whether men still have the image of God when it says in Ephesians 4:24 and Colossians 3:10 that salvation is the renewal of the image of him who created us. When we are saved, God destroys the image of Satan in us and recreates us in his own likeness when through the Spirit of Jesus Christ he regenerates us and again gives us righteousness, holiness, and true knowledge. Ephesians 4:24 and Colossians 3:10 tell us that the image of God consists of these three gifts: righteousness, holiness, and true knowledge. Until that image is renewed and recreated, fallen and depraved man has nothing of these qualities. Only those renewed in Christ have them.

Have you been renewed in the image of God? If you say Yes, do your deeds and speech show that you are *like* him? What a shame if they do not! What a shame to say we are saved and have the image of God, but continue to behave like the devil. On the contrary, what a wonderful testimony to the saving grace of God when we are like him—imitators of him as dear children (Eph. 5:1).

Adam's Relationship to the Human Race

Because Adam stood in a certain relationship to the human race, everything he did had consequences for us. What was that relationship?

Adam was our head or representative. We know this because we are held accountable for his sin (Rom. 5:12) in the same way that parents are often held responsible for the actions of their younger children because they represent them. We know it, too, from 1 Corinthians 15:45, where Christ, our representative before God, is called the "last Adam."

That Adam was our representative means he stood in our place so that all he did was done for us. Thus we are held accountable for what Adam did as though we ourselves had done it. In this way Adam's sin is counted as ours, and we are held accountable or guilty for it.

People often complain that this is unfair, but is it really? We know for one thing that such relationships are an integral part of our life here on earth. Parents represent and act for their children. Politicians act for everyone, so that when war is declared, everyone in the country is at war, even if some do not approve of the actions of their politicians. Most importantly, however, if men say it is not right and fair that Adam is our representative, then it is not right and fair that Christ is our representative, either. We may never forget that Christ takes Adam's place and acts as the representative of his people, so that what Christ did is accounted to them, and they are found righteous and blameless before God for his sake.

Further, we have the same nature Adam had, and he had the same nature as we do, though unfallen. We cannot say, therefore, that we would have done differently or better than he did. Moreover, Adam was perfect and righteous, which is another reason we may be sure that his choice would also have been ours. When Adam fell into sin, his sin was justly charged to us, and his fall, in perfect justice, became ours.

Adam was also our father; thus we inherit our human nature—depraved, corrupt, and fallen—from him. We are born dead in trespasses and sins because Adam himself died spiritually when he fell into sin. He produced children like himself (Gen. 5:3).

We are born dead in trespasses and sins, already suffering the penalty for sin, even before we do any evil. How can that be? The answer lies in our relation to Adam as representative. Before we are born or have done good or evil, we are already responsible for his sin and therefore are born suffering the penalty for sin, the same penalty that came on him. He died spiritually as punishment for his sin and became totally depraved. We are guilty of his sin and are born under the same penalty.

There is nothing that can so powerfully impress on us the hopelessness of our condition as this fact: we are guilty in Adam even before we have opportunity to do evil and are therefore born depraved and corrupt, already suffering the penalty for sin. Only an understanding of this will convince us that the remedy for sin must come from God. As long as we do not have a correct understanding of this, we will continue to think that the remedy lies within our own power or ability or will.

Merit

Many believe that Adam was on probation in paradise, and that by continued obedience he would eventually have merited eternal, heavenly life. We believe this to be unbiblical.

We know from 1 Corinthians 15:47–48 that eternal, heavenly life comes only through "the Lord from heaven," who is our Lord Jesus Christ. Apart from him, Adam would have remained earthy.

More importantly, though, the whole idea of merit is wrong. There is no room in Scripture for merit, either by man in his present fallen condition or in the perfection of paradise.

Man can never merit with God. The notion that he can, even in a state of righteousness, ought to be eradicated from our thinking—root, stem, and branch.

Even in a sinless state, no man has anything with which he can merit. To merit or earn anything, one must first have something of his own: time, talent, or strength that he can use to merit.

But no one has anything that is really his own. "What hast thou that thou didst not receive?" Paul asks in 1 Corinthians 4:7. Even Adam before the fall would have had to answer, "Nothing!" God himself says in Psalm 50:12, "The world is mine, and the fulness thereof." Whatever we might offer him as a basis for merit is already his own. Shall we offer that to him and think that he will be pleased?

This inability of man to merit anything with God is most clearly taught in Luke 17:10. There the Word of God compares man to a slave, who does not own his own life and therefore cannot earn anything. We learn that when we "shall have done *all* those things that are commanded" us, we are still "*unprofitable* servants." According to the little parable Jesus uses, we have not even earned God's thanks any more than the slave in the parable earns his master's thanks by doing his master's will. Notice, too, that verse 10 is not talking about our present fallen state, but about a situation where we have done *all that is commanded*. This is impossible for us, but it was possible for Adam before the fall. In other words, though addressed to us, this verse in Luke actually applies better to Adam in the state of righteousness! If Adam could not merit with God, how then can we?

It is necessary, therefore, that we get rid of this pernicious idea of merit—get it out of our doctrine, our practice, and our thinking. Only then will we realize the hopelessness of our natural condition. Only when we are sure that we cannot ever merit anything with God will we see our utter dependence on grace alone and stop putting any confidence in our own works or strength. Only then will we say, "Asshur shall not save us; we will not ride upon horses: neither will we say any more to the work of our own hands, Ye are our gods: for in *thee* the fatherless findeth mercy" (Hos. 14:3).

Paradise the First

One indication that Adam was the crown of creation, the best of all God's earthly works, was that God created a special home for him in a garden called paradise in the land of Eden. There Adam lived and worked. There he walked with God until he fell into sin.

It is difficult to imagine what that first paradise was like. We do not even know where it was or what the world was like in which it was planted. There was no death, no suffering, no pain in it. All was perfect and so very much different from the world in which we now live. Adam himself was perfect in that perfect home.

Adam threw all that away when he fell into sin. He lost a beautiful garden, which was a special gift of God, and he lost the place above all other places in which he could serve God and have blessed fellowship with him. That is part of the tragedy of his fall into disobedience. In barring him from the garden, God was punishing Adam for disobedience and showing him that as a sinner he had no right anymore to the fellowship of God.

It was from the first paradise that Adam and Eve were expelled when they sinned (Gen. 3:23–24). Though that paradise was earthly, their expulsion nevertheless pictured that there is no place for sin or for sinners in the heavenly paradise. By sin, they and their descendants were excluded from all life, from all fellowship with God, and from all the service of God. Only God's grace opens the way into the heavenly paradise.

To those who receive grace, the paradise to come is pictured in the first paradise. The two even have the same name (Rev. 2:7). The same tree grows there (Rev. 2:7; Rev. 22:2). There is no suffering, no pain, no tears, and no death in the second paradise, either (Rev. 21:4). The first paradise gives us a small glimpse of what heaven will be like and assures us that what Adam lost through sin, we regain through the work of Christ, our Lord and Savior.

The existence of that first paradise is a reminder that God already had something better in mind when he planted that garden in Eden. In that first paradise all things had begun their God-ordained history that would only end in the second, heavenly paradise. That was part of God's purpose to glorify himself through creation, sin, grace, and salvation, for nothing happens apart from his purpose. The first paradise was a promise and foreshadowing of the second.

Through Christ, and as a testimony to his power, the second paradise is better than the first. There will not even be the possibility of sin in the heavenly paradise. Best of all, God will *dwell* with his people forever and be their God (Rev. 21:3). There, too, they shall see Christ, their beloved. That is joy and bliss beyond comprehension.

Two Trees

When God created the garden of Eden as Adam and Eve's home, he put into it two special trees, the tree of life and the tree of knowledge of good and evil. That these trees were in the middle of the garden (Gen. 2:9) shows how important they were.

It is difficult to answer every question about those two trees, since so little information is given. There is the question, for example, whether or not the tree of life had the power in its fruit to give life to those who ate it. Other questions follow: If the fruit did have such power, did Adam and Eve need to eat of it only once, or did they need to eat of it repeatedly to have endless life? If the fruit of the tree of knowledge of good and evil would not itself have killed Adam and Eve like a poison (Gen. 3:6), that would seem to suggest that neither would the fruit of the tree of life automatically give life. However, verse 22 appears to say otherwise. But if the tree of life *did* have the power in it to sustain or to give Adam endless life, it was very different from the tree of knowledge, which did not have power in it to destroy life.

Perhaps we cannot answer all these questions, since Scripture says so little, but there is one thing that seems obvious about the two trees in the first paradise, and that is that they represented to Adam the *antithesis*. That antithesis is the separation and opposition between God and Satan, between good and evil, between the church and world, and between believer and unbeliever.

As far as God's people are concerned, their calling with respect to that antithesis is to say Yes to God and to God's law, and to say No to the devil and to sin. This is the essence of their spiritual separation from the world of sin in which they live (2 Cor. 6:14–18). This is always man's calling in relation to God.

In the garden the two trees set that same calling before Adam and Eve. By eating of the tree of life (the how and when makes no real difference), they would be saying Yes to God. By not eating of the tree of knowledge of good and evil, they would be saying No to the devil, to sin, and to disobedience. That was the reason they might not eat. There was no other reason for them *not* to eat of the tree of knowledge, for apart from God's command, it was "good for food" and "pleasant to the eyes."

Adam and Eve ate and failed and fell into sin. We continue in their sin whenever we say Yes to the devil and No to God and to God's law. Nevertheless, the calling they had, represented by those two trees, never changed. And because it did not change, redemption could come only through our Lord Jesus Christ, whose life was both a great Yes to God and to God's law, and an equally great No to all sin and to the devil, seen so clearly in his temptations in the wilderness. Thank God for the second Adam and for what he has done.

The Devil's Lie

One of the two special trees that God placed in the garden of Eden was the tree of knowledge of good and evil. Adam and Eve were forbidden to eat the fruit of that tree. When they did, they fell from God's favor into sin and death.

Why was the tree called "the tree of knowledge of good and evil"? That question must be answered because of the devil's lie (Gen. 3:5). The devil had said, "Ye shall be as gods, knowing good and evil," and Adam and Eve listened to him.

What the devil said was a lie. He always lies. We do *not* know good and evil by "tasting" evil and by disobeying God. Nevertheless, the devil still tells that lie, and men still listen. He tells men that they must "experience" evil, try it, in order truly to know it, and they are delighted to listen.

That, apparently, was the lie Jezebel was teaching in the church of Thyatira (Rev. 2:20–24). She was, we understand, teaching God's servants to commit fornication and to eat things sacrificed to idols (v. 20) in order, as she and her followers said, that they might *know* "the depths of Satan" (v. 24).

Christian parents hear that lie when they are told not to shelter their children from the evil world in which we live. Their children, they are told, must get out into the *real* world to find out what the world is like. They must experience it in order to know it, but that is not the way we or our children learn good and evil.

The truth is that we know good and evil only by *not* tasting evil—by forsaking it and fleeing from it. Think of fallen man. Having eaten of the tree of knowledge, he was *no longer able* to discern good and evil. Just as God knows evil by being wholly separated from it, so also do we.

Nevertheless, that was not *all* the devil meant. He meant, too, that Adam and Eve would have the right to *determine for themselves* what was good and evil. In that sense they would "know good and evil" by eating of the tree. They would then be *like God*, or so the devil said. Fallen man, in obedience to the devil, listened to that lie and continues to claim the right to decide for himself what is right and wrong.

God was referring to the same thing when he said, "The man is become as one of us." He meant that man had assumed for himself what belongs only to God, the right to determine good and evil. Having done so, man might no longer eat of the tree of life. He *could* no longer be allowed to put forth his hand to the tree of life and live forever as one who stood in open rebellion against God. So God banished him from the garden and from that tree of life.

All the evil that has come upon the human race has come because first Eve, then Adam, listened to Satan's lie. Having been told the truth in God's Word, let us listen to that lie no more, but know good and evil in the right way: by listening to what God says and by forsaking and separating ourselves from evil with all our heart.

The Tree of Knowledge of Good and Evil

We have explained the presence of the two special trees that God planted in the garden of Eden, Adam and Eve's first home. Now we should say something about the purpose of the tree of knowledge of good and evil in light of the Word of God in Deuteronomy 8:2–3. We believe that the tree of knowledge of good and evil represented the important spiritual principle taught in these verses: "And thou shalt remember all the way which the LORD thy God led thee these forty years in the wilderness, to humble thee, to know what was in thine heart, whether thou wouldest keep his commandments, or no. And he humbled thee, and suffered thee to hunger, and fed thee with manna, which thou knewest not, neither did thy fathers know; that he might make thee know that man doth not live by bread alone, but by every word that proceedeth out of the mouth of the LORD doth man live."

Let us begin by remembering that the fruit of the tree was itself good. There is no reason to think that what Eve saw when she looked at the tree was not true. It was "good for food," "pleasant to the eyes," and "a tree to be desired to make one wise" (Gen. 3:6), and so she had already begun to desire it, contrary to God's command. Why, then, had God forbidden the eating of it?

The answer is found in Deuteronomy 8:2–3. God was teaching Adam and Eve that man does not live by bread alone, but by the Word of God. There is more to life, God was saying, than mere physical existence; more to life than the life of the body, which is sustained by eating. Life for man is fellowship with the living God through obedience to God's Word.

As Homer Hoeksema says, "That tree offered bread to Adam, good bread, prepared from the earth. And yet it offered bread he might not eat! Instead comes the word of God, commanding him that . . . from this one tree he must abstain . . . By abstaining from the tree of knowledge of good and evil, Adam would exercise that other, higher, spiritual side of his life; he would obey in loving friendship and service of the Lord his God, and thus truly live."[2]

Adam's choice was to satisfy the lusts of the flesh rather than to obey God. He was the first (with Eve) whose god was his belly, the first to "mind earthly things" (Phil. 3:19). So men have lived ever since, satisfying the desires of the flesh and of the mind, not counting God's favor better than life. They are still trying to live by bread alone without the Word of God.

But where Adam fell, Christ stood. Not only did Christ tell us again that man does not live by bread alone (Matt. 4:4), he also stood to that principle, though perishing of hunger after forty days in the wilderness. Filling the wilderness with bread enough to satisfy all the hungry of the world by turning stones into bread was not as important to him as obedience to God. Would that the church today felt the same.

But what happened in the wilderness was really just the story of Jesus' whole ministry. Even his death was a testimony that for him, as for no other, obedience to God was more important than earthly life and the things that sustain it. He obeyed even unto death. And so he redeemed his elect among the fallen children of Adam.

The Tree of Life

The other special tree that God himself planted in the garden of Eden was the tree of life. This tree also was of the greatest possible significance to Adam and Eve.

There is the question whether that tree had the power in itself to give earthly life. The words God spoke when he barred Adam and Eve from eating of the tree (Gen. 3:22) would seem to suggest that it did, but even so, that was not the main significance of the tree.

The tree was there to represent to Adam and Eve the truth that life

---

2. Homer C. Hoeksema, *From Creation to the Flood,* Unfolding Covenant History: An Exposition of the Old Testament, vol. 1 (Grandville, MI.: Reformed Free Publishing Association, 2000), 119.

consists in obedience to God. Even the law testifies of that (Gal. 3:21), though it cannot itself give life. When Adam and Eve chose disobedience, it was impossible for them to continue to "live" in the true sense of that word. They had to die, and so among other things God took away from them the right to eat of the tree of life.

The tree of life represented to them the fact, very important and significant for us also, that obedience does not merely consist in forsaking evil—in *not doing* what God has forbidden. If that were true, then the drunkard who dries out but is not converted would be living in obedience to God, when in fact he is not.

There is always a positive aspect to obedience: what we described in an earlier chapter as saying Yes to God. Without that love of God and desire to please him, mere outward obedience is an abomination. Isaiah speaks of that when he says that offering a sacrifice without the love of God is no different in God's sight from slaying a man or cutting off a dog's neck (Isa. 66:3). Paul says the same thing when he reminds us that "whatsoever is not of faith is sin" (Rom. 14:23).

Those who do *not* love God, and do not say Yes to him with all their heart, mind, soul, and strength, do no good. Their outward conformity to God's law only shows that they know that law but do not know and love God. By such "obedience" they only increase their condemnation. True obedience is turning *from* sin, but it is also turning *to* God with all our heart and strength.

In the new creation there will only be the tree of life (Rev. 22:2). The tree of knowledge of good and evil will not be there. Sin and death and Satan will not be there, either, and our obedience will no longer consist in having to say No to them. Our obedience will be purely and completely the loving service of God himself.

For us, therefore, the tree of life represents Christ. Not only is he the source of our life everlastingly, as the first tree was meant to be the source of Adam and Eve's life, but also he is the one in whom our obedience to God is perfected. He is the one who said Yes to God on our behalf, even unto death. He is the one upon whom we feed and who nourishes our souls unto everlasting life so that we, too, may say Yes to God with all that we are and with all that we have. In the new creation, through feeding on him and enjoying him, there will no longer be the possibility of saying No to God.

Wonderful, is it not?

The Fall of Man

The most tragic event in all the history of the world was not the holocaust, not the world wars, not the great depression, nor any other such human or natural disaster, but the fall of man into sin. That one event is the explanation of all the misery, trouble, and suffering that is in the world. Except for the fall, there would be no death, no sickness, no war, no hospitals, no pain, and no alienation from God.

Let us note that it is *man's* fall that brought this all about. Let us not complain about God and suggest that if he is a God of love and mercy, such misery could not be. It is not God but man who is to blame for these things.

This misery has come upon us, not only because Adam sinned, but also because his sin was the sin of all (Rom. 5:12). Because he sinned, and we with him, death and the other consequences of sin came on everyone: "And so death passed upon all men, for that all have sinned."

That testimony of Scripture may not be destroyed by suggesting that the story of the fall as recorded in Genesis 3 is not historical truth. If we do that, we can no longer explain man's condition, the state of the world in which he lives, and the necessity of Christ's coming as the second Adam.

There are several other things we should know about the fall that are of abiding importance.

First, Eve sinned initially; for this reason the woman must be in subjection in the church (1 Tim. 2:11–14) and suffers in childbearing (Gen. 3:16).

Second, the first sin was committed by the instigation of the devil. By his lies and deceit he murdered Adam and Eve and their descendants (John 8:44); yet because they willingly listened to his lies, they, too, are responsible for the fall and its consequences.

Third, the fall of man is the reason also why man cannot blame God for his spiritual condition. Though all are born "dead" in sin, God had created man perfect and gave us a perfect representative in Adam. In Adam man willingly chose against God and threw away all the good gifts God had given him.

Fourth, the lie through which man fell is the same lie he still listens to and believes today: "Ye shall be as gods" (Gen. 3:5). In exalting his own "free will," in insisting that he is the captain of his own fate, in his godless teachings, philosophies, and ways of living, man pretends to be a law unto himself and denies God's sovereignty and rule. He shows that he still listens to Satan's lie.

Do you believe that *you* fell with Adam, that his fall is not only mankind's fall but yours also? If you do, you know why Christ alone can save us and why we must believe in him.

Sin and Its Consequences

Most would agree that the world is in terrible shape. Civil unrest is prevalent throughout the world. Crime continues to increase. We are involved in "wars" on drugs, terrorism, and violence. The creation itself is being ruined, and even the weather patterns of the world seem to be changing.

Some insist that the solutions to these problems must be found in radical changes in governments or in governmental policies, in environmental awareness, and in education. Others claim that vast sums of money must be committed to insure necessary changes. People must be assured of adequate education, housing, and other necessities of life. Only then will there be change for the better.

What so many refuse to see is that man has a "heart problem." This heart problem can be traced back to its beginning in the fall and disobedience of our first parents, Adam and Eve. These two were created perfect and capable of loving and serving God without sin.

However, Adam sinned in eating of the fruit of the forbidden tree (Gen. 3). Our first parents listened to the lie of the devil, who came to them in the serpent (Gen. 3:1–5; Rev. 12:9). Man believed that he could become as God.

What God threatened came on Adam for his sin: he died. This affected his physical existence, which ends in the grave; and it resulted in everlasting punishment in hell unless a way of deliverance were provided.

The consequences of this sin of Adam have had a devastating effect on all of mankind. Adam was the representative and first father of all. His one sin brought death upon all (Rom. 5:12). The sad result is that all are born spiritually dead and thus incapable of doing any good (Romans 3:10–19).

The heart problem of man has been called "total depravity," that is, the inability to do anything right in God's sight. Scripture speaks of a "stony heart" (Ezek. 11:19) and an "evil heart" (Jer. 16:12). A stony heart in relation to God is the cause of all man's troubles.

Those consequences of sin affect not only man's life in this world, but also his hope of the world to come. Except a person is first born again, he cannot even see the kingdom of heaven (John 3:3). If man's life is to be blessed again, there must be new life and a new or "clean heart" (Ps. 51:10), which must originate from God himself.

Only when God has finished his great work of grace, regenerating and renewing his people, will there be any hope of an end to the evil consequences of sin. Because of sin even this present world must be cleansed and the everlasting kingdom of Christ be brought in. Politics, education, and social reform will not do that.

Original Sin

The Bible teaches us that even if we have never sinned—never done anything wrong—we would still be counted sinners before God. This is the biblical doctrine of *original sin*.

When you hear of original sin, the reference is to Adam's sin and to the fact that God holds us responsible for that first sin of Adam. We are as guilty as he was of that first disobedience—so guilty that we are punished as he was. We are born dead in trespasses and sin, suffering the penalty that God announced in the beginning (Gen. 2:17).

You will find this doctrine of original sin in Romans 5:12. There we are reminded that when Adam sinned, death came on the whole human race. Notice that this verse does not say that death will come when all have sinned, but that it has already come upon all, because all sinned. At some point in the past, everyone sinned, even those yet unborn, and so they are born dead in trespasses and sins. When did everyone sin so that all are born dead in sin? The only possible answer, the answer of Romans 5:12, is that all sinned in Adam.

There are two parts to original sin. There is, first, that all sinned in Adam and are held guilty of his sin. This is usually referred to as "original guilt" and comes to every man because Adam represented all men before God. Second, being already guilty, even before birth, all men also come into the world suffering the punishment of sin, which is eternal death. They are *born* dead in trespasses and sins (Eph. 2:1). That part of original sin—the punishment that comes upon them at birth—is referred to as "original pollution" or "depravity."

Most people do not like this teaching because it seems to them so unfair. But it is really not unfair at all. In many other areas of our lives, we accept responsibility for the actions of others without thinking it unfair. When our political leaders make laws, we are held responsible for those laws. Parents are held responsible in many cases for the behavior of their children. This is simply part of human life. But even in salvation this holds true. We do not complain or think it unfair that Christ accepts responsibility for us and for all our sins as our Savior. Yet our salvation comes through him in the same way that sin came through Adam.

Original sin is a very important doctrine of the Bible, and it is of the greatest personal importance. It teaches us how completely lost we are as sinners and shows us that there is no possibility of salvation except in Jesus Christ. We learn from this doctrine that even if we never committed any sin, God would still be angry with us and punish us eternally. That leaves us with nowhere else to go but to the cross of Christ for help and salvation.

Do you know that you were born with original sin? Did you know that even your smallest children are infected with it from birth? Did you know that the only cure for this horrible "disease" is the work of Jesus Christ? That is the reason the Bible calls us to believe in him, and only in him, for salvation.

Total Depravity

Many of our readers are acquainted with the Five Points of Calvinism, sometimes also called "The Doctrines of Grace." These five truths, taken together, teach the sovereignty of God in salvation, in other words, that salvation is all of God and does not depend on our will or works.

The first of these Five Points is *total depravity*. It shows why salvation must be all of God and all of his grace.

The word *depravity* refers to our sinfulness and wickedness. We use the word to emphasize that we are *very* wicked in God's sight and in great need of his salvation.

When we describe depravity as "total," we mean three things.

First, *all men,* except Jesus, are depraved and wicked (Ps. 14:2–3).

Second, all men are depraved *in every part.* Not only their deeds are wicked in God's sight, but also their thoughts (Gen. 6:5), their wills (their choosing and desiring) (Eph. 2:3; Eph. 4:22), their emotions, and even their hearts (Jer. 17:9). That the will is depraved is especially important to know because it means that without grace *no one can choose* to be saved. Salvation must depend on God's will, not man's.

Third, all men are depraved in every part *completely.* The will, the heart, and the rest are not only partly depraved. Every part of man is totally depraved in that there is *no good at all* in any part. This is often denied, and the suggestion is made that though there is a great deal of evil in man, there is always a little good in him also: "some evil in the best of us and some good in the worst of us." Especially this suggestion is made regarding man's salvation. Man, it is said, cannot save himself, but he has sufficient good to *choose* to be saved.

We would not deny that much of what men do is judged good by other people. Yet God judges it all as evil. In his sight, no one can do any good, or even want to do any good. God judges by a higher standard than we do, and he requires that everything be done in faith and for his glory. If not, it is not good (Rom. 14:23; 1 Cor. 10:31).

God's judgment of the human race is recorded in Psalm 14, which is the only psalm repeated in Scripture (see Ps. 53). Psalm 14 clearly shows God's judgment of us: "The Lord looked down from heaven upon the children of men, to see if there were any that did understand, and seek God" (v. 2). And what is his judgment? "They are *all* gone aside, they are *all together* become filthy: there is *none* that doeth good, no, *not one*" (v. 3).

Ephesians 2:1 sums up the doctrine of total depravity by saying that we are *dead* in trespasses and sins. Our condition cannot be worse. Dead in sins, we have not the smallest stirring of any spiritual life. We are *totally* depraved.

When by grace we begin to understand this, we also begin to see our great need for the cross of Jesus Christ, for nothing else can save totally depraved sinners.

Man's So-called Free Will

At the time of the Protestant Reformation, Martin Luther wrote a book entitled *The Bondage of the Will.* This book was written against a man named Erasmus and his teaching that man's will is "free"; that is, that he has the ability to choose whether or not he will be saved. In his book Luther told Erasmus that this question about free will was the most important issue of the Reformation. He said to Erasmus, "[You] have not worried me with extraneous issues about the papacy, purgatory, indulgences, and such like—trifles, rather than issues… You, and you alone, have seen the hinge on which all turns, and have aimed for the vital spot."[3]

Over against Erasmus' teaching, Luther wrote that fallen man is not "free" to choose what is good and pleasing to God, but that his will—his ability to choose—is in bondage to sin. In spite of what Luther wrote, the teaching of Erasmus concerning free will has become the teaching of most of Protestantism today.

With Luther we believe that man's will is in bondage to sin and that he not only cannot do good, but that he cannot even *want* (will) to do it (Rom. 8:7–8). Especially man cannot do the great good of choosing God and Christ. We believe, therefore, that man cannot believe in Christ unless it is given him from above (compare with John 6:44).

We also believe that not man's will, but God's sovereign and eternal will (predestination) is and must be the decisive thing in salvation (Acts 13:48; Phil. 2:13). If man cannot choose to be saved, God must choose for him. This God does when he sovereignly determines who shall be saved and determines to give to the saved every blessing of salvation by his own sovereign and all-powerful grace.

The false doctrine of free will, then, denies many important truths.

First, it is *a denial of predestination.* Predestination means that God's *will* (God's choice) determines all things, including who will be saved (Eph. 1:3–6). The doctrine of free will teaches that man's choice is the important thing in salvation.

Second, it is *a denial of the biblical truth that saving faith is a gift of God* (Eph. 2:8–10). The teaching of free will says that faith is a person's own decision to trust in Christ.

---

3. Martin Luther, *The Bondage of the Will,* trans. J. I. Packer and O. R. Johnston (London: James Clarke, 1957), 319 in "Conclusion."

Third, it is *a denial of the truth that Christ died only for his people* (Matt. 1:21). Those who believe in free will teach that Christ died for all without exception and that their salvation now depends on their accepting him, that is, on their freewill choice.

Fourth, it is *a denial of the wonderful truth that salvation is by grace alone* (Eph. 2:8–10). The teaching of free will is that man must "do something" in order to be saved, whereas Scripture teaches that salvation "is not of him that willeth, nor of him that runneth" (Rom. 9:16).

Belief in the free will of man also shows itself in the kind of preaching and evangelism that is most popular today, the kind that begs sinners to accept Christ, that uses altar calls, appeals, decision times, raising of hands, and other such tactics to persuade people to accept Christ as their Savior. All these things presuppose that a person's salvation depends on his own choice.

Some may ask if there is a point of preaching the gospel to all. But the gospel is "the power of God unto salvation" (Rom. 1:16), the way in which God gives faith and repentance to all those whom he has chosen from eternity and redeemed in Christ. May it be that power unto salvation for many.

— *part 3* —

CHRIST AND HIS WORK

The Names of Our Savior

The Bible attaches great importance to the names of Jesus. In theology these names are so important that they are usually treated as a separate section.

The name *Jesus,* for example, is so important that it was given to Joseph by God's own messenger before Christ was born. The meaning of that name, as revealed by the angel, is a gospel in miniature in which every part of the name is a sermon (Matt. 1:21). It is by that name that men are saved (Acts 4:12).

The name *Christ* is so full of significance that Jesus pronounced Peter "blessed" for confessing it, telling him that the only way he could have known that name is by revelation from God (Matt. 16:17). That name confessed is the immovable foundation of the church (v. 18) and the proof of regeneration (1 John 5:1). Anyone who does not confess it is denounced in 1 and 2 John as an antichrist and a deceiver (1 John 2:22; 1 John 4:3; 2 John 7).

Likewise, concerning the name *Lord,* we are told that no one can say that Jesus is Lord but by the Holy Spirit, so great is that name (1 Cor. 12:3). And what is true of the name *Lord* is true of all the names of our Savior.

Jesus' names are important because, unlike our names, they tell us exactly *who* and *what* he is. They are part of God's revelation to us in Jesus Christ and are therefore a very important part of the gospel message, the good tidings of salvation. To know and confess these names is to be saved.

That is why there are so many names of Jesus and of God and of the Holy Spirit given in Scripture. Depending on how one counts, there are as many as 150 different names of Jesus in Scripture. What a blessing to know them all and what they mean!

However, it is not the mere repetition or meaningless chanting of the names that is blessed and brings blessing. The *knowledge* of what those names mean, learned from the Word of God, is what matters. Through that knowledge, our faith is strong; we know whom we believe and are persuaded of the saving power of Jesus (2 Tim. 1:12). There must be faith in his names—the faith that he is everything his names declare him to be. But without knowledge, faith is very weak.

This needs emphasis. There are many who think that the mere

recitation of these names has some kind of power. There is no basis in Scripture for this belief. The saving power of Christ's names is only through faith in him who is known and loved by those names, and faith must *know* from his names who and what he is.

Do you know Jesus' names? Do you know *him* by his names—know him personally and savingly? Do you love his names and love them enough to confess his names before the world? If you do, then you, too, like Peter, are blessed.

The Name *Jesus*

The name *Jesus* is special among all the names of our Savior. It is his *personal* name. Many of his other names are really *titles,* not personal names. This is true especially of names like *Christ* and *Lord. Jesus,* however, is the name that was given him by his own Father and the name by which he is known and loved in the family of God. It is the name above all others by which we talk to him and about him.

When we remember the meaning of the name *Jesus,* we realize how wonderful this name is. His personal name in the family of God is one that means "Savior" or "Jehovah saves." Think of it. Every time we speak to him or about him personally we are saying that he and he alone is Savior, God's Savior.

The meaning of the name *Jesus* was revealed by the angel Gabriel when he announced the birth of Jesus to Joseph: "Thou shalt call his name JESUS," the angel said, "for he shall save his people from their sins" (Matt. 1:21). What a wealth of meaning there is, therefore, in that one name!

Because Jesus' personal name refers to Jehovah (the *Je-* is a shortened form of the name *Jehovah*), the message of the angel concerning the name *Jesus* means that it is *Jehovah* who saves. No one else can. Jesus is *God's* Savior, not only because he comes from God, but also because it is God alone who saves through him.

Jesus' name speaks, too, of the certainty of salvation for all who believe in him. He *shall save* his people! He is a sure and certain Savior, and he is that because he comes from God and brings God's great salvation.

His name even speaks of the fact that he saves those, and those only, whom the Father gave to him, namely *his people.* He is not the Savior of all men without exception. To some that seems a terrible truth, but to those who understand it, it is a blessed and wonderful truth. That he saves some only means that he is not one who only tries to be a Savior and fails with many, but one who surely and infallibly saves all those who are his own by gift of God.

Jesus' name reminds us, too, that he is a Savior from *sin.* Many do not want such a Savior. They only want someone who will fill their bellies, heal their bodies, and solve their present problems. But those who by grace know themselves to be sinners before God and who pray, "God be merciful to me a sinner," like the publican in the temple, not daring to lift up their eyes (Luke 18:13), find in Christ their heart's desire and the assurance that there is a way of escape, of pardon, and of peace with God.

What a blessing to know him as Jesus! Truly there is "none other name under heaven given among men, whereby we must be saved" (Acts 4:12). May many know that name, not as the name of a mere man who lived several thousand years ago, but as the name of God's Son, their Savior.

The Name *Christ*

The name *Christ* is not the same kind of name as Jesus. Jesus is the personal name of the Savior, but Christ is a *title.* Like other titles—President, Prime Minister, Member of Parliament, and Congressman—it describes the *position and work* Jesus has in the kingdom of God.

For this reason Jesus is sometimes called *the* Christ in the same way that someone else might be called *the* President. The difference is that Christ is unique. There never was, nor ever will be, another Christ.

Christ means "anointed one" (*Messiah* means the same and is the Old Testament equivalent of the name *Christ*). It refers to Jesus' special appointment and ordination by God to do the work of God's kingdom. He was publicly anointed with the Spirit at the time of his baptism (Matt. 3:16), as was foretold in Isaiah 61:1–3, where his work as the anointed one is also described.

What is Christ's position and work in the kingdom of God?

It is that of a *Prophet, Priest,* and *King.* The Heidelberg Catechism, one of the great Reformation creeds, asks, "Why is he called Christ, that is, anointed?" The answer given is, "Because he is ordained of God the Father, and anointed with the Holy Ghost, to be our chief Prophet and Teacher, who has fully revealed to us the secret counsel and will of God concerning our redemption; and to be our only High Priest, who by the one sacrifice of his body, has redeemed us, and makes continual intercession with the Father for us; and also to be our eternal King, who governs us by his Word and Spirit, and who defends and preserves us (in the enjoyment of) that salvation he has purchased for us."[1]

This reference to Christ's prophetic, priestly, and kingly offices in the name *Christ* is the reason the name is so important. It is the foundation of the church (Matt. 16:18), for the church cannot exist without Christ's work as Prophet, Priest, and King. The name *Christ*, confessed, is the proof of regeneration (1 John 5:1), for no one can believe in him unless Christ has spoken to him as Prophet, sacrificed for him as Priest, and delivered him from Satan as King.

To confess that Jesus is Christ is not merely to speak the name, but to say that he is *our* chief Prophet and Teacher, *our* only High Priest, and *our* eternal King. It is an acknowledgment that we will be taught by him alone, ruled by him alone, and blessed by him alone. No wonder, then, that no one can say that Jesus is the Christ except by a gift from heaven.

That Jesus is Christ means, too, that he is the only one who can hold these offices and perform the work that belongs to them. We need not that any *man* teach us (1 John 2:27). We need no other priest or sacrifice! We acknowledge no other King, for he is King of kings and Lord of lords. He is unique.

Confessing that Jesus is the Christ, we seek salvation in him alone.

The Name *Lord*

A most important name of our Savior is the wonderful name *Lord*. Like the name *Christ*, Lord is not a personal name, but a title of honor.

This title is important because it reminds us that Jesus is God. One

---

1. Heidelberg Catechism, Lord's Day 12, Q&A 31.

should need no further proof of his divinity than this: that he is identified in Scripture as *the Lord*. "My Lord" and "my God" are really one and the same confession (John 20:28).

The title *Lord* emphasizes especially Jesus' sovereign *ownership* of all things. As Lord he not only rules over all with sovereign authority and power, but all things *belong* to him and are his servants as well.

It is as *the Lord* that God says in Psalm 50:12, "The world is mine, and the fulness thereof." That means, as the psalmist confesses to God in Psalm 119:91, that "all are thy servants." That lordship, God has given to Jesus (Acts 2:36).

There are two sides, though, to the lordship of Jesus. On the one hand, he holds rightful ownership of all things as their Creator, ruling them with sovereign might according to his purpose. This aspect of the lordship of Christ is sometimes called *the rule of his power*. As Lord of all, he sovereignly uses all things, even against their own will, for his own purposes.

But there is also what is called *the rule of his grace*. In this sense he is Lord only of his people, and he is that by right of purchase. His people belong to him, not merely as do the sun, moon, and stars, but as a purchased treasure: "They shall be mine, saith the Lord of hosts, in that day when I make up my jewels" (Mal. 3:17). Jesus exercises that lordship over them not by mere power, but by the sweet influences of his grace. He rules them not with a rod of iron (Ps. 2:9), but with a shepherd's staff (Ps. 23:1).

This is the aspect of his lordship that can be confessed only through the Holy Spirit (1 Cor. 12:3). If I confess his lordship in this way, I not only acknowledge that he is Lord, but also that he is *my* Lord. Then I confess that I belong to him and am precious in his sight, not because of what I am or what I have done, but because of the blood he shed for me.

Furthermore, I am then confessing that all I have belongs to him as well. Nothing I have is really my own—not my family, not my time, not my possessions, not even my body: "For ye are bought with a price: therefore glorify God in your body, and in your spirit, which are God's" (1 Cor. 6:20). Belonging to him with all I am and all I have, I must use all things in his service and for his glory and kingdom.

Do you make that confession that Jesus is Lord—*your* Lord? Do you live and use everything as belonging to him? Then he is indeed your Lord and your God.

The Name *Only Begotten Son of God*

Only begotten Son of God! What a wealth of glorious truth there is in this name of our Savior! Everything else we believe about him depends on the truth of this name. If he were *not* the only begotten Son of God, he would be nothing to us.

This name is part of the biblical truth that Jesus Christ is God, equal in all things to the Father. Though many today deny it, even the unbelieving Jews of Jesus' day understood what he was claiming. When he called himself the Son of God, they took up stones to kill him for blasphemy (John 8:59; John 10:30–42). They understood far better than many do today. The cults, oneness doctrine, and other anti-trinitarian teachings read the name *only begotten Son of God* and do not even recognize what it means. It ought either to be the truth to them, or the most horrible blasphemy, for the name *only begotten Son* teaches his divinity even more powerfully than the name *Son of God*. It shows that among all God's children, Jesus is unique, the eternal and natural Son of God.

The truth expressed in this name *only begotten Son* is often compromised by the modern Bible versions. Not only do they retranslate many important verses like 1 Timothy 3:16 so that they make *no* reference to Christ's divinity, but they also retranslate this name, usually as "only son" (Revised Version, Revised Standard Version, English Standard Version) or "one and only Son" (New International Version), something that is not even true. Jesus is *not* the only son of God; he is the "*only begotten* son" (John 3:16, 18). We are sons of God also, but we are not "begotten." We are sons "adopted" by grace for Christ's sake.

We must understand that not only is this name an exact and literal translation of the Greek, but it is *the* name with which the church of Christ has defended the truth of his divinity against all comers. It ought not, therefore, be tampered with by those who claim to be retranslating the Word of God, even if their efforts are legitimate—although we believe they are not.

Another aspect of the great truth that Jesus is God's only begotten Son is that his sonship is the basis and reason for ours. For this reason he is also called the "firstborn" (Heb. 12:23) or "first begotten" (Heb. 1:6). In Scripture the firstborn is the one who opens the womb (Ex. 13:2). As firstborn in the family of God, Jesus is the one who opens the way out of the "womb" of death and the grave for all his brethren when they are reborn into God's family as sons and daughters. Without him we would be as children who come to birth, but could not be brought forth. Looking ahead to his work as firstborn, every firstborn was specially dedicated to God in the Old Testament.

Like the other names of Christ, this is not a name that can be confessed abstractly. The only way for me or for you to confess this name is to say that the *only begotten Son of God* is *my* God. And to say that he is my God is to find in his divinity, as it is uniquely expressed in this name, a sure foundation for believing in him and hoping in his mercy.

The Name *Son of Man*

Jesus is not only the Son of God; he is also the *Son of man*. This name *Son of man* emphasizes the real *humanity* of our Savior.

It is the name Jesus uses for himself, and it is found most often in the gospel according to Luke, just as we would expect. In the same way that John emphasizes the wonderful truth that Jesus is God and uses the name *Son of God* most often, so Luke emphasizes the truth that Jesus is like us in all things except sin, and uses the name *Son of man*. Luke's emphasis on the humanity of Christ is also why the story of Christ's birth and childhood is told most fully by Luke.

That Jesus is the Son of man means that he was born into this world as we are, that he lived and died here, that he is "one bone and one flesh" with us, and that he is as really and truly part of the human race as we are. It even means that he was "in all points tempted like as we are, yet without sin" (Heb. 4:15).

That Jesus is fully and truly man is as important as the truth that he is God. If he were not a man, like us in all things, he could not be our Savior. As a man he takes Adam's place (1 Cor. 15:45 – 47) and represents us before God. As our representative, he takes our sins upon himself, assumes full responsibility for them, and makes atonement for us.

If he were *not* man, he could not have suffered and died. If he were not fully human, he could not in justice have taken our place on the cross and been punished for our sins, for man must suffer for man's sin. If he were not like us in all things, he could not be a merciful and sympathetic

High Priest who is "touched with the feeling of our infirmities" (Heb. 4:15).

As a man, Jesus is the one in whom dwells all the fullness of the Godhead *bodily* (Col 2:9). He is therefore the one through whom and by whom we know the invisible and all-glorious God, the one in whose face shines "the light of the knowledge of the glory of God" (2 Cor. 4:6). "He that hath seen me," Jesus says, "hath seen the Father" (John 14:9).

There is, then, great comfort for believers in the name *Son of man*. The name is Jesus' own way of telling us that he has lived here on earth, suffered the same things we suffer, been tempted in all points as we are, died our death, and been raised again to eternal glory. It assures us that he knows our needs, not only as the one who knows all things, but also as the one who himself has had those same needs "in the days of his flesh" (Heb. 5:7). It convinces us that he is able to help us in all our weaknesses and infirmities, since he knows them all firsthand. It is the assurance that man has made atonement for man's sin and that Christ's death has saving power. As the Son of man, Jesus truly is our Elder Brother.

The Name *Immanuel*

The name *Immanuel,* or *Emmanuel,* is found only twice in Scripture, in the promise of Isaiah 7:14 and in its fulfillment in Matthew 1:23.

The name means "God with us," the *-el* ending being the Hebrew word for "God," and the rest of the name meaning "with us." This is, in fact, the interpretation of the name given through the angel Gabriel by God himself in Matthew 1:23.

The name was first announced in the Old Testament to King Ahaz by the prophet Isaiah in Isaiah 7:14. It was announced as part of the sign God was giving Ahaz, a sign to assure the faithful in Judah that God had not forsaken them in a very difficult time and that he never would forsake them.

Later, when the prophecy of Isaiah was fulfilled in the birth and naming of Christ, God showed how he would be with his people and why he would never forsake them. He would be with them *in Immanuel,* and never forsake them *for Immanuel's sake.*

The name *Immanuel,* therefore, means that Jesus is God and man in one person. In him, God is with us in the closest possible way, taking our human nature into union with himself. Thus the name *Immanuel* is the fulfillment of all God's covenant promises to be the God of his people and to dwell with them.

Indeed, Jesus as Immanuel is himself the realization of that covenant of friendship and fellowship. Through the union of the divine and human natures in himself, Jesus makes us partakers of the divine nature (2 Pet. 1:4), and as the only begotten Son of God, he dwells with us and in us in unbreakable union (Gal. 2:20), so that he is one bone and one flesh with us (Eph. 5:30).

As Immanuel, Jesus is the true tabernacle or temple of God and fulfills the promise of Revelation 21:3: "And I heard a great voice out of heaven saying, Behold, the tabernacle of God is with men, and he will dwell with them, and they shall be his people, and God himself shall be with them, and be their God." That is the reason there is no temple in the new Jerusalem, for "the Lord God Almighty and the Lamb [as Immanuel] are the temple of it" (v. 22).

The name *Immanuel* also refers to the *work* of Christ, for God cannot be "with" sinners except through atonement for sin. The name, then, is a reminder that "God was in Christ, reconciling the world unto himself" (2 Cor. 5:19). God is with us in Immanuel as the one who comes to us in our lost condition, takes our sins upon himself, and thus removes all our sins in order to redeem and deliver us from them.

What a blessing that name *Immanuel* is, therefore, to all who believe in it. In one word, it is the whole gospel message, teaching us about our Savior and about the blessedness of salvation in him.

A Name above Every Name

There are many names for our Savior recorded in the pages of Scripture. All of them are given to us by God to teach us the glory and power of Jesus as Savior. Some of the most important names we have already studied: Jesus, Christ, Lord, only begotten Son of God, Son of man, and Immanuel.

His many other names are important also. They emphasize various things about him. Names such as *rose of Sharon* and *lily of the valleys*

(Song of Sol. 2:1) emphasize his beauty as the Savior. Names like *Lion of the tribe of Judah* (Rev. 5:5) and *prince of the kings of the earth* (Rev. 1:5) remind us of his kingly power.

Other names, such as *son of David* (Matt. 1:1), *root of David* (Rev. 22:16), *Head* (Col. 2:19), and *bridegroom* (Matt. 9:15), show him in his relationship to the church, in both the Old and New Testaments.

There are also names that speak of the Savior's humiliation, such as *root out of a dry ground* (Isa. 53:2), and others that speak of his exaltation, like *Lord of glory* (1 Cor. 2:8). There are names that tell of his divinity: *image of the invisible God* (Col. 1:15), *Wonderful, Counselor, The mighty God, The everlasting Father* (Isa. 9:6), *the Word* (John 1:1), and *Alpha and Omega* (Rev. 1:8). Other names emphasize his humanity: *firstborn* (Col. 1:15), *first begotten of the dead* (Rev. 1:5), and *son of David* (Matt. 21:9).

Many of the Savior's names describe his work: *Lamb of God* (John 1:29), *The Prince of Peace* (Isa. 9:6), *the good shepherd* (John 10:11), and *Governor* (Matt. 2:6). Some of them emphasize what he is to us in his work: *Sun of righteousness* (Mal. 4:2), *messenger of the covenant* (Mal. 3:1), *the way, the truth, and the life* (John 14:6), *the bread of life* (John 6:48), and *the faithful witness* (Rev. 1:5).

We learn from these names that Jesus is eternal, almighty, unchangeably faithful, and all-glorious; that he sees, knows, and rules over all things; and that he is God manifest in the flesh, the only Savior of his people. Indeed, everything we know about him is comprehended in one or another of his names. This is the reason they are such an important part of God's revelation of him to us.

In every one of his names, we see that he has "a name which is above every name" (Phil 2:9). By his names we learn that there is no other Savior, and so we are encouraged to put our faith and trust in him alone. In this way we who know his names find him altogether lovely, the fairest of ten thousand, and we learn to say of him, "This is my beloved, and this is my friend" (Song of Sol. 5:16).

Christ's *Real* Human Nature

A most precious truth concerning our Lord is that he is like us in all things except sin (Heb. 4:15). That he is like us means that he has our human nature in addition to his divine nature. He is *both* God and man in one person.

When we speak of Christ's human nature there are a number of important truths that we emphasize, five especially. He has a *real, complete, sinless,* and *weakened human nature,* and he has a *central human nature* out of the line of the covenant.

Each of these truths is of the greatest possible importance for our salvation.

That Christ has a *real* human nature needs to be emphasized over against the teaching of some in the early church and in some cults today that Christ only *appeared* in the form of a man, but did not in fact have a real, human body of flesh and blood and a real human soul as we do. His humanity, it is said, was only an appearance—something like an angel appearing in the form of a man.

But if Christ did not have a real human nature, our salvation is not real either. If his human nature was only an appearance, so was his suffering and death, and so is our salvation. The reality of our salvation depends on the reality of his human nature. Hebrews 2:14, 15 says, "Forasmuch then as the children are partakers of flesh and blood, he also himself likewise *took part of the same,*" and then the verse shows why this was necessary for our salvation by adding, "that through death he might destroy him that had the power of death, that is, the devil; And deliver them who through fear of death were all their lifetime subject to bondage."

The Bible teaches the reality of Christ's human nature not only by emphasizing that he was like us in everything, even in being tempted (Heb. 4:15), but in many other ways as well. The reality of his human nature is taught in all those passages that speak of Jesus' being born, growing, learning, obeying, eating, drinking, being tired, weeping, suffering, and dying. They all tell us that he really was a man, like us in all things. To doubt the reality of his agony in Gethsemane, his pain at Peter's denial and Judas' betrayal, and his anguished abandonment on the cross is not only to doubt his own truthfulness, but also to doubt our salvation by these sufferings.

Christ is therefore bone of our bone and flesh of our flesh (Eph. 5:30), able to represent us before God and to lay down his life as a sacrifice for our sins. He is a man in order to pay for man's sin and to bring us to God in himself.

Christ's *Complete* Human Nature

We have pointed out that there are five truths that need to be believed about Christ's human nature: that it was real, complete, sinless, weakened, and central out of the line of the covenant.

We now look at the wonderful truth that Christ had a *complete* human nature, which means that when Christ was born in our flesh, he was not born with a human body only. He also had a human soul or spirit (Luke 23:46; John 12:27), a human mind (Phil. 2:5), a will (John 6:38), a heart (Matt. 11:29), and everything else that belongs to our human nature.

He is not half man and half God, but fully man and fully God; yet he is only *one* Christ. That is the wonder, the mystery, and the glory of his incarnation.

This truth has been denied in the history of the church. Some tried to explain the incarnation by saying that Christ had only a human body and that his divine nature took the place of the human mind or the human soul. By analogy, therefore, he would be like a creature that had a human mind in an animal's body. In that case Christ would not have a complete human nature, but only part of it.

It is of the utmost importance, however, for us to believe that Christ had a complete human nature. Our salvation depends on it!

Christ had to take on himself every part of our human nature, because *every part* needed to be redeemed. The biblical truth of total depravity says that we are corrupt and depraved *in every part.*

Our body is vile (Phil. 3:21), our soul is lost (Matt. 16:26), our will is in bondage (Rom. 6:16), our mind is carnal, full of enmity against God so that it cannot be subject to the law of God (Rom. 8:7–8), and our heart is deceitful above all things and desperately wicked (Jer. 17:9). There is no part of our human nature that is good.

Christ therefore took upon himself our complete human nature so that he might suffer in it, making atonement for sin in every part. In that way he redeemed us, heart and mind and soul and strength, from the dominion and power of sin and made us, with all we are, the servants and sons of the living God.

Christ is a *complete* Savior. Thanks be to God for him. Surely there is no other besides him.

Christ's *Sinless* Human Nature

We have presented the first two of five truths that need to be believed about Christ's human nature. We have looked at the wonderful teachings that he has a *real* and a *complete* human nature. This time we turn to the important truth that Christ has a *sinless* human nature.

That he is sinless is taught most clearly in Hebrews 4:15. It is also taught in Isaiah 53:9, Luke 1:35, and 2 Corinthians 5:21. Hebrews 4:15, however, raises the question whether Christ was able to sin, since he was tempted like us in all things. In other words, does the sinlessness of Christ mean only that he *did not* sin, or does it mean that he *could not* sin?

Some have said that Christ's temptations could be real only if it were possible for him to sin in his human nature. That he did not sin was only because he was also God. In the face of such teaching, we must emphasize the truth that it was *not possible* for him to sin. We must remember that it is not a *nature* that sins, but a *person*, and Christ is only *one* person, the Son of God. As a divine person, he could not sin. To say that it was possible for him to sin in his human nature is to say that *God* could sin, for *personally*, even in our human nature, he is the eternal Son of God. This, we believe, is one of the truths being taught in 2 Corinthians 5:21, which says that he *knew* no sin, and in Hebrews 7:26, which says that he was "holy, harmless, undefiled, *separate* from sinners."

That Christ was without sin also means that he was without original sin, the sin we have from Adam (Rom. 5:12). In this respect, too, he was undefiled. The virgin birth of Jesus and that God was his Father, also the Father of his human nature, guaranteed that among all Adam's descendants, Christ alone was born pure and holy.

He not only had no original sin; he had no actual sin, either. During his whole life, from the time he was born, Christ never broke God's commandments, never erred in the least thing, and never spoke an idle word that did not glorify God. He was perfect.

In sum, therefore, his sinlessness means that he was without original sin, without actual sin, and without the possibility of sin. This, as Hebrews tells us, is the reason he could be our Savior.

As the sinless one, he did not need to offer sacrifice first for his own sin, but was able to offer on our behalf a perfect sacrifice (Heb. 7:27). He therefore could be made sin in our place so that we might be made the righteousness of God in him (2 Cor. 5:21).

Christ's sinlessness, then, is the guarantee that his righteousness is perfect, and that it is for us. All that he merited by his death he did not need himself; he earned it for us, who are in such great need of it.

Christ's *Weakened* Human Nature

We now look at the fourth great truth about Christ's human nature: that he who now has a glorified human nature had a *weakened* human nature while on earth. His human nature, besides being *real, complete,* and *sinless,* was *weakened.*

Because Christ had a weakened human nature, during his earthly lifetime he was subject to all the evil results of sin, though not to sin itself. He was subject to sickness, hunger, sorrow, pain, weakness, and even to death, just as we are. He was "touched with the feeling of our infirmities" (Heb. 4:15).

Romans 8:3, which says that Christ came in the likeness of sinful flesh, also teaches this truth. Since it cannot mean that he was himself sinful, it can only refer to the fact that he was subject to all the evils that sin has brought upon us, namely, to the infirmities of our sinful flesh.

Christ did not, then, come in the likeness of *sinless* flesh. He was not like Adam, first created and standing in all the glory and splendor of his first estate. He was made like us who have lost that estate and brought upon ourselves not only depravity and guilt, but also the curse of God.

That is an important truth. Disease, suffering, sorrow, and death are all the results of our sin and of God's curse upon sin. Christ's bearing of our infirmities is part of his being made a curse for us. He took all our infirmities upon himself by way of taking our curse upon himself and carrying it away from us. What a comfort to us, therefore, are all his infirmities!

Isaiah said all this when he prophesied of Christ and called him "a man of sorrows, and acquainted with grief" (Isa. 53:3). His sorrows, Isaiah said, were to be explained thus: "Surely he hath borne *our* griefs and carried *our* sorrows...He was wounded for *our transgressions,* he was bruised for *our iniquities.*" By his sorrow, pain, and grief "the chastisement of *our* peace was upon him" (vv. 4–5).

It was not only Christ's death that had atoning power, but also the suffering he endured during his whole life on earth. He confessed this when he said, "For my life is spent with grief, and my years with sighing: my strength faileth because of mine iniquity, and my bones are consumed" (Ps. 31:10).

There is further comfort for us in Christ's afflictions and sufferings; they mean that he knows our trials and sufferings from firsthand experience. He has gone through them, and we cannot say that no one really understands our trials. Christ understands.

In this way, too, our Savior's weakness, pain, sorrow, and suffering are all part of our salvation. May we not only behold and see that there is no sorrow like his (Lam. 1:12), but believe.

The Temptations of Christ

Hebrews 4:15 teaches us that Christ had both a *weakened* human nature (he was "touched with the feeling of our infirmities" and "in all points tempted like as we are") and a *sinless* human nature ("yet without sin"). These truths we have explained already. Together, these two truths raise questions about Christ's temptations. How could he be tempted if he was sinless? How could the temptations be real if it was not *possible* for him to sin? And if he could not sin, did he really have a weakened human nature that was like ours in everything?

That Christ's temptations *were* real is clear from Scripture. When they were finished, he needed the ministry of angels (Matt. 4:11). He had a weakened human nature that suffered in temptation as we do. That does not answer the question, however, how the temptations could be real if he could not sin.

Some say that it was possible for Christ to sin in his human nature, but not in his divine nature. This, we believe, is an unacceptable answer. It ends by saying what we *must not* say: that he was not perfect. Even if it were true that he was able to sin only in his human nature, it was nevertheless *he,* the only begotten Son of God, who was able to sin. Such talk is blasphemous.

Without pretending to be able to explain the great mystery that "God was manifest in the flesh" (1 Tim. 3:16), we believe that Scripture does help us to understand Christ's temptations. We should understand that the New Testament really uses just one word where we have two words in English: "temptation" and "trial." By using just one word, the Bible teaches us that temptation and trial, which seem so different to us, are two sides to the same spiritual struggle against Satan and sin. When Satan *tempts* us, God is at the same time *trying* us.

That is a tremendous testimony to God's sovereignty over sin and Satan, a testimony we make every time we pray to God, "Lead us not into temptation." It is also helpful in understanding Christ's temptations.

It means that when Christ was being tempted by Satan, he was also being tested by God. When we think of his temptations in that way, it is somewhat easier to understand that he could be tempted without being able to sin, and to understand why he was so tempted.

Christ's temptations were a great spiritual battle against sin and Satan, a test sent by God to prove to us that Christ was, in fact, without sin. From that point of view, it is not necessary even to think of the possibility of his sinning and yet to see that his temptations were still real and difficult—that he was tempted in all points as we are.

It is important for us to understand this. Christ's sinlessness in the struggle against Satan is part of our encouragement in the same battle. We must look to him lest we grow "wearied and faint" in our minds (Heb. 12:2–3).

Christ's *Central* Human Nature

We have learned that Christ had a *real*, a *complete*, a *sinless*, and a *weakened* human nature. In addition a few theologians speak of a fifth characteristic: his *central* human nature.

By this, nothing more is meant than that Christ was born of the flesh and blood of Mary, that he was a Jew of the line of David, of the seed of Abraham according to the flesh. So, too, he was a true son of Adam, our own flesh and blood.

This seems self-evident, but it has been denied in church history. Some taught that Christ brought his human nature with him from heaven and that by his birth and conception he merely passed through

Mary's womb like water through a tap. Or they taught that his human nature was specially created in her womb so that he was not genetically and physically her son.

This was taught by some Anabaptists at the time of the Reformation, and more recently by the neo-orthodox theologian Karl Barth.[2] Both Barth and the Anabaptists held such views in the interest of preserving Christ's sinlessness. If Jesus was not born of human ancestry, they claimed, then there was no possibility that he was tainted with human depravity.

It is not necessary to hold these views, however, in order to believe that Christ was wholly without sin. His conception by the Holy Spirit guaranteed his sinlessness, as Luke 1:35 teaches.

Indeed, to hold the view of the Anabaptists and of Barth is to deny that Christ was like us in all things except sin (Heb. 2:14; Heb. 4:15), even in his conception and birth. As Berkhof says, "If the human nature of Christ was not derived from the same stock as ours but merely resembled it, there exists no such relation between us and Him as is necessary to render his mediation available for our good."[3]

To say that Christ was not genetically and organically, by real conception and birth, a son of Abraham is also to cut him off from the covenant made with Abraham and his seed, and from the promises of that covenant. These promises, then, do not belong to him and cannot be fulfilled in him. Nor is there any possibility that New Testament Christians who are in him by faith have any interest in those promises. To cut Christ off from Abraham and David is to cut both him and us off from the Old Testament and its promises.

Let us hold, therefore, to the precious truth that Christ, by the incarnation, is truly a member of the human race and by natural descent a true son of Mary and through her of Abraham and his descendants. Our salvation and our place in the covenant as children of Abraham depends on it.

---

2. Karl Barth (1886–1968) was a modern Swiss theologian who worked in Germany over the period of the two world wars. His theology is known as dialectical or crisis theology and is characterized by paradoxes and reformulation of almost all fundamental Reformed doctrines. Notable among his heretical teachings are the notion that God is unknowable, the idea of "encounter" as the way in which God reveals himself, and a rejection of the historicity of Scripture.

3. Louis Berkhof, *Systematic Theology*, Part 3, "The Doctrine of the Person and Work of Christ," "New" Edition (Grand Rapids, MI: William B. Eerdmans Publishing Company, 1996), 334.

The Eternal Generation of Christ

Defending the full divinity of Christ—that he is equal to the Father in all things—includes a defense of his *eternal generation.*

"Generation" refers to a father begetting a son. A mother conceives, but a father generates. The generation of Christ means that he, as the Second Person of the Trinity, is the *Son* of God and that the First Person is his *Father.* Another word for "generated," therefore, is the word *begotten.* In relation to the Father, Christ is the only "begotten" Son.

In our human experience generation means that a son comes after his father and has a beginning. Eternal generation means that as the Second Person of the Trinity, Christ is begotten—generated—by the First Person of the Trinity, but *from eternity,* or without a beginning. Because his generation is eternal, the Second Person of the Trinity is not *after* the First Person or inferior to his Father.

We are not speaking here of Christ's birth in the flesh. He is the Son of God in that respect also, born in our human nature by the overshadowing power of the Holy Spirit. As the Son, born in our flesh, he does have a beginning and is inferior to the Father. It is as the Second Person of the Trinity that he is *eternally* generated.

The Athanasian Creed puts it this way: "For the right faith is that we believe and confess that our Lord Jesus Christ, the Son of God, is God and man. God, of the essence of the Father, begotten before the worlds; and man, of the substance of his mother, born in the world ... Equal to the Father as touching his Godhead, and inferior to the Father as touching his manhood."[4]

The eternal generation of Christ is a truth that needs emphasis today. It seems to be the fashion among some to deny it. Whatever their reasons, they are really denying the Trinity. If Christ is not eternally generated as the Son, he has a beginning. If he has a beginning, he is not eternal. If he is not eternal, he is not fully and really God. If he is not fully God, he is no Savior to us.

Denying the eternal generation of Christ is part of the old heresy of Arianism. Back in the early history of the church, this heresy taught that Christ was *a god,* but not equal to the Father, just as the cults teach today. The Arians insisted that the name *only begotten Son* implied that

---

4. Athanasian Creed, verses 30–31, and 33.

Christ had a beginning and was not eternal like the Father; that he was, therefore, not equal to the Father.

Eternal generation is clearly taught in Proverbs 8:22–30, where Wisdom, the speaker, is Christ, the Son of God. He says there, "I was set up from everlasting, from the beginning, or ever the earth was...Then I was by him, as one brought up with him" (vv. 23, 30). Similar ideas are found in Micah 5:2, 1 Corinthians 1:24, and Colossians 1:15. Let us hold to Scripture, therefore, and not allow the enemies of the truth to take away our confession that Christ is our Lord and our *God*.

The Virgin Birth of Christ

One of the fundamentals of our faith is the virgin birth of Christ. Both the reality and significance of Christ's humanity are inseparably connected with belief in his virgin birth.

Because this truth is fundamental, it has been often denied. Some in the early church, called the Gnostics, denied Christ's virgin birth. It is still under attack today.

Some modern Bible versions, such as the Revised Standard Version, attack the virgin birth of Christ by retranslating the word *virgin* in Isaiah 7:14 as "young woman." The Mormons deny it with their blasphemous teaching that Christ was born of sexual relations between the Father and Mary. Many today think the virgin birth was only a legend about Jesus that the early church believed, but that is no longer credible today. All of these attacks only serve to show how important the doctrine is. The devil does not waste his time attacking matters of no consequence.

The virgin birth of Christ is important, first, because it is a testimony to Christ's real humanity. Although Christ did not have a human father, he was nevertheless born as we are. If he had not been, he would not be like us in all things except sin (Heb. 2:17; Heb. 4:15).

Also, the virgin birth, with emphasis on the word *virgin*, is a confirmation that although Jesus was born a man of the flesh and blood of Mary, he was born "not of the will of the flesh, nor of the will of man, but of God" (John 1:13). As Isaiah pointed out long ago (Isa. 7:14), the virgin birth is a sign that Jesus is indeed Immanuel, *God with us*.

Faith in the virgin birth does not require belief in the *perpetual* virginity of Mary, as Rome teaches, or as the Swiss reformer Zwingli taught. It is not the virginity of Mary, either before or after Christ's birth, that guarantees Christ's sinlessness, but his conception by the power of the Holy Spirit. Luke 1:35 clearly teaches this: "The Holy Ghost shall come upon thee; . . . *therefore* also that holy thing which shall be born of thee shall be called the Son of God."

That a virgin birth is difficult to understand should not surprise us. It is part of the wonder and miracle of grace. When ordinary human conception and birth remain a mystery, how can we expect to understand fully the miracle of Christ's coming into the world? Its being scorned should not surprise us either. Christ's virgin birth belongs to his work as our Savior, and only faith can receive him and the truth concerning him.

May that miracle of Christ's virgin birth point us to the even greater miracle of what he did in the flesh when he suffered, bled, and died for the sins of all those whom the Father had given him.

The Union of Christ's Two Natures

The mystery of the incarnation is not so much that our Lord is true God or true man, but that he is *both*. According to 1 Timothy 3:16, God manifested in the flesh is the great "mystery of godliness." Because it is a mystery, it is something we cannot fully understand.

There are, however, some analogies (comparisons) that can be used to help us understand how the two natures of Christ are united in one person. These analogies are not perfect (no analogy can be), but as Charles Hodge says, "There is . . . enough resemblance to sustain faith and rebuke unbelief."[5]

The best analogy is that of the union of soul and body. Even the Athanasian Creed makes use of this analogy when it says, "For as the reasonable *soul* and *flesh* is one man, so God and man is one Christ."[6]

This analogy has the following points of similarity to the union of Christ's two natures.

---

5. Charles Hodge, *Systematic Theology,* vol. 2 (London: James Clarke, 1960), 380.
6. Athanasian Creed, verse 37.

First, as soul and body are two "substances" in man—one material and the other immaterial—so Christ has two natures—one finite and creaturely and the other infinite and divine.

Second, as soul and body constitute one person, so the two natures of Christ are united in one person. In the activities of both soul and body, there is one man acting, thinking, and willing; so also in Christ there is but one person acting in and through the two natures.

Third, as soul and body remain distinct, so the two natures of Christ remain distinct and do not mix to form some kind of hybrid that is neither truly God nor truly man. They are not joined like copper and zinc are joined to make brass—something entirely new. Christ remains fully and really God, and fully and really man, not half God and half man.

Fourth, as the attributes of soul and body are both ascribed to the same person (the *person* may be wise in spirit and tall in body), so the characteristics of both Christ's divine and human natures are ascribed to him personally. Just as apparently inconsistent statements can be made about a person—he is spirit and he is dust—so to Christ both the perfections of the divine nature and the limitations of the human nature are ascribed. He is all-knowing and yet does not know the day or hour of his second coming; he is eternal and yet has a beginning in time; he is almighty and was weak.

The Athanasian Creed expresses this last point very beautifully when it says that Christ is "God, of the essence of the Father, begotten before the worlds; and man, of the substance of his mother, born in the world...Equal to the Father as touching his Godhead, and inferior to the Father as touching his manhood. Who although he is God and man, yet he is not two, but one Christ,"[7] one Christ to be worshipped and adored.

The Inseparable Union of Christ's Two Natures

In speaking of the mystery of the incarnation of our Lord Jesus Christ, one thing that needs to be stressed is that he *continues* to be true God and man. The union between the divine and human is an *inseparable* union.

---

7. Ibid., verses 31 and 33.

Some sincere Christians have the vague and unbiblical notion that after the resurrection, Christ ceased to be human. He took on our human nature when he was born in Bethlehem and left it behind again when he arose from the dead, so they think. In fact, his rising from the dead proves that he is still a man like us. Insofar as he is God, he cannot die and does not need to rise again from the dead.

It is in his human nature, therefore, that he also ascends into heaven. God has no need to ascend, for he is everywhere present. As *man* he is seated at the right hand of God, makes intercession, and returns for judgment at the end of all things.

We must remember that if he is not still human like us, we have no part in him. Then what Scripture says of him is no longer true—that he is "made like unto his brethren," and that he is a "merciful and faithful High Priest in things pertaining to God" (Heb. 2:17). Indeed, if he is not still made like unto us, we are no longer his brethren.

Nor does Christ's human nature become divine through the resurrection. If that were the case, he would no longer be our Elder Brother, the one who ever lives to make intercession for us. As one who knows and is touched with the feeling of our infirmities, he now makes that intercession and makes it as one who is like us in all things except sin. As man, he represents us before God and obtains for us all blessings.

Christ's human nature is glorified and changed through the resurrection as ours also shall be when we rise from the dead in the last day and go to meet him. His human nature was not left behind when he died, or changed into the divine. He is still the Son of *man*.

Because Christ still has his human nature, he will come again in that human nature at the end of the world, even as he went away from us when he ascended to his Father. As God, of course, he is everywhere present and is still with us until the end of the world. But we shall not see him as a man and meet him face-to-face until he returns.

Hard to understand? Indeed it is, but that is only because Christ's incarnation and the union of his two natures is a work of God, whose ways are always too high for us. It is part of the miracle of our redemption by his grace.

It is hard to understand, indeed, but gloriously comforting, for it means that "we have our flesh in heaven as a sure pledge that he, as the head, will also take up to himself, us, his members."[8]

The Personal Union of Christ's Two Natures

The union of the two natures of Christ is a *personal union*. This, too, is part of the mystery of our Lord Jesus Christ.

When we say that it is a personal union, we mean, first, that he is only one person. There are not two Christs, one human and one divine, but only one who was born in Bethlehem, suffered and died on the cross, and rose again the third day.

We also mean that personally Christ is the only begotten and eternal Son of God. He is not a human person and a divine person, but the one divine, eternal person who came in our flesh and took our human nature to be his own. Nor is he a human person; he has taken our human *nature* as his own, but he *is,* as a person, the Second Person of the Trinity. This is often denied, especially by those who only believe that he *became* divine.

This is the hardest part of the doctrine of Christ to understand. It means that the only begotten Son *personally* suffered and died on the cross, and that the *person* who said, "My God, my God, why hast thou forsaken me?" was God himself. What an awesome truth!

It does not explain the mystery to say that Christ did these things in or according to his human nature, for it was *he,* the only begotten and eternal Son of God, who did them. How incomprehensible are the ways of God!

It is important to believe that Christ is personally the Second Person of the Trinity, because only as such could he make atonement for sin and bring us an everlasting righteousness. Only the Son of God could pay for all the sins of his people by dying on the cross. Only the Son of God could suffer all the eternal wrath of God against sin in six short hours. Only the Son of God could bring us an everlasting righteousness, the righteousness of God himself (Rom. 3:21–22), a righteousness that cannot be destroyed or lost again.

---

8. Heidelberg Catechism, Lord's Day 18, Q&A 49.

Only because Christ is personally the Son of God are his work and his death of saving value for us. What man cannot do, *God* does in the person of his Son.

It is important, too, that Christ is personally the Second Person of the Trinity as the one who was incarnate of the virgin Mary. If nothing else, it reminds us that the miracle of the incarnation and of our salvation is that God became man, not that man became God.

The words of 1 Corinthians 8:6 sum this all up very beautifully: "But to us there is but one God, the Father, of whom are all things, and we in him; and one Lord Jesus Christ, by whom are all things, and we by him." May God give us grace to make that confession our own and to keep it as our confession always.

The Distinction between Christ's Two Natures

When speaking of Christ as God and man, we must be careful not to confuse his two natures. This has been done in the history of the church. Some, for example, have called Christ the God-man, teaching that he is not any longer truly God or truly man, but a kind of hybrid of the two. An analogy would be the mixing of the metal sodium with the poisonous gas chlorine to produce sodium chloride (table salt), something that is neither metal nor gas.

The problem with this old heresy is that it obliterates the distinction between the human and the divine. That error is still around today, though it is not called by the same name. Many blur the distinction between human and divine by teaching that Christ was God only in the sense that as a good man he became divine. According to this view, Christ reached divinity by realizing all the potential of his humanity. Isaac Watts, the writer of many hymns, believed this.

A blurring of the distinction between human and divine is the error, too, of those who promote a gospel of "positive thinking" and of modernism: that people must put away all thoughts of sin and guilt and learn to think positively about themselves, thus realizing their potential as human beings just as Christ did. Salvation, then, consists in the growth of men and women into a kind of perfect humanity, which is the same, it is said, as being divine.

In maintaining the distinction between human and divine in Christ, we must be very careful with our language and not go beyond what Scripture itself says about Christ's two natures. We say, for example, that Christ died on the cross, or that he suffered and died "according to his human nature," but we do not say that *God* died on the cross. Or we say that Christ was forsaken of God "according to his human nature," but we cannot say that God was forsaken of God.

We have biblical warrant for this kind of language, too. We find it used in passages like Romans 9:5, where Scripture says that Christ is come of the Jews "as concerning the flesh."

We must therefore maintain that Christ our Lord, in one person, is eternal, omniscient, omnipotent, and the Creator of heaven and earth, while at the same time he is fully and truly man with all the limitations of the human nature. This is the wonder of the incarnation, the great mystery of godliness, and the hope of our salvation (Eph. 4:9–10).

We can understand the mixing of two substances to produce a third, but to understand fully how the two natures of Christ can be forever united in one person and yet remain distinct is beyond our comprehension. It shows us that the incarnation of Christ is a wonderwork of God.

God's Covenant in Christ

The union of Christ's two natures is very important as far as some of the most precious promises in Scripture are concerned. He is the fulfillment of those promises, because he is *Immanuel,* "God with us."

We refer to such promises as those of 2 Peter 1:4: "That by these ye might be partakers of the divine nature"; 2 Corinthians 6:16: "I will dwell in them, and walk in them"; Ephesians 3:19: "That ye might be filled with all the fulness of God"; Ephesians 5:30: "For we are members of his body, of his flesh, and of his bones"; and Galatians 2:20: "I am crucified with Christ: nevertheless I live; yet not I, but Christ liveth in me: and the life which I now live in the flesh I live by the faith of the Son of God, who loved me, and gave himself for me."

All these promises presuppose what John Calvin called the "mystical union" between God in Christ and his people. That this union is more than just a figure of speech is clear from the passages themselves and even from the way faith is described in Scripture. Faith is, literally, faith *in* Christ or even *into* Christ.

These passages describe, therefore, the closest possible fellowship between God and his people: fellowship in which God's people are actually joined and united to him and share his own blessed life. They are received into his family and become, by grace, partakers of the divine nature. Wonderful, is it not?

This union is realized in Christ himself. He is, on the one hand, our own flesh and blood; on the other hand, he is also really and fully God in one person. In him God and man meet and are united, for we are *in him* by faith, while in him also dwells all the fullness of the Godhead bodily (Col. 2:9–10).

Christ is, by virtue of his incarnation, Immanuel (God with us), not only because God visits us in him, but also because God comes to dwell with us and live in closest fellowship with us through him.

Christian marriage is a picture of this, since man and woman in marriage become "one flesh." In fact, in Ephesians 5, where Paul talks about Christian marriage and says that man and woman become one flesh, he adds, "This is a great mystery: but I speak *concerning Christ and the church*" (v. 32).

The marriage of God and his people in Christ whereby they become one flesh is the realization of God's covenant of grace. God's covenant is a covenant of friendship and fellowship in which God promises to be our God and to make us his people. It is realized when we are one with God in Christ.

So we wait for the wedding feast of the Lamb, not merely as a picture of heaven's joys, but as the consummation of our union with God in Christ, which will be the realization of all our hopes and the beginning of all our joys.

The Three Offices of Christ

When we speak of Christ's offices, we are saying that he is our great *Prophet* (Acts 3:22–26), our only *High Priest* (Heb. 7:24–28), and our eternal *King* (Rev. 17:14).

With these three offices Christ is unique in Scripture. No one else except Melchizedek held all three offices (Heb. 7). During the kingdom years it was forbidden that the kings of Israel and Judah serve as both priests and kings. One of Judah's kings, Uzziah, was stricken with leprosy for trying, as king, to perform the functions of a priest (2 Chron. 26:16–21; compare with 1 Sam. 13:8–14).

A man might be a priest and a prophet, like Samuel, or he might be a king and a prophet, like David, but he could not be both king and priest. Only Melchizedek held both offices, and he was a unique picture of Christ. There is no one like Christ.

Because there is no other like Christ, we must have no other besides him—no earthly priest or prophet, and no king but Christ. His claims put to shame the claims of all those who say today that they are prophets or priests or supreme rulers in the church of Jesus Christ. The church has no head but Christ, no prophet but the living Word of God, no priest but the merciful Son of God, the one who offered himself a sacrifice for the sins of his people. Of these things we will speak later.

However, before we look at Christ's prophetic, priestly, and kingly offices, we must understand what an office is. First, it is *a position of service.* With his offices Christ is identified in Scripture as the Servant of Jehovah, especially in the prophecy of Isaiah (Isa. 52:13; Isa. 53:11). As Servant of Jehovah he comes to do God's will and work (Luke 2:49; John 4:34).

An office is also *a position of authority.* In his three offices Christ has all authority in heaven and on earth (Matt. 28:18). The words he speaks as Prophet have such authority that those who do not hear him will perish. His rule as King is supreme over all. His work as Priest, both in making sacrifice and in blessing us, is a saving work, because he was given authority by God to make the one sacrifice that atones for sin and to bless with all the riches of salvation those whom God had given him.

Finally, an office is *a mediatorial position.* As Prophet, Priest, and King, Christ is our Mediator. He "stands between" God and us, not only to make a priestly sacrifice for sin that satisfies the demands of God's justice, but also to bring us God's Word as Prophet and to rule over us in God's name as sovereign King.

His name *Christ,* the same name as the Old Testament name *Messiah,* shows us all this. That name means "anointed one" and refers to the fact that Christ is anointed and appointed by God the Father, through the Holy Spirit, to be our Prophet, Priest, and King.

Truly there is none like him. Let us listen to no other, bow to no other, and trust in no other sacrifice but his. Then we can say in truth that to us he is the Christ, the Son of the living God.

Christ, Our Chief Prophet

We sometimes forget that Christ is not only our great High Priest, who offers one sacrifice for sin, but that he is also our Prophet and King. These offices are of equal importance to his priestly office.

As our Prophet he is the one who brings us the Word of God. He does this first by *being* the living Word of God (John 1:1ff.). As the living Word he reveals God to us (John 1:14; John 14:9)—all the grace, mercy, and love of God, but also the holiness, justice, and wrath of God.

Christ also functions as our Prophet in speaking the Word of God to us. He does this in the preaching of the gospel. In commissioning and sending faithful preachers, he makes himself heard by his people (John 5:25; John 10:27) so that though they have not seen him, they love and obey him (John 20:29). This is one of the most important truths in Scripture concerning the preaching: that in the preaching God's people hear the voice of Christ through the work of the Holy Spirit. That is what makes preaching the very power of God unto salvation (Rom. 1:16). That is why faith comes by hearing (Rom. 10:17).

Because Christ speaks with such power, we need no other prophet, nor may we seek or follow any other besides him. The claims of those today who say they are prophets, and who claim to be able to speak infallibly or to reveal the will of God, are put to shame in Christ's presence and are a denial of his unique prophetic office. Before Christ came, other prophets were needed, but now that he has come as the living and abiding Word of God, there can be no others.

Because Christ's work as Prophet is so important, Moses told of his coming long before his birth (Deut. 18:15; Acts 3:22–25). Moses said concerning Christ's prophetic work, "Him shall ye hear in all things whatsoever he shall say unto you" (Acts 3:22).

The people did not always hear and heed Moses, and that is why Moses spoke of a better prophet to come. He who comes *makes* himself heard. As the Son of God, he speaks with such power that the sinner cannot but obey when he calls. When he calls to faith and repentance, his powerful voice creates faith and repentance in the hearts of his people. When he speaks, the dead hear the voice of the Son of God and live (John 5:25). That is why Moses said, "Him *shall* ye hear *in all things.*"

Sinners are "dead" and cannot hear Christ until he speaks with such power to them, but this does not destroy the accountability of those who perish in their sins: "Every soul, which will not hear that prophet, shall be destroyed from among the people" (Acts 3:23).

We can hear Christ only when he speaks his powerful, creative word in our hearts. Indeed we *must* hear him lest we perish. As *the* Prophet he demands our attention. We must "give the more earnest heed to the things which we have heard, lest at any time we should let them slip" (Heb. 2:1).

Christ, Our Only High Priest

The great work of Christ as our only High Priest is the work of offering himself as a sacrifice for sin. He is the Priest making the sacrifice as well as the offering itself.

Making sacrifice for sin is not the only work that Christ does as our Priest. If it were, his priestly work would be finished. Yet Hebrews 7:28 says that he is consecrated forevermore. His work was no more finished when he had offered that only atoning sacrifice than the work of the priest in the Old Testament was finished when he had offered the burnt offering on the great altar in the temple. Thus he is pictured in Revelation 1, exalted and glorified and *still* performing the work of a priest. His robe, girt with a golden girdle, is the garment of a priest.

Christ's work as High Priest continues in two things especially. It continues, first, in the intercession he makes for his people before God. This was symbolized in the Old Testament when the priest went with fire from the great altar into the temple to offer incense on the golden altar that stood before the veil. That incense, sweet smelling and rising into God's presence, was a picture of the sweet prayers of Christ as they mingle with our prayers and rise into God's presence, where they are accepted and answered.

Because that incense symbolized the intercession of Christ, the priest had to burn the incense with fire from the great altar on which atoning sacrifice had just been made. That incense pictured the acceptableness of the prayers of God's people as those prayers came before God himself through Christ's intercession. The coals from the altar of burnt offering pictured the only reason our prayers are acceptable, namely, Christ's sacrifice.

Christ's work as Priest also continues in the blessings he pours out upon his people. The outpouring of the Spirit and the Spirit's blessings are the work of Christ as our heavenly High Priest.

This was symbolized in the Old Testament when the priest finished the work of making sacrifice and intercession and brought to the people the blessing of God that had been obtained (Num. 6:22–27). He did this at the door of the tabernacle or temple when he blessed the people in the name of the Lord (Luke 1:22). This Christ does from the heavenly sanctuary when he blesses us in God's name.

To do this, Christ first had to enter into heaven itself. This was symbolized in the Old Testament when the high priest, once a year, went into the most holy place to bring before the mercy seat the blood of atonement. When Christ appears in the presence of God for us (Heb. 9:24), he brings his blood before God. This is the basis for the intercession he continues to make and the blessing he continues to obtain for his people.

All those who believe in Christ have such a High Priest—one who offers a perfect sacrifice, makes perfect intercession, and is able to obtain for them the blessings of God. Trust no other priest but him!

Christ, Our Eternal King

The third office of Christ is his kingly office. There are several things we need to learn about his office and work as King.

We must know that there are two aspects to his kingly office—his rule over the wicked world and his rule over his people. The first is called *the rule of his power,* the second *the rule of his grace.*

By the rule of his power, he sovereignly controls all the actions and even the thoughts and hearts of wicked men, using them for his purposes and kingdom. He exercised this power when he said with kingly authority to Judas, "That thou doest, do quickly" (John 13:27). He sent Judas to do the work of darkness in order that he might be crucified and shed his blood for the salvation of his people. He revealed the same power when he made those who captured him in the garden go backward and fall to the ground (John 18:6) in order to show that he went willingly to the cross.

This kingly power is exercised *against* and *in spite of* the will of those who rebel against Christ. They rise up and take counsel together against him (Ps. 2), but he laughs them to scorn and uses them, even in their rebellion, for his own good pleasure.

But he also rules by grace. Through the rule of his grace, he rules in the church and among his people. This rule he exercises *in and through* the will of his people. By his grace he changes their will and causes them to love and serve him willingly. This aspect of his rule is described most beautifully in Psalm 110:3: "Thy people shall be willing in the day of thy power."

The difference between these two aspects of Christ's rule is most clearly seen in the fact that he rules the wicked with a rod of iron and with it, breaks them in pieces (Ps. 2:9). He rules his people with a shepherd's staff, guiding them to peace (Ps. 23:4).

We must also remember, however, that as King he rules not only *over* his people; he also rules *for* them, *fighting* for them and leading them in battle. As King, he is the Conqueror and Victor over all his enemies, the one who has overthrown the whole power and kingdom of darkness, the one in whom we are more than conquerors (Rom. 8:37).

This victory he has already obtained. The victory is not yet to be won, but by his cross is fully accomplished (John 19:30; Col. 2:14–15). "The kingdoms of this world *are* [present tense] become the kingdoms of our Lord and of his Christ" (Rev. 11:15). His *is* the kingdom, the power, and the glory, forever (Matt. 6:13).

We must acknowledge Christ as King so that the victory may be ours also. We do this by honoring the rule of his grace in our hearts. Let us, then, kiss the Son, whom God has set as King, lest he be angry and we perish from the way (Ps. 2:12).

The States of Christ: His Humiliation and Exaltation

Good Reformed theology will usually include a discussion of the *states* (sometimes called *estates*) of the Mediator Jesus Christ. The Westminster Shorter Catechism, for example, says, "Christ, as our Redeemer, executeth the offices of a prophet, of a priest, and of a king, *both in his estate of humiliation and exaltation.*"[9] What are these states of humiliation and exaltation?

The word *state,* or *estate,* refers to our *legal status*—that we are either guilty or innocent before the law. Here it has to do with Christ's work. During the first part of his work, which is called the state of humiliation, his legal status before God was that of a guilty sinner. During the second part, his state of exaltation, his legal status was that of one justified before God.

In the state of humiliation—the time from his birth to his death—Jesus was counted guilty before God. In the state of exaltation, including his resurrection, his ascension, his glory at God's right hand, and his return for judgment, he is counted as one justified or innocent.

Christ himself was never guilty of any sin, nor did he ever need to be justified personally. But as the Sin-bearer, the one upon whom the Lord laid the iniquity of us all (Isa. 53:6), he was *counted* and *dealt with* as a guilty sinner, suffering the full punishment for sin, and then, also on our behalf, dealt with as justified and innocent.

Isaiah 53 indicates this when it says that "he was numbered with the transgressors; and he bare the sin of many" (v. 12). Christ himself says in Psalm 69:5: "O God, thou knowest my foolishness; and my sins are not hid from thee"—not as having any sin personally, but as the one who bore our transgressions.

Because Christ was numbered "among the transgressors," he was also "smitten of God and afflicted" (Isa. 53:4). It pleased the Lord, as Judge, to "bruise him [and to] put him to grief" (v. 10). In his suffering, his trial, and his death on the cross, he was treated by his own Father as though he himself were the sinner whose place he had taken, until finally he cried out, "My God, my God, why hast thou forsaken me?"

As the Sin-bearer, Christ also needed to be justified, not for his own sake, but for ours, whose sins he bore. Of this the Word speaks in Isaiah 53:11 when it calls him God's *righteous* servant, for righteousness and justification are the same thing. He was "made unto us... righteousness" (1 Cor. 1:30).

This is the heart of the gospel and one of the most amazing truths of

---

9. The Westminster Shorter Catechism, Answer 23.

Scripture: that the Son of God was willing to be numbered with the transgressors for our sake (Isa. 53:12), and that his own Father was willing to deal with him on that basis in order that we might be redeemed. Wonderful Savior, indeed! And wonderful the love that sent him!

Christ's Lowly Birth

The circumstances of Christ's birth are nearly all we know of his early life, and the emphasis is all on his birth into poverty, rejection, suffering, and persecution. Bethlehem, the stable, the manger, the swaddling clothes, the shepherds, the flight into Egypt—all tell the same story.

Why is the story of his birth told in such detail, and why is there so much emphasis on his *lowly* birth? It is because his lowly birth is the first step in his state of humiliation. It is at birth, first of all, that he is dealt with by God on our behalf as a guilty sinner.

The story is not told to arouse our sympathy or to convince us that no one ever suffered such poverty and rejection as he did. The story is not a story with a social moral, not a call for social reform and for an end of poverty and suffering. It is part of the gospel, and it is recorded in Scripture to show us that Jesus is the Savior.

Scripture itself tells us the reason for his lowly birth when it says that he was "made . . . to be sin for us, who knew no sin; that we might be made the righteousness of God in him" (2 Cor. 5:21). All his lowliness, humiliation, and poverty were part of what he suffered as the one who bore the sins of his people in order to redeem them.

Scripture teaches this most clearly in 2 Corinthians 8:9: "For ye know the grace of our Lord Jesus Christ, that, though he was rich, yet for your sakes he became poor, that ye through his poverty might be rich." There is no doubt but that his becoming poor is a reference to his incarnation and to all the circumstances of it. This, the Word of God says, happened so that we, through his poverty, might be rich, not with earthly riches, but with all the riches of salvation that are in him (Eph. 1:3).

His suffering, *all of it,* is our salvation. His humiliation is our exaltation, his lowliness our glory. He was our Savior not only on the cross, but all his life long. What a Savior!

It was necessary that he be our Savior from birth. Just as we are *born* sinners, corrupt and depraved (Ps. 51:5), so he had to be born suffering the punishment of sin. Just as our whole life from birth to death is under the dominion of sin, so our whole life must be redeemed by his life of suffering, which climaxed in his shame and sorrow and in the shedding of his blood on the cross.

The story of his birth, therefore, is not simply a touching tale, not a matter of mere pious sentiment, but the gospel. Hearing of his birth, we repeat the words of old Simeon when he saw Christ in his infancy: "Lord, now lettest thou thy servant depart in peace, according to thy word: For mine eyes have seen thy salvation, Which thou hast prepared before the face of all people; A light to lighten the Gentiles, and the glory of thy people Israel" (Luke 2:29–32).

Christ's Life of Suffering

Christ's life of suffering is the second step in his state of humiliation. Our Lord Jesus Christ suffered so many things during his earthly life that it sometimes seems that his life was nothing but suffering. Indeed, there is no more apt way to describe his life than to say, "He suffered."

He endured poverty, so much so that he said to a would-be disciple, "The foxes have holes, and the birds of the air have nests; but the Son of man hath not where to lay his head" (Matt. 8:20). In the end they took the little he had away from him, parting his garments and casting lots for his robe.

He was "despised and rejected of men" (Isa. 53:3), "hated without cause" (John 15:25), a stranger unto his brethren (Ps. 69:8), contradicted by sinners (Heb. 12:3), cast out by his own (John 1:11), forsaken and denied by his disciples (Matt. 26:56, 74), and "numbered with the transgressors" (Isa. 53:12).

He was accused of being a friend of publicans and sinners, of blasphemy, of being in league with Satan, of being a danger to national security (John 11:47–50). His kingly claims were despised, and Caesar was chosen before him as king; even the vile criminal Barabbas was preferred to him. Many times his own people, the Jews, tried to kill him.

In the end his enemies spit in his face, slapped him, mocked and ridiculed him, whipped and crucified him. How he suffered!

In all this suffering, however, it was not the shame, humiliation, rejection, and pain that mattered so much, but that he suffered for our sins and under the wrath of God. This the Word of God teaches us in Isaiah 53:3–6.

When Christ was despised and rejected, when he became intimately acquainted with grief, it was not only that *we* esteemed him not, but also that he was smitten of *God* and afflicted (v. 4). So in *all* his suffering he was "wounded for our transgressions and bruised for our iniquities." In all his suffering God was laying on him "the iniquity of us all" (v. 6). In that respect there was no one whose sorrow was like his (Lam. 1:12).

This was necessary for our redemption. Not only did Christ have to pay the penalty for our sins by dying on the cross, but because our whole life is lived in sin, he had to suffer all his life long. And by obeying sinlessly in all that suffering, he made restitution, repaying that which we had not paid, the great debt of obedience we owe to the glory of God. Of this, Christ himself speaks in Psalm 69:4: "Then I restored that which I took not away."

Hebrews 5:7–9 sums it all up: "Who in the days of his flesh, when he had offered up prayers and supplications with strong crying and tears unto him that was able to save him from death, and was heard in that he feared; Though he were a Son, yet learned he obedience by the things which he suffered; And being made perfect, he became the author of eternal salvation unto all them that obey him."

Christ's Death on the Cross

The third step in Christ's state of humiliation is his death. The death of Jesus on the cross and the shedding of his blood is the central event of history and the heart of the gospel. Paul indicates this in 1 Corinthians 2:2 when he says, "For I determined not to know any thing among you, save Jesus Christ, and him crucified"; and again, in Galatians 6:14:

"But God forbid that I should glory, save in the cross of our Lord Jesus Christ."

The cross was many things. It was the judgment of this world. Jesus himself says that in John 12:31, and the darkness, the earthquake, and the rending of the temple veil show it. The judgment of God revealed at the cross was so evident that those who were there went home beating their breasts (Luke 23:48).

The cross, too, continues to be a stone of stumbling and a rock of offense to those who do not believe. At the cross, Christ was laid not only as the chief Cornerstone, but also as a stone of stumbling (1 Pet. 2:6–8).

It is the cross, therefore, that makes division between faith and unbelief, between election and reprobation. The cross and "Jesus in the midst" (John 19:18) show clearly that the reason one person believes and not another is not in man but in Christ's cross and in the purpose of God that is revealed through Christ.

The blood of the cross is the reconciliation of *all things* in heaven and earth (Col. 1:20), but above all, the cross is our reconciliation to God, payment for our sin, atonement, and redemption (vv. 21–22). At the cross all of Jesus' suffering and humiliation reached its climax, especially during the three hours of darkness. During that time, bearing our sins, he went to face God the Judge. What happened during those few hours is far beyond our comprehension.

Only one brief word comes to us out of the darkness: "My God, my God, why hast thou forsaken me?" During that time the Son of God was forsaken of his Father and so suffered all that our sin deserves. He was forsaken that we might be accepted of God and never be forsaken of him. Suffering all the wrath of God for our sins, he delivered us from that wrath so that we shall never experience what happened during those three hours of darkness, nor what it means to face God as an angry and implacable Judge.

Last, the death of Jesus Christ on the cross is the source of our sanctification, as Paul tells us in Galatians 6:14: "By whom the world is crucified unto me, and I unto the world." It is the reason we suffer persecution (Gal. 6:12). It is even a symbol of the self-denial that we must practice for his sake (Matt. 10:38). It is the source of every blessing we have in this life and in the life to come. Let us, then, know nothing but Christ, and him crucified.

Limited Atonement

Calvinists believe in limited atonement, that is, that Christ did not die for all men but only for the elect. By *limited* atonement, however, is not meant that the value or power of Christ's death and blood are limited, but only that he died for a "limited" number of people.

It is better to speak not of *limited* atonement, but of *particular* atonement. The word *particular* emphasizes the biblical truth that Christ died only for some particular persons, and not for all without exception.

We believe in particular or limited atonement because of the many passages of Scripture that teach that Christ died not *for all* but *for many* (Isa. 53:11; Matt. 20:28; Matt. 26:28; Heb. 9:28); that is, he died *for his people* (Isa. 53:8; Matt. 1:21), *for his sheep* (John 10:14–15, 26–28), and *for the church* (Acts 20:28).

We do not believe that the passages that speak of "all" or of "the world" in any way contradict those that speak of a limited number. The Word of God cannot contradict itself. What such passages teach is that Christ died for all men *without distinction,* not for all men *without exception.* In other words, such passages teach that Christ died for *all kinds* of men (1 Tim. 2:1–6), for all who are in him (1 Cor. 15:22), or for the "world" of his own people, that is, for his elect from every nation (compare John 3:16 and John 17:9).

Limited atonement alone exalts Christ as Savior. The idea that Christ died for all men, but that many are still not saved debases Christ's saving work. That teaching really says Christ did not do enough by his suffering and death for our salvation and that something more is needed (usually a person's freewill choice). It says that Christ died for all, but that some still go to hell. If that were true, Christ's blood was shed in vain for some, and his death was useless for them. Then his death was not really a ransom, an atonement, or a satisfaction for sin, nor did it reconcile us to God.

If Christ died for all men, and yet some are still not saved, and if the difference is their freewill choice, then the thing that really matters in our salvation is not Christ's death, but our choice. Then our salvation depends not on him, but on us. God forbid that we should think such things about Christ's death or about ourselves.

The teaching that Christ died for his elect people, those whom the

Father had given him, means that he did all that was necessary for their salvation by his suffering and death, and that nothing more is needed. Then his death really is atonement, reconciliation, full payment for sin, ransom, and satisfaction. Then he really does save, and save completely, those for whom he died.

Limited atonement says that Christ does not simply make salvation available. He *is* a Prince and a *Savior.* Thanks be to God!

Christ's Descent into Hell

Another step in Christ's humiliation is his going to hell. In the Apostles' Creed the early church confessed that Christ "descended into hell." There has always been controversy about this confession, especially since "descended into hell" follows the creed's statement that he "was crucified, dead, and buried."

Many have taught that Christ actually went to the place called hell after his death and before his resurrection. They point to 1 Peter 3:18 – 20 as proof. These verses, however, are speaking about something that took place "by the Spirit" and after the resurrection. What is more, the idea that Christ was in hell after his death contradicts his own word to the dying thief: "*Today* shalt thou be *with me* in *paradise*" (Luke 23:43).

Others teach that if the descent into hell means anything, it refers to the time that Christ was in the grave. This explanation corresponds most nearly to Psalm 16:10, the one passage of Scripture where Christ is spoken of as being in hell: "For thou wilt not leave my soul in hell; neither wilt thou suffer thine Holy One to see corruption." The second part of verse 10, referring to corruption, and the previous verse, which refers to Christ's flesh, might suggest that Psalm 16:10 is talking about Christ's burial.

The Westminster Larger Catechism says, "Christ's humiliation after his death consisted in his being buried, and continuing in the state of the dead, and under the power of death till the third day; which hath been otherwise expressed in these words, *He descended into hell.*"[10]

However, the word *hell* in Acts 2:31, where Psalm 16:10 is quoted, is

---

10. The Westminster Larger Catechism, Answer 60.

a word that *in every other case* in the New Testament refers to the place of eternal punishment. There must be a sense, then, in which Christ was not only in the grave, but in hell, though not necessarily in the place itself.

When and how did that happen? We believe that Christ was in hell in this sense: during his suffering on the cross, he experienced in our place what the Heidelberg Catechism calls "the anguish and torments of hell."[11]

He certainly expressed that in his words from the cross: "My God, my God, why hast thou forsaken me?" (Mark 15:34). To be cast out of God's presence and to be forsaken of him is what hell is all about. This is what Christ suffered.

But whether Christ's descent into hell refers to his burial, or to what he endured on the cross, or to both, it reminds us of his inexpressible suffering and that he has, by his suffering and death, delivered our souls from the lowest hell. By those same sufferings he has also earned for all of his people a place in everlasting glory in the presence of God and of the holy angels. There he, and we with him, will enjoy everlasting glory and blessedness.

Christ's Burial

Christ's burial is usually considered to be part of his humiliation. Acts 2:24 tells us why. It was not until he was raised that the "pains of death" were loosed. Until then he continued "in the state of the dead, and under the power of death."[12]

His burial was a necessary part of his work, because by it he showed that he had suffered and conquered all our death. It is only because he was buried and in the grave that we can say, "O grave, where is thy victory?" (1 Cor. 15:55) and believe that we shall not be left forgotten in the grave (Ps. 31:12).

It is in Christ's burial, too, that his victory over sin and death begins to show itself. Acts 2:31 points to this when it says, "Neither his flesh did see corruption."

---

11. Heidelberg Catechism, Lord's Day 16, Q&A 44.
12. The Westminster Larger Catechism, Answer 50.

Those words can only mean that when Christ was in the grave, his body did not begin to decay and rot as ours do. Acts 13:36–37 says this about Christ in contrast to David (and all others): "For David, after he had served his own generation by the will of God, fell on sleep, and was laid unto his fathers, and saw corruption: But he, whom God raised again, saw no corruption."

From that viewpoint, Christ's three days in the grave show that he had conquered all the power of death by his death on the cross. He had done that by paying for sin, which is the "sting of death" (1 Cor. 15:56). Apart from sin, neither death nor the grave has any power. That is the reason, too, why death could not hold Christ (Acts 2:24). So completely had he conquered that death could not even bring on him its ordinary corruption.

In Acts 13:37–38 the apostle Paul says that because Christ saw no corruption, we may know that there is forgiveness of sins through him. We do not have to wait, therefore, until the resurrection to learn that his work is finished and that full atonement has been made for us. His burial already proclaims it.

Because Christ was buried and saw no corruption in the grave, we can be sure that someday we also shall be incorruptible: "This corruptible must put on incorruption." When that happens, the saying will have been brought to pass, "Death is swallowed up in victory" (1 Cor. 15: 53–54).

We may not ever forget that Jesus died on the cross and was raised again the third day. But neither may we forget that he was "crucified, dead, *and buried.*" In this, too, he shows himself to be our Savior. And what a Savior he is, that even the corrupting power of the grave, the stink, the decay, the ugliness, and all that they represent are overcome by him. He has destroyed completely the spiritual corruption of sin for us, so that even in death our bodies shall only be "asleep in Jesus."

Christ's Resurrection

Christ's resurrection is the first step in his state of exaltation. It is also one of the great works of our redemption. Without the resurrection, even the cross is not complete. The Word of God reminds us of this in

1 Corinthians 15:17: "If Christ be not raised, your faith is vain; ye are yet in your sins."

Without the resurrection we would be still in our sins in two ways and for two reasons. We would still be in our sins both legally and actually.

First, that we would still be in our sins *legally* means that without the resurrection we would not be justified and have our sins forgiven.

Why? Because justification is a work of God himself as Judge. He must pass the sentence that justifies us. He does this in raising Christ from the dead and thereby accepting and approving Christ's finished work on our behalf. The resurrection is therefore the sentence of the everlasting and unchangeable Judge of heaven and earth sealing our justification.

Think of it this way: On the cross Christ said, "It is finished"; God said, "It is finished," in raising Christ from the dead. Thus God passes the sentence that legally justifies us before him.

That is what Romans 4:25 means: "... And was raised again for our justification." This is why the Bible emphasizes in so many passages that *God* raised Christ from the dead.

Second, without the resurrection we would also still be in our sins *actually.* If Christ had not been raised, we would have no one to give us the gift of faith, and through faith, the forgiveness of sins and deliverance from all our sins. We would still be living as we once did, in our sins. As our *living Lord,* Christ gives us both forgiveness of sins and deliverance from sin. He gives us both peace and holiness.

That does not tell all the blessedness of Christ's resurrection, however. The resurrection is also the means of our access to God. As the first begotten of the dead (Rev. 1:5), Christ is the one who *opens the way* into the presence of God and into the favor of God. That was always the work of the firstborn or first begotten—he opened the way for all the other children (Ex. 13:2; Ezek. 20:26). Christ opens the way for us out of death into life and into the presence of God.

Further, Christ's resurrection stands as the sure pledge that we also shall be raised. His resurrection and ours are inseparable, as Paul demonstrates in 1 Corinthians 15:16. Because he lives, we shall live also.

Christ's resurrection, therefore, is at the heart of the whole scheme of redemption and cannot be denied without overthrowing all that we believe. Believe it, then, and rejoice in him who lives forevermore. He who believes in Christ crucified and raised again shall never die.

Christ's Ascension into Heaven

The *ascension* is the second step in Christ's state of exaltation. The importance of his ascension as part of his redemptive work is best seen by looking at the event in the Old Testament that foreshadowed it. That event was David's bringing of the ark to Jerusalem.

At least four Psalms, 24, 47, 68, and 132, celebrate this important part of Israel's history and make clear that it foreshadowed Christ's ascension. This is especially interesting because the Psalms mention the resurrection of Christ only very briefly, although we would probably judge the resurrection to be of greater importance than the ascension.

How did the bringing of the ark to Jerusalem, the event celebrated in these Psalms, foreshadow Christ's ascension? In four ways.

First, the ark was brought "up" to Jerusalem, just as Christ ascended up to heaven (2 Sam. 6:12; Ps. 68:18; Ps. 132:8; Eph. 4:8).

Second, in David's time the ark (itself typical of Christ as the one in whom God dwells with his people and reveals himself to them) entered its final resting place after a long pilgrimage. So also, by his ascension, Christ entered into heavenly rest after his life and work on earth were finished (Ps. 132:8, 13–14; Heb. 4:10).

Third, by the bringing up of the ark, David was confirmed in his kingdom, having obtained the victory over all Israel's enemies. In like manner, Christ at his ascension is crowned with glory and honor and revealed as King of kings and Lord of lords, he also having conquered all his enemies and ours (Phil. 2:9–11; Ps. 24:7–10; Ps. 68:1, 18, 23).

Fourth, through the victories of David and the following peaceful reign of Solomon, God fulfilled the promises he had made to the Jews in the Old Testament regarding the land of Canaan (1 Kings 8:56). In the same way God fulfills the promises made to us through the ascended Christ, who from heaven through the Spirit gives us all the benefits of his finished work (Ps. 68:19; Ps. 132:15–16).

The ascension, therefore, *completes* the resurrection. In his ascension Christ himself receives the benefits and rewards of his finished work, and as our risen Lord, he begins to pour out upon us those same benefits, just as David did when he gave gifts to all Israel at the time the ark was brought to Jerusalem (2 Sam. 6:19; Ps. 68:18; Eph. 4:8–13).

The ascension, then, is the promise of God that we shall also be in heaven with him. Because Christ has ascended on our behalf, we have already been made to sit together in heavenly places in him (Eph. 2:6).

The ascension of our Lord is no small thing in the work of redemption, but an essential and necessary part of that work. It causes us to say with rejoicing, "God is gone up with a shout, the LORD with the sound of a trumpet. Sing praises to God, sing praises: sing praises unto our King, sing praises...He is greatly exalted" (Ps. 47:5–6, 9).

Christ Seated at God's Right Hand

The third step in the state of Christ's exaltation is his sitting at God's right hand. The Bible tells us that this happened at the time of his ascension (Eph. 1:20). It, too, is part of his redemptive work as our Savior and Mediator.

Since according to his divine nature Christ *is* God, his being seated at God's right hand must have reference to his human nature. *In our flesh and as a man,* he was raised from the dead, ascended to heaven, and is now at the right hand of the Father.

We know that God has neither "body, parts, or passions."[13] Thus he cannot have a physical and fleshly "right hand." We learn from Scripture that to be at the right hand of someone great and mighty is to have a place of high honor, great power, and blessing (Gen. 48:8–22; 1 Kings 2:19; Matt. 25:33–34). That Christ is seated at God's right hand, therefore, must refer to his exaltation to a position of the highest honor, glory, and power. At God's right hand he is the Lord of lords and King of kings.

His being *seated* there must refer to his kingly glory and power. Seated at God's right hand, he is *enthroned* in majesty. He has been set there as King by God himself, and his power there is God's power. In one passage Christ is described as *standing* at God's right hand (Acts 7:55), an obvious description of his readiness to come again in glory to receive his own and to avenge their blood, but ordinarily we read that he is *seated* there. He will remain seated until he stands up once more to come for his own and to bring them to himself.

All this honor and glory is Christ's reward for his finished work, the

---

13. Westminster Confession of Faith, Chapter 2, Article 1

reward that was promised him by the Father from the very beginning (Phil. 2:9; Heb. 1:3). It is important to realize, though, that he receives all this and is exalted and honored *in his human nature.* As the Son of God he does not need to be and cannot be exalted, but as man he *is* exalted on our behalf.

The honor, glory, power, and blessing that he receives, he receives for us, his people, and gives it to us through the outpouring of his Spirit. That is what Peter meant on Pentecost when he said, "*Therefore* being by the right hand of God exalted, and having received of the Father the promise of the Holy Ghost, *he hath shed forth this,* which ye now see and hear" (Acts 2:33).

By that same glory and power, he not only sheds forth what he received, but prepares our hearts to receive it, gathers us into his church, prepares a place for us in his Father's house of many mansions, and subdues all our enemies. And at his Father's right hand, he makes continual intercession with the Father for us. Whom would the Father hear if not his own beloved Son, and him seated at his own right hand?

Thinking of the ascension of Christ, we must say, "Him hath God exalted with his right hand to be a Prince and a Saviour" (Acts 5:31).

Christ's Second Coming

The last step in Christ's exaltation is his coming again. The time and circumstances of Christ's return are the subject of much dispute among Christians. There can be no doubt, however, that his return is the hope of everyone who loves him and who has received salvation from him.

His return will mean that we will see him whom we love face-to-face. For nearly two thousand years he has been away, and only when he returns will we see him again.

When Christ comes again, our relationship with him will be consummated. Then the great wedding supper of the Lamb and his bride, the church, will begin, and he will take his church to himself (Rev. 19:6–9).

Then the church will be united with no divisions and with no sea to separate us one from another (Rev. 21:1). All things will be gathered in one—in him (Eph. 1:10).

In that day all things will be renewed and changed, for there will be new heavens and a new earth in which righteousness dwells (2 Pet. 3:13). The effects of sin and the curse will be gone, and paradise shall be ours again—only this time a *heavenly* paradise.

Then, too, God's covenant with his people will be realized finally and forever. In Christ "the tabernacle of God is with men, and he will dwell with them, and they shall be his people, and God himself shall be with them, and be their God" (Rev. 21:3). That is perfect covenant life.

When Christ returns, all our present sorrows and trials will be finished. "God shall wipe away all tears from their eyes; and there shall be no more death, neither sorrow, nor crying, neither shall there be any more pain" (v. 4).

More importantly, there will be no more sin when Christ returns. The devil and those who serve him will be cast out, and all our present sinning will be finished. What a great day that shall be!

In fact, the very possibility of sin will be gone for God's people. "When he shall appear, we shall be *like him;* for we shall see him as he is" (1 John 3:2). Even our vile bodies shall be changed and fashioned into the likeness of his most glorious body (Phil. 3:21).

Then, too, God's purpose to glorify himself in all the work of his hands will be realized. Those who love God think not only of themselves and their glory when they think of Christ's return, but also of the glory of God. When Christ comes and delivers up the kingdom to the Father, then God shall be all in all.

What a hope! Is it yours?

—————— *part 4* ——————

THE COVENANT
AND SALVATION

The Nature of the Covenant

What is the covenant? Scripture speaks of it often, and it is necessary, therefore, to know what Scripture is talking about.

Most would define a covenant by speaking of a contract or an agreement. They say that God's covenant with man is of the same sort as a human covenant, such as that between Abraham and Abimelech (Gen. 21:27–32), with various duties, promises, and penalties.

Such a covenant is made by two parties or sides, depends to some extent on each, and can be broken by either. Adam, so it is said, was the original covenant-making party with God, but now that Adam has fallen, Christ has replaced him.

God's covenant with men is *not* that kind of covenant. Man can never be a party with the living God in making such a covenant. Because God is God and man is a creature, owing his very existence to God, there are no duties man can assume by way of a special agreement besides those duties that he is already obliged to perform. The creature cannot make a contract with the Creator.

Nor can man ever merit anything with God in such a covenant by his own works or by fulfilling certain conditions. When he has done all that is required of him, he is still an *unprofitable servant* (Luke 17:10). Certainly man could not merit eternal life in the covenant, as some teach. Eternal life comes only through him who is the *Lord from heaven*, our Lord Jesus Christ (1 Cor. 15:47–48).

Scripture teaches that the covenant is not an agreement, but a sovereignly established *bond* or *relationship* between God and his people in Christ. This is clear from the often-repeated words of Scripture through which God reveals his covenant: "I will be thy God, and ye shall be my people" (Gen. 17:8; Ex. 6:7; 2 Cor. 6:16; Rev. 21:3).

These words, found in slightly different forms, become a kind of covenant formula throughout Scripture. They show us that a particular passage is speaking of the covenant.

Other passages actually describe such a relationship between God and his people. Genesis 5:22–24, Genesis 6:9, Genesis 18:17–19, Psalm 25:14, John 17:23, James 2:23, and 1 John 1:3 are a few such passages. All of them show that God's covenant is the blessed relationship of fellowship and friendship that he establishes with them by grace alone and through the saving work of Jesus Christ.

This relationship is sovereignly established by God: he makes and guarantees the relationship. In no sense does the covenant depend on man as a second party, but it is wholly the work of God and all of grace, that is, of undeserved favor. The covenant is always a covenant of *grace*.

The Covenant with Adam

There is only one passage of Scripture that speaks explicitly of a covenant with Adam, which is Hosea 6:7: "But they like men have transgressed the covenant: there have they dealt treacherously against me." The word *men* in verse 7 means either "man" or "Adam" (they are the same word in Hebrew). However one translates it, the verse speaks of a covenant with Adam by referring either to a covenant that Adam transgressed personally or that mankind transgressed in him.

We believe that this covenant with Adam was not a separate covenant, but the first revelation of the one, everlasting covenant of grace. Certainly if the covenant is everlasting, there can be only one covenant, and Adam, too, was in that covenant.

This first revelation of the covenant showed what the covenant is all about. In it God revealed that he is the divine Friend of his people and that he lives with them in blessed fellowship. In the first revelation of the covenant, God revealed man's calling in the covenant, the calling to live in thankful, not meritorious, obedience.

That this was only a revelation of the one covenant is clear from the fact that Scripture speaks of our being *reconciled* to God after Adam transgressed (2 Cor. 5:18–21). The word *reconciliation* is very much a covenant word and implies not only a previous relationship that has been damaged, but implies also that the relationship *has not been completely destroyed.* It is possible to speak of reconciliation only where the previous relationship has not been ruined entirely, and where it is being restored and renewed.

If it were not so, we would have to speak of God's being frustrated and having to change. His first covenant and purpose would have been utterly ruined, and he would have been frustrated, made to change his purpose, and forced to start over again with a new covenant.

How could the covenant with Adam—before he fell into sin—be a covenant of *grace*? We should remember that grace is undeserved favor. All that Adam was and all that he had were by the undeserved favor of God. What had Adam done to deserve anything when God established his covenant with him? What could he *ever* have done to deserve anything from God when he owed his whole existence to him?

It was grace, too, that maintained the covenant relationship and insured that it would not be destroyed by Adam's fall. As soon as Adam fell into sin, God came to him and put enmity between the devil and the woman, thus renewing the covenant relationship of friendship between himself and Adam (Gen. 3:15). Our "first parents" had chosen the friendship of the devil, but God, who had chosen them to be his own, would not allow them to continue as friends of Satan. In order that his covenant with them might continue, he clothed them with the skins of animals, himself offering the first sacrifice and pointing to Christ, who was to come (v. 21).

God's dealings with his people are always and only of grace. There is no other basis on which the eternal God can deal with us.

The Covenant with Noah

We believe that the different covenants of the Old Testament are, in fact, only different revelations of the *one* covenant of grace. If the covenant is everlasting, there can be only one covenant (Gen. 17:7).

In each of these revelations, God showed something new and wonderful about his covenant of grace. Thus in the first revelation of the covenant to Adam, God showed that his covenant was a covenant of *friendship*.

After Adam, the next great revelation of the covenant was to Noah. In that revelation of his covenant, God showed its *universal* character, that the covenant would embrace the whole of the world he had created. The covenant, you see, is made not only with man, but also with "every living creature of all flesh" (Gen. 9:15). It is a covenant with the day and with the night (Jer. 33:25). The universality of God's covenant, therefore, is not a universality that embraces all things or all men *without excep-*

tion, but it does embrace all things *without distinction,* so that in the end, all kinds of created things will be renewed and represented in the new heavens and earth.

That covenant is well symbolized by the rainbow as it arches over the whole of God's creation. It is a covenant that will finally be consummated in the new heavens and new earth. It is a covenant in which even the creature "shall be delivered from the bondage of corruption into the glorious liberty of the children of God" (Rom. 8:21).

That revelation of the covenant was given in the days of Noah because it was then that God destroyed the earth. He made it clear, however, both in his judgments and in the covenant with Noah, that the destruction of the earth then or in the future would not be the end of the earth, but only its cleansing and the beginning of its renewal. It will be the same at the end when God destroys this present world with fire.

This, we believe, is one of the reasons why the Bible, in speaking of God's purpose, speaks of the *world* (the cosmos) (John 1:29; John 3:16–17). The whole of God's world finally will be redeemed and saved, though not every single creature or person.

This must be so. God will not allow his purposes to come to nothing. He will not allow man, by his sin, to steal away from him the world that he created for his own glory. He saves his world.

All of this is very important in understanding a passage like Isaiah 11. Reading such a passage, many conclude that there will be a future *earthly* kingdom before Christ's return in which some of the effects of sin will be overcome, but Scripture promises no such thing. It is speaking of the new heavens and the new earth in which righteousness will dwell—a kingdom in which the wolf will indeed dwell with the lamb, a kingdom in which "the creature itself also shall be delivered . . . into the glorious liberty of the children of God" (Isa. 11:6; Rom. 8:21). What a glorious day that will be!

The Covenant with Abraham

Scripture shows clearly that the covenant with Abraham is the same as the covenant with Israel. When God made his covenant with Abraham, he made it also with his seed (Gen. 17:7), and when God established his covenant with Israel, he made it clear that he was only keeping the covenant that he had already made with Abraham, Isaac, and Jacob (Ex. 3:15, 16).

This is important because it means that what was true for Abraham in the covenant was also true for Israel. And since *all who believe* are the true seed and children of Abraham, what was true for Abraham is also true for us.

There are several notable features about the covenant with Abraham. The first and most important is that this covenant with Abraham, and thus also with Israel, was very much a covenant of grace. The great revelation of the covenant in Genesis 15 displays this.

To understand Genesis 15, one must know that in those days a human covenant was sealed not by drawing up a contract and having it legally attested, but by those who were making the covenant walking together between the cut-up pieces of an animal or animals. Jeremiah 34:18 also describes this solemn ceremony, which was used only for important matters and was a warning that anyone who violated the covenant deserved to be cut in pieces and his body cast out as food for the beasts and birds. God threatened Israel with that when they broke a covenant they had made among themselves (Jer. 34:19–20).

Since a human covenant is between equals, it is also an agreement—a bilateral or two-sided covenant—and therefore all those who were involved in making the covenant walked together between the pieces of the animals. God's covenant is different, because God and man never act as equals in the covenant. The covenant between God and Abraham, according to Genesis 15, was very much a one-sided (unilateral) covenant, established by *God alone*. When God covenanted with Abraham by walking between the pieces of the animals, Abraham was fast asleep. Abraham had nothing to do with the making of that covenant. In no sense did it depend on him. It was truly a covenant of *grace*.

By passing between the pieces of the animals, God declared symbolically that he alone would suffer the consequences of any covenant breaking, as indeed he did in the death of his Son (Isa. 53:8; Gal. 3:13). For our sins in the covenant, God, in Christ, suffered the penalty by being cast out and cut off. Christ expressed that when he cried, "My God, my God, why hast thou forsaken me?" Thus the covenant of grace revealed to Abraham was fulfilled in Christ.

The Covenant and the Land Promise

Genesis 15 shows clearly that God's covenant with Abraham—and through Abraham also with true Israel and with us—is a covenant of grace. That same chapter, however, reminds us of another notable feature of the Abrahamic covenant: it involved a promise of *the land*.

The land promise, however, is very often misunderstood and leads many to look for some future restoration of the nation of Israel in the earthly land of Canaan. We believe this to be a vain hope.

The covenant with Abraham shows just how vain that hope is. If the covenant with Abraham as a land covenant involved the promise of an earthly land, then that promise was *never* fulfilled to Abraham himself.

The Word tells us in Acts 7:5 that God gave Abraham *no* inheritance in the land, not so much as to set his foot on. Yet as verse 5 says, God promised it not only to Abraham's seed, but also to *him*. There cannot be, in our estimation, clearer proof that the land promise and all such promises in the Old Testament had a *spiritual* fulfillment. The promise of the land was always essentially the promise of a *heavenly* inheritance, and not really the promise of any earthly land or inheritance.

Hebrews 11:8–16 confirms this. When Abraham, by faith, left Ur to go to the *land God had promised him,* he "looked for a city which hath foundations, whose builder and maker is God" (v. 10). Isaac and Jacob, too, always "confessed that they were *strangers and pilgrims on the earth*" (v. 13) and declared that they were seeking "a better country, that is, an *heavenly*" (v. 16). In fact, if they had been looking for an earthly inheritance, they might have had opportunity to go back to the land from which they first came (v. 15), but that was not their hope. Nor is it ours.

Because the land promise to Abraham was really a promise of spiritual and heavenly things, all the true children of Abraham (Rom. 3:28–29; Rom. 4:16–17; Gal. 3:29), those who believe in Abraham's God, both Jews and Gentiles, shall enjoy the fulfillment of that promise and of all the other promises of the covenant that God made to Abraham and his seed. Not one shall fail to obtain what was promised—not Abraham himself, not those believing Jews who were scattered after the captivity and never returned to Canaan, and not the Gentile believers who are also true children of Abraham by faith.

Thus all Abraham's children inherit with Abraham something far better than the hills and rivers and cities of the earthly land. They enter that blessed inheritance of which Hebrews 12:22–24 speaks, and there is none better.

The Covenant with Israel

That God had a covenant with Israel is clear from Scripture. How that covenant is to be understood is a matter of much dispute.

The great question is whether the covenant with Israel was a different covenant from the one God establishes with his people in the New Testament, and how the Old Testament (old covenant) and the New Testament (new covenant) are related to each other. Are they *old* and *new* in that they are *different kinds of covenants* made with two different groups of people, or are they older and newer revelations of *one covenant*?

Dispensationalism answers such questions by teaching that the old and new covenants are completely distinct from one another and that they concern different groups of people, have different promises, and have different fulfillments. In its most extreme forms, it even teaches different ways of salvation for Israel in the old covenant and for the church under the new covenant, the *Scofield Study Bible* notes being an example of this teaching.[1]

There are those who reject dispensationalism, but who still hesitate to completely identify the two covenants. Some find a difference between the promises of the old and new covenants and their fulfillments (premillennialism and postmillennialism). They say that at least some of the old covenant promises have an earthly fulfillment in distinction from the promises of the new covenant, which are spiritual and heavenly.

The Baptists make some distinction between Israel and the church, especially as regards the covenant *and its sign*. They would say, for example, that Israel is not the church but only a type of the church, and they would refuse to identify circumcision and baptism as the signs of the old and new covenants, respectively.

Others make a disjunction between law and grace. They teach in one

---

1. C. I. Scofield (1843–1921), orig. editor, and Doris W. Rikkers, cont. editor, *Scofield Study Bible, King James Version* (New York: Oxford University Press, 2003). Scofield's work was first published in 1909.

way or another that the law has no place in the life of a new covenant believer. This error is called antinomianism.

In contrast to all of this, the Reformed faith insists that there is only one covenant; one covenant people, Israel being the church of the Old Testament (Acts 7:38); one sign of the covenant, circumcision and baptism being essentially the same (Col. 2:11–12); one Savior and one way of salvation (Acts 4:12); one promise of eternal life in Christ (Acts 2:38–39); and one spiritual fulfillment of all that belongs to the promise (Heb. 11:9–10, 13–16). It insists, too, that there is unity between law and grace under both covenants (Rom. 7:12).

The Reformed faith insists on a complete unity of the two testaments (covenants) as a reflection, finally, of God's own unity. No more than there is division in God can there be any essential division between the old and new covenants.

One People of God

Many would vehemently dispute the teaching that Israel is the church of the Old Testament and that therefore God's covenant with Israel is the same covenant that he has with his church in the New Testament. For this reason we need to prove our doctrines carefully from Scripture.

That Israel and the church are the same is clear. True Israel in Scripture is not an earthly people and a carnal nation, but *the spiritual people of God,* as is the church.

In Romans 9:6–8 the Word of God tells us that "they are not all Israel, which are of Israel." Scripture therefore makes a clear distinction between those who are only *of Israel* and those who truly *are* Israel. Everyone who belonged to the nation was *of Israel*, but only those who were born by the power of the promise (born again by the living Word of God) were counted as the seed, that is, as children of Abraham and children of God. They were a spiritual people.

Romans 2:28–29 confirms this in a remarkable way. It says plainly that *they are not Jews* who are Jews only outwardly. A person is a Jew who is one inwardly, that is, one who is circumcised in heart and spirit (compare with Col. 2:11).

This should mean, according to the biblical definition of a Jew, that even the believing Gentiles are counted as children of Abraham and as Israelites. That, too, Scripture teaches. Romans 4:11–16 makes it clear that Abraham is not only the father of believing Jews, but of believing Gentiles as well. He is the father "of us all," that is, of one spiritual people. Galatians 3:7 plainly says, "Know ye therefore that they which are of faith, the same are the children of Abraham."

In fact, the New Testament makes it clear that believing Gentiles are more truly Jews and more truly circumcised than unbelieving descendants of Abraham. Those who are Jews only according to the flesh are called in Philippians 3:2 "the concision," or mere "mutilators," because though circumcised outwardly, they are unspiritual. Jesus also had made it clear that some of the Jews were neither true children of Abraham, nor children of God (John 8:33–41ff.). In contrast, the Philippians, who were Gentiles, are called "the circumcision," because they "worship God in the spirit, and rejoice in Jesus Christ, and have no confidence in the flesh" (v. 3).

There are other passages that teach this as well. Galatians 4:1–7 tells us that the church of the Old Testament and New Testament are one by comparing them to *one person,* growing from infancy to maturity. Galatians 3:16, 29 shows that there is only *one* Seed: Christ and those who are in him. Hebrews 12:22–24 identifies Jerusalem, Mt. Zion, and the church of the firstborn. To come to one is to come to all.

This identification of Israel as the spiritual people of God is critical. Our participation in all the blessings and promises of the covenant depends upon it. Only true Jews have any right to the promises and to what was promised. Those promises are not for all who have the name, of either Jew or Christian, but only for those who believe. A true Jew is one who believes—anyone who believes. Do you?

The Law and the Covenant

The unique feature of the covenant with Israel was, of course, the giving of the law at Mt. Sinai. What is the relationship between the law and the covenant?

Fundamental to an understanding of this relationship is Galatians 3:17–21. This passage shows, first, that the covenant with Abraham four hundred years before the giving of the law is the covenant that was "confirmed in Christ," that is, the one everlasting covenant of God; and, second, that the giving of the law could not disannul this covenant (v. 17). In fact, the law is not even *against* the covenant (v. 21).

Exodus 24:7 goes so far as to call the law "the book of the covenant," the book in which God makes known his covenant with his people. If the covenant to which it belonged is the covenant that was confirmed in Christ—the same covenant to which we belong—then the law is still the book of the covenant, though much has been added to that book since then.

According to Galatians 3:19, this written law was added to the covenant because of transgressions, until Christ should come. This means that the law, by revealing sin, shows us our need for Christ. It was "our schoolmaster to bring us unto Christ, that we might be justified by faith" (v. 24) in him.

Romans 10:4 says much the same thing. It does not say that Christ is the *end* of the law in the sense that he takes the law away, but that he is the *end* of the law by being its *goal and purpose*. The law was given with Christ as its goal, and it accomplishes its purpose when, by discovering sin, it shows true Israel their need for Christ and for justification through faith in him.

That the law continues to have this function Paul clearly shows in Romans 7:7: "I had not known sin, but by the law." Galatians 3 also proves this when it says that the law was not only the Jews' schoolmaster, but "ours also" (vv. 23–24).

We have no difficulty, therefore, in saying that the law was and is part of the covenant. It certainly was part of the covenant in the Old Testament, as Galatians 3:19 reminds us. That it still belongs to the covenant is clear from the fact that the same law continues to be to us a schoolmaster to lead us to Christ. What has changed is our relationship to the law as covenant people, but that is another subject entirely, the subject of Galatians 4:1–7.

This is not to deny that there were "rudiments of the world" attached to the law and elements that were purely ceremonial (Col. 2:20–23). These have ceased, but even in the Old Testament they were part of God's covenant in that they pointed to Christ and functioned as a "schoolmaster" to bring Israel to Christ.

The point is that there is but one covenant, a covenant that is not in conflict with the law, a covenant of grace in Christ to which all true Israel belongs. God's law was not, is not, and never will be against God's covenant.

The Law's Function in the Covenant

We have shown from Galatians 3:17–21 that the law was given as part of the covenant of God and that it still remains part of the covenant. This is to say, of course, that law and grace are not against each other. The law is not against the covenant or its promises (v. 21). We have also shown that in the covenant the law has the function, first, of discovering sin (vv. 19, 24). With this few would disagree.

But that is not the only function of the law as "the book of the covenant" (Ex. 24:7). In the covenant the law also functions as a guide for the life of thankful obedience that Christians are called to live as God's covenant people.

Because of this function of the law, the believer calls the law "a lamp unto my feet, and a light unto my path" (Ps. 119:105; Prov. 6:23). It is a sure and safe guide along life's pathway.

For this reason the law is also called "the perfect law of liberty" and "the royal law" (James 1:25; James 2:8, 12). This royal law is not a new law but the ten commandments, as we see from James 2:8, 11. As the royal law of liberty, given by the King of kings, it defines and sets boundaries to our liberty, thus keeping our liberty in Christ from becoming licentiousness (Gal. 5:13–14).

Even in the Old Testament, God first gave the law to a people whom he had already redeemed and brought forth from bondage in Egypt (Ex. 20:1–2). He did this not to bring them back into bondage, but to set bounds about their life as his own covenant people, and to organize their life so that they might better serve him and show their gratitude to him for so great a deliverance.

This is always the case. In a free country, liberty is guarded by law. It is law that sets bounds to liberty so that liberty is not destroyed by every man doing what is right in his own eyes. When law is discarded and every man does as he pleases, as often happens today, finally a person does not even have the liberty to leave his own house and walk the streets without fear.

It is the law, therefore, that gives structure and order to the life of God's covenant people. It defines their relationship to him so that he is glorified by their life. The law is able to do this because it reveals the nature and attributes of God and so shows us the nature of a God-glorifying life.

The law does *not* bring men into a covenant relationship with God, nor does it give the necessary grace to live a God-glorifying life. This they have from Christ (Gal. 3:24). Nevertheless, it is still the book of the covenant, revealing how God's covenant people may please him and be thankful to him, in word as well as in deed.

This is not to deny, however, that the believer's relationship to the law has been changed by the coming of Christ. He is no longer *under the law*, but *under grace*.

The Covenant with David

The last great Old Testament revelation of God's covenant was that made to David (2 Sam. 7). As a revelation of the covenant, it also had some notable features.

We have here again the covenant formula that shows the covenant with David still to be the one, everlasting covenant of God, in spite of different circumstances. In this covenant God promises to be the God of his people and to take them as his own (v. 24). This is always the purpose of the covenant.

The revelation of the covenant made to David is unique, however, in several respects. It brings together covenant and kingdom and shows that they are very closely related. God promises to establish David's kingdom and his throne forever (vv. 12–13), a promise that is fulfilled in Christ, the King of kings (Luke 1:32–33).

In showing that covenant and kingdom belong together, God teaches David and us some important truths. The relationship between covenant and kingdom shows the orderly structure of the covenant. In that covenant God's people are citizens of a kingdom, each with his proper place under God's own rule. The "throne" of which God speaks (2 Sam. 7:13) is really always God's throne, even when a man like David sits on it.

This connection between covenant and kingdom also reveals the spiritual nature of the kingdom. There are many today who have the same earthly and carnal conception of the kingdom that the Pharisees had at the time of Jesus' ministry. They think that the whole world is, or will be, the kingdom of God; that the kingdom is here on earth before Christ's return and is composed of a society dominated by Christians. Or they think that the kingdom will be an earthly Jewish state modeled after the kingdom of Israel in the Old Testament and that it will be set up prior to the return of Christ.

God makes clear that these conceptions are wrong by connecting the coming of the kingdom with the promise of the covenant. The kingdom is neither a Jewish state nor a Christian society, but the orderly dwelling of God with his people in fellowship. At the center of that kingdom, therefore, is God's house, the temple (v. 13), the great Old Testament picture of the church as the body of Christ (John 2:18–21).

It is in the work of Christ that we see the fulfillment of these covenant promises to David. He establishes and enters his kingdom not by world dominion or by the establishment of a Jewish state, but in the way of suffering and shame (2 Sam. 7:14; Ps. 89:30ff.). It is not armies and weapons and governments that must be defeated, but sin.

The words that hung over Christ's head on the cross, therefore, marked the fulfillment of the promises made to David, although those who put it there meant it in mockery. In his suffering Christ was *the King* of the Jews, that is, of all true children of Abraham. Christ is the one who delivers them from their spiritual enemies and earns for them a place in paradise, in his own heavenly kingdom.

The New Covenant

The New Testament is called the new covenant in Hebrews 8:6–13. In fact, the word *testament* is the same word as *covenant.* According to Hebrews 8, this new covenant replaces the old.

From Hebrews 8:6–13 many conclude that there is some essential difference between the old and new—that they are different covenants. The Baptists come to this conclusion in their defense of believer's baptism, saying that the covenant sealed by circumcision is not the same as the covenant sealed by baptism. The premillennialists come to a similar conclusion in defense of their belief that there is still a special earthly future for Israel (one covenant promise for Israel, another for New Testament believers).

We believe that the new covenant replaces the old only as a newer and fuller revelation of the one everlasting covenant of God. The differences are only differences of administration. Hebrew 8 itself makes this clear.

First, verse 10 uses the ordinary covenant formula—I will be their God; they will be my people—to show that the new covenant is not essentially different from the old. The relationships are still the same in both the old and new covenants.

Second, the reference to "my laws" in verse 10 confirms this. In the new covenant the law is not removed, but *rewritten* on different tables: the fleshy tables of the heart (2 Cor. 3:3). Law and covenant still go together. In fact, the giving of the law, though now differently written, *is* the making or declaring of the covenant, both in Deuteronomy 4:13 and in Hebrews 8:10.

Third, in both the old covenant and the new, according to Hebrews 8:11, the essential thing is knowing the Lord, though there is a difference in *how* we know him. This verse speaks of the New Testament as a time of realization and fulfillment. It is a time, therefore, in which God's people know him directly and not anymore through the mediation of priests and Levites (Mal. 2:5–7).

The new covenant, then, is not something completely different, but new in the same way that the heavens and earth shall be new when Christ comes again. The heavens and earth are not *annihilated,* but *renewed.*

The passing of the old covenant does not, therefore, bring in an entirely new covenant, but a better revelation of that one covenant in which God is the God of his people and takes them to be his own. It is the last and fullest revelation of the covenant through the coming of the things promised, rather than through the pictures and types of the old covenant. To the new covenant belongs the law, not as a kind of bondage, but as a help that shows how we may better glorify and thank the great God of our salvation in word and *deed.*

That new covenant is "better," as expressed in Hebrews 8:6, and more glorious, because it brings us Christ instead of just the types of

Christ. Only the final consummation of the covenant will be more glorious.

The Old and New Covenants Compared

We have shown from Hebrews 8:6–13 that the old and new covenants are not two separate and different covenants. At all essential points they are the *same.*

The differences between them are only in what we call *administration,* or administrative details. It is only in respect to these details that one is "old" and the other "new," and that the old perishes and passes away. A new president is a change of *administration* and therefore is a new government in that limited sense, not a change in the type of government or in the constitution.

How, then, are the old and new covenants different? According to Hebrews 8, in three ways.

First, there is a change of mediator (v. 6). Christ replaces Moses. This is not an essential difference, however, because Moses was a *type* of Christ. In Hebrews 3:5 Moses is even called "a testimony of those things which were to be spoken after." Also, in Deuteronomy 18:15, Moses himself speaks of Christ as a "Prophet...like unto me." This difference, therefore, is only administrative.

Second, there is also a change in the way the law is written (Heb. 8:10). As we have pointed out, the law itself is not taken away; it is simply rewritten on fleshly tables of the heart instead of on tables of stone. This, too, is only an administrative change, though it has great significance for the New Testament believer. Something rewritten is not something different and separate from what went before.

This second point is especially important because in both Deuteronomy 4:13 and Hebrews 8:10, the giving of the law is called the giving of the covenant. One cannot, then, argue that although the law was the same, the covenants are different. They are *identified* in both Deuteronomy and Hebrews.

Third, the new covenant also brings a fuller and more complete revelation. This is what Hebrews 8:11 is talking about. This fuller revelation is of such a kind that all God's people know the Mediator *directly,* and not any longer through the intervention of earthly mediators. There is not under the new covenant the need of teachers like the priests and Levites of the Old Testament (see Mal. 2:6–7 for proof that they, especially, were the teachers of the Old Testament).

This is also an administrative change. The new covenant does not bring a *new* (different and separate) revelation of God, but a better revelation (Heb. 8:6), that is, one that is completed and that reveals the realities only prophesied under the old covenant.

There is only one, everlasting covenant of God.

The Consummation of the Covenant

One reason we do not believe that the covenant is an agreement or contract by which salvation is brought to God's people has to do with the consummation of the covenant. The consummation of the covenant is its final realization and glory in the everlasting and heavenly kingdom of Christ our Lord.

If the covenant were a contract or agreement to bring salvation, then at the consummation, when we receive the fullness of our salvation, the covenant would be set aside or discarded in the same way that any other contract would be finished when all that had been contracted was completed.

But this cannot be. For one thing the covenant is *everlasting*. It is not something that is useful only for a time and then set aside, as a contract or agreement would be.

We believe, therefore, that the covenant is a relationship or bond between God and his people in Christ. That relationship is described in Scripture by the covenant formula: "I will be your God, and ye shall be my people."

If that is indeed the essence of the covenant—that God is ours and we are his—then in heaven the covenant will not be left behind or abandoned but fully realized. That is what heaven is all about—that we will be with God to glorify him and to enjoy him forever.[2]

That is exactly how Revelation 21:3 describes the glory of the new

---

2. Answer 1 of the Westminster Shorter Catechism is "Man's chief end is to glorify God and to enjoy him for ever."

heavens and the new earth. When all is new, there will be no more tears, no more death, no more crying or sorrow or pain. How wonderful that will be!

But even more wonderful is that which the voice from heaven foretells: "Behold, the tabernacle of God is with men, and he will dwell with them, *and they shall be his people, and God himself shall be with them, and be their God.*"

Notice that this passage has in it the same covenant formula that is used throughout Scripture: "I will be your God, and ye shall be my people." There is nothing more desirable or wonderful than that!

Notice, too, that the passage speaks of God's tabernacle. In the Old Testament that was the place of his covenant, the place where he dwelt with his people and revealed himself as their God (Ex. 29:42–46).

That Old Testament tent was a type and shadow of better things, for it pictured the Lord Jesus Christ himself, in whom and through whom God dwells with us and is our God, and by whom he reveals himself to us in all his glory. In Christ he meets with us and speaks with us. In Christ he dwells among us. That is the everlasting blessedness of God's covenant.

The Covenants Summarized

We believe that we have shown from Scripture that the different covenants mentioned in Scripture are not separate covenants, but different revelations of the one everlasting covenant of God. We now wish to summarize what we have written earlier by listing the different covenants and what each of them shows as a revelation of that one covenant.

The first revelation of the covenant was to Adam in paradise. That covenant might be called *The Covenant of Life,* since it revealed the essential character of the covenant. It showed what the covenant was, revealed God as the sovereign Lord of the covenant, and clearly delineated man's place in the covenant (Gen. 1; Gen. 2; Hos. 6:7).

The second great revelation of the covenant was to Adam after the fall. That covenant could be called *The Covenant of Promise.* It revealed God as the faithful, covenant-keeping God who maintains his covenant with his people by the power of sovereign, redemptive grace (Gen. 3, esp.

v. 15). In it Christ is revealed as the promised Seed and the great Sacrifice (vv. 15, 21).

The third important revelation was to Noah. The covenant is best remembered as *The Covenant of Creation.* In it God revealed the universal character of his covenant, to include not all men, but all creation as well (Gen. 9:1–17). In it Christ is revealed as Reconciler and Lord of all creation (Gen. 9:15–16; Col. 1:20).

The fourth revelation was to Abraham. That covenant could well be called *The Covenant of the Family,* since it showed more clearly than ever before that God's covenant is very much a family covenant (Gen. 15; Gen. 17). The Father reveals to Abraham through his Son that he, God, will be the God of believers and their children.

The fifth great revelation was to Israel. Since the giving of the law was the main feature of that revelation, that covenant should be called *The Covenant of Law.* In it God revealed that law and covenant are not opposed, but belong together (Ex. 19; Ex. 20; Gal. 3; Gal. 4). He showed Israel that it is the law that defines and sets boundaries for our lives as God's covenant people.

The sixth and last revelation in the Old Testament was that to David, and it might well be remembered as *The Covenant of the Kingdom.* In it God revealed especially the orderly structure of his covenant (2 Sam. 7; Ps. 89), as well as the unique place of Christ as sovereign Head and Lord of the covenant.

The whole New Testament itself is called in Scripture *the new covenant,* not because it is an entirely different covenant, but because it is a new revelation of the covenant, not of types and shadows, but of the realities to which those types pointed (Heb. 8). Here, finally, Christ comes with all his blessings and fulfills the types and shadows.

Now we still wait for the day of the consummation of the covenant, when the covenant will be realized in all its fullness. Then the tabernacle of God will be with men; he will dwell with them and be with them as their God, and they shall be his people (Rev. 21:3).

The Order of Salvation

When in theology we speak of the "order of salvation," we are speaking of the different parts of salvation as they are applied and given to God's people by the Holy Spirit. In other words, the "order of salvation" describes the work of God's Spirit *in* us.

The closest thing we have to an order of salvation in Scripture is Romans 8:30, but that is not an order of salvation in the strict theological sense. For instance, it speaks of predestination, which is not part of God's work *in* us, but something he did *for* us before the foundation of the world.

A typical order of salvation is that followed by the Westminster Larger Catechism: union with Christ, effectual calling, justification, adoption, sanctification, and glorification. Others would propose a different order. Many, for example, would include regeneration and faith. In any case, the purpose of such an order is to try to understand the relationship between these different parts of our salvation, all of which are described in Scripture.

Several things must be remembered in speaking of such an order.

We must remember that this is only an attempt to understand these biblical concepts and is in no sense to be understood mechanically, as though we first receive one blessing, then the next, and so on. The fact is that in our experience many of these blessings are received at the same time. Also, many of them are not one-time spiritual happenings. Sanctification, for example, is something that begins when a person is first saved and continues to the very moment of death. The application of salvation does not take place all at once, but is something lifelong—something finished only when we are finally with Christ in heaven. This is, of course, denied by those who believe in perfectionism and entire sanctification; they tend to see the application of salvation as a one-time thing.

In a Reformed order of salvation, there are several things that must be emphasized and cannot be changed. Regeneration and effectual calling must come before faith, or we have faith as a work of man, which is Arminianism. Faith itself must come before justification to maintain the great Protestant truth of justification by faith alone. Finally, justification must precede sanctification, or we have the Romish doctrine of justification by works.

All this is only to say that the one thing any order of salvation must teach is that also in its *application,* salvation is entirely the work of God himself through the sovereign operations of the Holy Spirit. It is all of grace, and therefore is "of the LORD" (Jonah 2:9).

Irresistible Grace

In studying the order of salvation, we find that *grace* runs through the entire order like a golden thread. The grace that produces and guarantees each step of the order is *irresistible.*

This must be emphasized. We must not think that the first part of the order is all of grace, but that the last part of the order of salvation is of works. Regeneration is not God's work and sanctification our work.

Nor is it true that the first part of the order is of grace alone and the last part of the order is both grace and works together. While it is true that we become active in faith, conversion, and sanctification, these do not depend on us or merit anything with God. They, too, are all of God and all of grace (Rom. 9:16). It is God who works in us both to will and to do of his good pleasure (Phil. 2:13).

Nor should we think that only *part* of the order is by irresistible grace. Our *activity* in conversion and sanctification does not imply that the work of the Spirit and the grace by which we are converted and sanctified can be resisted. *All* of salvation is by irresistible grace.

Grace is irresistible in the very nature of the case, because it is *God's* grace. Since he is almighty, his grace also is almighty. Not only in providence, but also in salvation, "none can stay his hand, or say unto him, What doest thou?" (Dan. 4:35).

Many ignore and set aside this great truth today. The doctrine of common grace—that there is a certain grace shown to all men—really teaches that there is a kind of grace that is resistible. So does the doctrine of the well-meant offer of the gospel, which teaches that God graciously offers salvation to all who hear the gospel, even though that grace is rejected and resisted by many. In defense of the precious doctrine of irresistible grace, we should have nothing to do with either of these teachings.

Irresistible grace does not mean, however, that God brings people to heaven kicking and struggling and resisting all the way. Irresistible grace does not *compel* but *impels;* in other words, by it, God changes us in heart and mind and will so that we love him, seek him, obey him, and persevere in obedience, even to the end.

The Canons of Dordt, which are the original Five Points of Calvinism, say that this grace of God "does not treat men as senseless stocks and blocks, nor takes away their will and its properties, neither does violence thereto; but spiritually quickens, heals, corrects, and at the same time sweetly and powerfully bends it; that where carnal rebellion and resistance formerly prevailed, a ready and sincere spiritual obedience begins to reign."[3] That is a beautiful description of *irresistible grace.*

Only irresistible grace can overcome our natural depravity. Only such grace can guarantee that we are "kept . . . through faith unto salvation ready to be revealed in the last time" (1 Pet. 1:5). Only irresistible grace, therefore, can give us good hope in believing and the comfort of knowing that *nothing* can separate us from the love of God that is in Christ Jesus our Lord. Irresistible grace is assuring grace.

Regeneration

We begin our study of the actual "order of salvation" by looking at regeneration. Since regeneration means "rebirth," we believe that it describes the beginning of our new life as Christians and is first in the order of salvation.

In describing this first work of grace as a *rebirth* (John 3:3), Scripture is emphasizing the truth that it is wholly a work of God, done without our aid—even without our first being aware of it. No more than a newborn infant has anything to do with being born into the world do we have anything to do with our rebirth into the kingdom of God.

In fact, Scripture does not only imply this, but plainly teaches it as well (John 1:13): "Which were born, not of blood, nor of the will of the flesh, nor of the will of man, but of God." Note that neither the sinful will (the will of the flesh), nor human willpower in any sense (the will of man), has anything to do with this rebirth.

Without regeneration as a first work of grace, no one can even *see* the kingdom of God (John 3:3). Jesus does not say "no one *will*" but "no one *can.*" It is as impossible for the unregenerate sinner to have anything to do with the kingdom of God as it is for the fish of the sea to live on the dry land.

Scripture describes this first work of grace as a rebirth as well as the gift of a *new heart* (Ezek. 36:25ff.); a *circumcision of the heart,* that is, a cutting away of sin in the heart (Col. 2:11–13); a *baptism,* which is a

---

3. Canons of Dordt, Heads of Doctrine 3 and 4, Article 16.

washing away of sin (Titus 3:5); a *spiritual quickening,* a being made alive, or a resurrection from spiritual death (Eph. 2:1); a *new creation* in Christ Jesus (v. 10); and *a translation from the kingdom of darkness to the kingdom of God's dear Son* (Col. 1:13).

Each of these descriptions reminds us that regeneration is both a sovereign work of the Almighty and wonderful. Who else can raise the dead and create things? As the Canons of Dordt describe this, "It is evidently a supernatural work, most powerful, and at the same time most delightful, astonishing, mysterious, and ineffable [incomprehensible]; not inferior in efficacy [power] to creation or the resurrection from the dead."[4]

Perhaps the most wonderful description of regeneration, however, tells us that it is the giving of Christ's life to a lost sinner (Gal. 2:20; Col. 1:27). The new life that is given us in regeneration is the new, resurrection life of Christ himself, a life that cannot die again (John 11:25–26).

It is *new* life. One who has it cannot possibly continue to behave and speak as he once did. He is no longer spiritually dead, but alive. Death only lies there and rots, but life breathes and moves and speaks. We who are regenerated must, therefore, in spite of the continued presence of our sin and old nature, reckon ourselves to be alive unto God through Jesus Christ our Lord, and yield ourselves unto God as those who are alive from the dead (Rom. 6:11–13).

Calling

If regeneration (spiritual rebirth) can be compared to the planting of the seed of the new resurrection life of Jesus Christ in our hearts, then *calling* can be compared to the rain and sunshine that fall on that seed and cause it to grow and bear fruit.

Calling is sometimes referred to as "efficacious calling." This only means that the calling is a powerful work of God that always brings about the desired *effect,* namely, salvation. Efficacious calling is really part of "irresistible grace."

When we speak of calling in the order of salvation, we are not referring to the preaching of the gospel through which that call comes and

---

4. Ibid.

that is heard *without* saving power by many. Matthew 22:14 uses the word *called* in that sense when Jesus says, "Many are called, but few are chosen." Instead, we are referring to the work of the Spirit in the hearts of those whom God has chosen, by which the preaching of the gospel brings them to salvation and keeps them in it.

This needs emphasis. Efficacious calling does not only begin salvation in us; it also brings about our *whole* salvation. It calls us powerfully and irresistibly to repentance (Matt. 9:13), faith (Rom. 10:17), holiness (1 Thess. 4:7), fellowship with Christ (1 Cor. 1:9), liberty (Gal. 5:13), assurance (Eph. 4:4), and finally, also to glory with Christ (1 Pet. 5:10; Rev. 19:9). The call, therefore, must continue to come to us all our lives. It must come not only as a call to holiness and assurance, but also as a call to repentance and faith. As long as we sin and are weak in faith, we must be called to repentance and faith.

We say this to counter a common notion. Many have the idea that the call is only for the unsaved, so that often the minister has no call—nothing to say—to those who have already been saved, though they are as greatly in need of the calling as the rest.

We wish especially to emphasize that it is *Christ* who calls (John 10:3, 16, 27) with the voice of almighty God (Rom. 4:17). By the work of the Spirit, that call is applied to the hearts of some so that they hear Christ calling, know his voice, and come to him as sheep to their Shepherd. Is that not wonderful?

John 10:3 says, "He calleth his own sheep *by name.*" The call is not general, but very specific. It implies that Christ already knows his sheep. And indeed he does, for they were given him by the Father before the foundation of the world (Eph. 1:4–6).

When Christ calls his sheep by name, however, they do not hear their natural names, Mary or William. They hear their *spiritual names,* the names they have received by the very first work of God's grace in their hearts: names such as *Thirsty One* (Rev. 22:17), *Hungry One* (Isa. 55:1), *Laboring and Burdened One* (Matt. 11:28).

Indeed, it is the calling that *makes* sinners hungry, thirsty, burdened by sin and guilt, and finally willing also to come to Christ. That is why it is referred to as the *efficacious* call. Christ's word in calling is a creative word that brings into existence the thing called for.

What a blessing and a joy, then, to hear Christ's voice calling and to know that he calls us to himself.

Calling and Preaching

Efficacious calling is sometimes referred to as *internal* calling, because it involves the sovereign and irresistible work of the Holy Spirit in the *hearts* of God's people. It is distinguished from the external calling, the preaching of the Word.

Scripture makes it clear that not all who hear Christ calling in the preaching of the gospel hear him calling internally by the work of the Holy Spirit in the heart. Thus not all are saved under the preaching of the gospel.

In other words, that some are saved under the preaching of the gospel, and others are not, is not due to some difference in them, but to a difference in God's work. That is why Matthew 20:16 and Matthew 22:14 say, "For many are called [outwardly], but few are chosen." The passage does not say, "Many are called, but few respond," for that would leave the impression that the difference lies in us. Instead, the difference lies in God's choosing some and not others. According to that choice, he calls some both outwardly and inwardly, but not others.

Although Scripture uses the word *call* to refer to both an outward and an inward call, we must remember that the inward call comes *through the outward,* that is, through the preaching. Indeed, that is why the same word is used to describe both.

We see this in Romans 10:17: "So then faith cometh by hearing, and hearing by the word of God." This verse is summing up what verses 10 – 14 say. There an inseparable connection is made between *believing unto salvation* and *hearing a preacher.*

This is why the church must preach the gospel to the ends of the earth. It is the means by which God calls those whom he has chosen to salvation and by which, through the Spirit, he works inwardly in them.

We would stress, too, that because the Holy Spirit works through preaching, the preaching of the gospel *is its own power.* It is "the power of God unto salvation to every one that believeth" (Rom. 1:16; see also 1 Cor. 1:18, 24). It does not require eloquence, begging, or other sorts of gimmicks to make it effectual.

Because Christ speaks in the preaching, and because the Spirit works through preaching, the preaching of the gospel is always a *power,* though not always a power unto salvation. Where Christ speaks and the

Spirit works, it is impossible to remain unaffected. Either one is saved or one is hardened under the preaching of the gospel (2 Cor. 2:14–17). No one can be neutral.

Thus through the preaching of the gospel, God's purpose is realized and the merits of Christ made effectual. Not one of the elect is lost, nor one drop of the precious blood of Christ wasted. The preaching is not wasted on those who are not saved, either. It is therefore a very serious thing to come under the gospel. Even those of us who are already saved by it should "give the more earnest heed to the things which we have heard, lest at any time we should let them slip" (Heb. 2:1–3). The gospel will always be a savor either of life unto life, or of death unto death.

Call, Not Offer

There are many who prefer to speak of the gospel as an "offer" rather than a call. It is interesting, to say the least, that Scripture *never* uses the word *offer* to describe the gospel. We have no objection to the word *offer* as such. In its older sense it means only that in the gospel there is a "showing forth" of Christ. The Westminster Larger Catechism, for example, defines an offer of Christ as a "*testifying* that whosoever believes in him shall be saved."[5]

In its modern sense, however, the word *offer* suggests and is used to teach that God loves all men and wants to save every one of them, that he makes an effort to save all of them in the gospel, and that whether or not a sinner will be saved is dependent on the will of that sinner. These teachings are all contrary to Scripture.

Scripture does not teach that God loves all men (Ps. 11:5; John 13:1; Rom. 9:13), nor does it teach that God is trying to save all of them (Isa. 6:9–11; Rom. 9:18; 2 Cor. 2:14–16). Certainly it does not teach that in saving sinners God can be frustrated by their unwillingness, or that he waits, cap in hand as it were, for them to *accept* his salvation (Ps. 115:3; John 6:44; Rom. 9:16; Eph. 2:8–9). For these reasons we prefer not to speak of the gospel as an "offer."

---

5. The Westminster Larger Catechism, Q&A 65.

A call is different from an offer. It reminds us of the sovereignty of God. He, as King, summons sinners to believe and obey the gospel. It even intimates that he actually does bring some to salvation by his sovereign call. When we remember that it is *God* who calls, it is not difficult to understand this. He is the one who "calleth those things which be not as though they were" (Rom. 4:17).

That call is heard in the preaching of the gospel. It is made effectual to salvation by the inward work of the Holy Spirit, so that some not only hear, but also obey that call. By the Spirit's work it is *God in Christ* who calls, not the preacher. The preacher is only an instrument.

That is the reason the ungodly are condemned for disobedience when they refuse to heed the call. By their unbelief they do not refuse a mere man, but the living God himself as he speaks through his only begotten Son. That is serious.

It is also the reason the preacher must bring nothing but Scripture. Those who hear must hear God's Word, not the preacher's notions, philosophies, political commentaries, etc. The preacher must even be careful that he does not obscure the sovereign call of God by adding all sorts of unnecessary begging or "hard sell" tactics, leaving the impression that God waits upon the will of sinners.

It must be clear in the preaching of the gospel that God sovereignly demands faith and repentance of sinners—that he, the Almighty, the Judge of heaven and earth, requires obedience and will punish disobedience. By such preaching sinners are saved, and God is glorified.

The Essence of Faith

When we think of faith, we usually think of the *activity* of believing and trusting in God and in his Son, the Lord Jesus Christ. Faith *is* believing and trusting, but before that it is something else. Faith in its deepest reality and essence is *union with Christ.*

This is suggested in the Heidelberg Catechism, which speaks of true faith in terms of "ingrafting into Christ,"[6] and in the Westminster Larger Catechism, which says that faith is not only assent to the truth of the

---

6. Heidelberg Catechism, Lord's Day 7, Q&A 20.

promise of the gospel, but also a *receiving and resting upon Christ* for salvation.[7] In distinction from the activity of faith, this ingrafting into Christ, this receiving and resting upon him, is sometimes referred to in theology as the "power of faith," or the "principle of faith."

Scripture teaches that faith is union with Christ in such passages as John 17:20–21, Galatians 2:20, and Ephesians 3:17. This union is also shown in the very way that Scripture speaks of faith. In the New Testament, for example, the Greek uses several different expressions, most of which imply that faith brings us into living contact and union with Christ. Scripture speaks most often of believing "*in* Christ." What else can that refer to but that we are, through faith, bone of his bone and flesh of his flesh (Eph. 5:30)? Scripture speaks also in the Greek of believing "into" him (John 3:16, 18; Col. 2:5), or of believing "on" him (Rom. 9:23; Rom. 10:11) or "upon" him (Acts 11:17; Acts 16:31).

All these passages imply close personal union and fellowship with the Son of God. Even those passages that speak simply of believing Christ imply that we are close enough to him by faith that we can actually hear him speaking and know and trust what he says (John 14:11; 2 Tim. 1:12). Such is the nature of true faith.

This, then, is what distinguishes true faith from all its counterfeits. In many other ways a counterfeit faith mimics a true faith, but there is one thing that cannot be mimicked, and that is being *in Christ* by faith.

To see faith as union with Christ is also to see that faith *must be* a gift of God. If we only speak of the *activity* of faith, we may begin to think that faith has its origin in us and in our will. But when we remember that faith is, first of all, *union* with Christ, it is clear that faith must be God's work and gift. Are we able to unite ourselves to Christ? No more than a branch can graft itself into the tree!

This understanding of faith explains many other things as well. It explains how in justification the righteousness of Christ becomes ours *through faith*. It explains how faith is the victory that overcomes the world, for it is not some inherent power in faith that overcomes, but the fact that faith puts us into Christ and so brings us into union with Christ's victory over sin, death, the world, and Satan.

What a marvelous thing, then, to be able to say that we have faith. To say it is to confess that by a wonderful and sovereign work of God,

---

7. The Westminster Larger Catechism, Q&A 72.

we live in Christ and he in us, nevermore to be parted from one another.

Faith and Knowledge

In speaking of the activity of faith, we believe that faith includes *knowing*. There have always been those who wish to separate faith from knowledge and to see faith as "blind" acceptance or trust. This is especially common today.

Roman Catholicism has always taught that faith and knowledge can be separated, especially in its teaching about implicit faith (faith without any intellectual content). This, according to Rome, is the faith of many or most laymen.

Modernism and neo-orthodoxy teach this also, as do the charismatic and other anti-doctrinal movements. They do not actually deny that faith includes knowledge, but they separate faith and knowledge by denigrating and speaking scornfully of doctrine and teaching.

Sadly this inclination is also found among some Reformed theologians and teachers. They, too, do not explicitly deny that faith is knowledge, but end up doing so nonetheless when they promote paradoxes and contradictions as part of their theology.

These are the people who say that God loves all men in the gospel, but that he does not love all men in election; that he wants to save all men according to his revealed will, but does not want to save all men according to his secret will; and that he well-meaningly offers salvation to all, yet has not determined to give faith to all. Such talk is irrational and anti-intellectual. No one can *understand* such contradictions. They can only be implicitly accepted, and faith then becomes a blind leap, not a matter of knowing!

This opposition to knowledge and doctrine is also contrary to Scripture. In John 17:3 Jesus defines saving faith as "knowing" God and Jesus Christ whom God sent. This *knowledge*, Jesus says, is eternal life, not merely trusting, but knowing.

In 2 Timothy 1:12 Paul speaks of his own faith as a "persuasion," but he says that he is persuaded because he first knows. Indeed, it is impossible to be persuaded that Jesus Christ is able to keep us unless we first know that he is the only begotten Son of God, the one come in the flesh who suffered and died on the cross for our sins.

We may not despise knowledge. By itself, knowledge is profitless; there must also be *trust*. But Scripture makes it clear that knowledge is nevertheless a good thing. In 2 Corinthians 4:6–7 "the light of the *knowledge* of the glory of God in the face of Jesus Christ" is called our treasure (see also Luke 1:77; Eph. 1:17; Eph. 4:13; Phil. 3:8; Col. 2:3; 2 Pet. 1:2–3). There is no confidence in *not knowing*.

Faith without knowledge truly is a leap into the dark. But God is not in the dark. He dwells in the light. Neither is our Lord Jesus Christ to be found by a leap into the dark. He is the *Light of the World,* and to believe in him we must come to the light. That light is the light of the knowledge of the glory of God in the face of Jesus Christ (2 Cor. 4:6).

Faith and Trust

It is clear from the various ways faith is described in Scripture that saving faith includes different "acts." In these descriptions we can see that there is a certain development and growth of faith as it is given to and exercised by believers. Luke 17:5, for example, says, "The apostles said unto the Lord, Increase our faith."

Although Christ is always the object of faith, faith involves *looking* to him (Isa. 45:22), *coming* to him (Matt. 11:28), *fleeing* to him for refuge (Heb. 6:18), *receiving* him (John 1:12), *putting* him *on* (Rom. 13:14), and *giving oneself up* or *yielding oneself* to him (2 Cor. 8:5).

All of these describe especially a second activity of saving faith: that of *trusting* in Christ. We have already said that one principle act of saving faith is knowledge. Trusting is another. These two elements of saving faith are mentioned in relation to one another in 2 Timothy 1:12: "I *know* whom I have believed, and *am persuaded* that he is able to keep that which I have committed unto him against that day." As this verse points out, trusting or being persuaded is founded on knowledge. The very word *persuade* emphasizes this. One is persuaded by truth and by reasonable and sound arguments.

We cannot trust or be persuaded if we do not know. We cannot trust Christ for salvation unless we know that he is God manifest in the flesh

(1 Tim. 3:16), the one who gave his life as a ransom for many (Matt. 20:28).

This second element of saving faith—trusting in Christ—emphasizes the *personal* nature of saving faith. It is this trust that makes the knowledge of faith not only a "knowing about" but also a matter of really "knowing" God himself personally as he reveals himself through Jesus Christ.

Without this element of trust, there would be no difference between saving faith and the "faith" of demons (James 2:19), for the demons "believe" that there is one God, and they tremble. Nor are demons the only ones who believe in this sense. Many have been taught the truth of the Word and can find no argument against it, yet they have never *trusted* God or Christ.

Trust, as an element of saving faith, allows a person to see not only that the Word is true, but also that it is true for himself. Trust, therefore, can be described in terms of yielding oneself to Christ or in terms of resting in him (Matt. 11:28). It involves the complete abandoning of self and the surrender of the soul to him by the power and grace of the Spirit.

There are those who wish to speak of faith solely in terms of knowledge or of intellectual assent. We, too, believe it necessary to emphasize knowledge over against the reliance on "feeling" and the resistance to sound doctrine that are so popular today. Nevertheless, in light of Scripture's own teaching, we do not believe it is adequate to describe faith solely in terms of its intellectual activity. It is also, as Paul says in 2 Timothy 1:12, a matter of committing oneself to Christ and so finding peace and rest in him. Without that, we are nothing and have nothing.

Justification

What is justification? Sadly there are few today who even know what the word means, and fewer still who know the blessedness of the justified, though the doctrine of justification is one of the fundamentals of the Christian faith.

To understand what justification is, we should know, first, that its synonym is *righteousness.* To be justified and to be righteous are the very same thing.

Second, we should see that justification is a *legal* term. In justification we have to do with God as *Judge* (Heb. 4:13). Justification is a *sentence* of the supreme Judge, from whose sentence there is no appeal (Job 40:8).

Third, justification therefore involves our *legal status* (state, estate): our standing before the law and before God (Ps. 130:3). That legal status or standing determines whether we will enjoy certain rights and privileges, or be punished.

When sentence is passed by any judge, there are only two possible "standings": guilty or innocent, unrighteous or righteous. In the justification of sinners, God as Judge declares them *innocent* of any wrongdoing or crime (Num. 23:21; 2 Cor. 5:19).

The wonder of justification is that *sinners* are found innocent by God. Those who are justified have committed and do commit every sin, and commit their sins against the Judge himself (Ps. 51:4; Rom. 5:18, 21).

The sentence by which God justifies them is like the laws of the Medes and the Persians: it cannot be altered, for God does not change. Yet God does not lie in passing such a sentence (Num. 23:19). His sentence is true and just.

That means that the sinner cannot possibly be justified and found innocent before God because of his own worthiness or works (Rom. 3:28; Rom. 4:6). The cause for justification—and there must be a cause—is the perfect obedience of Jesus Christ and his suffering and death.

Jesus stands as the substitute for those whom the Father gave him. His suffering and death are the punishment for their sins (Isa. 53:5), and by his perfect obedience he makes restitution, "restoring that which he took not away" (Ps. 69:4).

Think of a thief who must atone for his crime, not only by being punished, but by repaying what was stolen. Christ not only suffers the punishment for our crimes but also repays to God the debt of God-glorifying obedience that we did not pay.

Christ does all this for his own. His obedience, suffering, and death are charged to their account, or as Scripture says, are "imputed" to them (2 Cor. 5:19), so that before God it is as though they never had sin or committed any actual sins.

What a wonderful thing it is, then, to be justified. Nothing can compare with knowing that there is "no condemnation" for us with God. All other blessings and privileges and their enjoyment depend on this. As Paul says, "I have suffered the loss of all things, and do count them but dung, that I may win Christ, And be found in him, not having my own righteousness, which is of the law, but that which is through the faith of Christ, the righteousness which is of God by faith" (Phil. 3:8–9).

Justification by Faith

When Scripture speaks of justification *by faith,* it is teaching several very important truths.

Justification by faith shows how the sinner is *actually* justified before God. It explains how God's justifying sentence as Judge is applied to the sinner, so that he passes from a state of guilt to innocence.

When we are justified by faith, our faith is counted (imputed) to us for righteousness (Gen. 15:6; Rom. 4:5). God as Judge accepts that faith as our righteousness or innocence.

He does this, however, not because faith itself is worthy, or because faith and the obedience of faith are somehow accepted as a substitute for perfect obedience to his law. Rather, faith is counted as righteousness because of its own character. As we have seen, faith in its deepest reality is a *bond of union* with Christ. That explains how we are justified by faith. Faith is counted as our righteousness not because it is a substitute work or because it is worthy in itself, but because it brings us into contact with Christ and his perfect righteousness.

Truly, therefore, we are justified by the righteousness, obedience, holiness, and works of Christ, which become ours *through* faith. And it is only by faith that we can be justified. Nothing else but faith lays hold on Christ and his righteousness. And nothing but Christ's righteousness will ever find acceptance with God for our justification.

Nor is faith another work. Justification by faith does not mean, as many believe, that God as Judge has decided that instead of demanding all the works of the law, he will demand just one thing of us—one work—and that is faith.

Faith is not something we produce, not something that has its origin in us, as many teach. Believing is not a decision that the sinner makes; he can make no such decision as long as he is lost in his sins. The faith by which we are justified is itself the gift of God. He provides not only the righteousness that we need in order to be justified, but also the means or way by which that righteousness becomes ours.

Our justification, therefore, is wholly the work of God. From him are all things necessary for our justification. The righteousness that justifies us, the Person who provides that righteousness, and the means by which we receive righteousness are all God's gifts.

The fact that justification is *by faith* means, therefore, that it is *not by works*. We are called to do good works; they are even ordained for us (Eph. 2:10), but we do them as proof of and in thankfulness for salvation received, not to earn or merit salvation. Our works have *nothing* to do with our standing before God. Only Christ's works can change our standing and justify us.

As Scripture says, "Where is boasting then? It is excluded" (Rom. 3:27). "For of *him*, and through *him*, and to *him*, are all things [including our justification]: to whom be glory for ever" (Rom. 11:36). Free, gracious justification, given through the gift of faith—what a blessing! And what a gracious God who so justifies unworthy sinners.

Justification and Election

While we do not believe that God's people are *actually* and fully justified in eternity (before the foundation of the world), we do believe that there is a very close relationship between election and justification. God's people are justified *by faith*, not *by election*. Nevertheless, their justification cannot be separated from their election.

First, having chosen his people to be his own, God also *decreed to justify them*, and them only. He decreed that they should be holy and *without blame* (Eph. 1:4), which is the decree of their justification.

Second, insofar as they are chosen in Christ according to God's eternal love, God also *saw* them and viewed them in eternity as justified and without guilt. Having foreseen them without sin, God also set his love upon them. In giving them to Christ in eternity, God gave them to him as those whom he eternally saw without sin.

Numbers 23:21 is especially important here. Note that it uses the past tense of the verb: "He *hath not beheld* iniquity in Jacob." The same past tense is used in Romans 9:13: "Jacob *have I loved.*" This language has always been understood by those who believe in sovereign grace to refer to God's eternal decrees.

Numbers 23:21 is the answer to Balak and Balaam's attempts to curse God's people. Though Christ had not yet come, and the blood of atonement had not yet been shed, God's people could not be cursed because of what God had decreed in eternity.

It is in this sense alone that we are willing to speak of "eternal justification," or better, of "justification *from* eternity." It is of the utmost importance to emphasize this eternal background to justification.

To separate justification from God's eternal decree of election is to end with a justification that is available to all, if only *they* will believe. This is a conditional justification that in some way depends on the sinner's response to the gospel. That is not the free, gracious justification of which Scripture speaks.

It is according to the decree of election, therefore, that justification is made available in the death of Jesus for the elect, and for them only. According to that same decree of election, they and they alone are given the gift of faith by which that justification becomes their own.

There is no justification or righteousness possible for the non-elect. No forgiveness is available for them. What does not exist, either in God's decree or in the cross of Christ, cannot be offered to them without doing violence to Scripture's teaching concerning the truthfulness and unchangeableness of God.

Such a close connection between election and justification exists that we know our election by way of our justification. Experiencing through faith the forgiveness of sins, we also know that we have this forgiveness from him who "*hath* not beheld iniquity in Jacob" nor "perverseness in Israel" (Num. 23:21).

Praise be to his name who sovereignly justifies his people.

Justification and the Atonement

As we have seen, justification may not be divorced either from election or from the cross. Grounded in the atoning work of Jesus on the cross, justification harks back to eternity past.

This is of the utmost importance. What is not decreed by God cannot possibly come to pass in time, such as the justification of the non-elect. And what is not purchased and obtained for all by the death of Christ on the cross is not available to all.

There is, therefore, no justification (righteousness or forgiveness) to "offer" to those who are non-elect. The gospel must be preached to all; the righteousness of God in Christ must be declared (Rom. 3:25–26). All who hear must be called to faith with the sure promise that those who believe will be justified before God. But that promise, as becomes evident in time, is only for those whom God has chosen and for whom Christ died on the cross. The promise of justification, therefore, is only for the elect, and it is surely fulfilled for them in that God graciously gives them the faith by which they are justified (Eph. 2:8–9).

That Christ died *only* for the elect is the doctrine of particular redemption (limited atonement). It is the clear teaching of Scripture. The death of Christ *secures* the justification of God's elect (Isa. 53:11; Rom. 3:24; Rom. 5:9, 19). It does this because Christ by his suffering and death substituted his perfect obedience for their disobedience and endured the punishment of their crimes.

In this way Christ earned for them a perfect righteousness (innocence) that is acceptable to God, the Judge. That righteousness becomes theirs *through* faith, whereby their guilt is removed and they are received once again into God's favor and presence. Christ's work, then, is the *ground* of their justification.

It is even possible to speak of Christ's death as the justification of God's people in an objective sense (Rom. 5:19). By his death everything that separated them from God is taken out of the way, and a righteousness is earned for them that God accepts and approves (Isa. 53:11).

It is therefore not a general righteousness that Christ earned, but a righteousness decreed and purchased for particular persons. It is a righteousness that belongs to them by the price Christ paid on the cross. There is no other righteousness but this (Rom. 10:1–4).

Sovereign, gracious, particular election and particular atonement together guarantee the actual justification through faith of all those whom God has given to Christ. A justification that is available to all conditionally is a justification divorced from election and the cross—a justification that justifies no one.

Adoption

Adoption is very often not included in the order of salvation. The reason is not that Scripture does not speak of it, but that it is a benefit of justification. It is therefore understood to be included in justification.

Indeed, adoption is the first and greatest of the benefits of justifiction. When our sins are freely pardoned and we are made righteous in Christ, God not only receives us, but he also receives us as his *own dear children.*

Scripture speaks often of our adoption, of the fact that we are by grace children of God, and that he is our Father. It is not inappropriate, then, to speak of adoption as a topic by itself.

Adoption, like justification, has several steps. It can be traced back to the counsels of eternity and has its completion in the new heavens and earth. The steps are these.

First, God sets his love on us and chooses us from eternity to be his children (Rom. 8:29; Eph. 1:5). Remember, God does not choose us because we are or will be fit to be his children, but so that we may be his children. We are predestinated *unto* the adoption of sons.

Second, in Christ's suffering and death God provides a legal basis for our sonship, for we would have no right to his fatherly love and care and no right to dwell in his house without that legal foundation (Gal. 4:4–5; Eph. 2:13). We might think of it this way: our adoption papers are written and sealed with the blood of Christ.

Third, we are actually received into God's fellowship and family through the work of the Spirit, so that we experience his love and care for us (Gal. 4:6–7). Speaking of the coming of the Holy Spirit, John 14:18 says literally, "I will not leave you orphans; I will come to you."

At this point in adoption, God does a wonder that transcends the earthly practice of adoption. God by the Spirit causes us to be born again in his own image and likeness so that we are like him, something that can never be true of our own adopted children (Eph. 4:24; 1 John 3:1–2).

Fourth, because "it doth not yet appear what we shall be" (1 John 3:1), there will be in the judgment day what Scripture calls "the manifestation of the sons of God" (Rom. 8:19). Then all will see what we are in Christ, and we will be received into our eternal home to dwell there with our Father forever. In that day our bodies will also be adopted, that is, redeemed from the presence and power of sin (v. 23). For that we wait.

Predestinated eternally, prepared in Christ, possessed through the Spirit, and perfected in eternity—what a marvelous and gracious work of God is our adoption. As John says, "Behold, what manner of love the Father hath bestowed upon us, that we should be called the sons of God" (1 John 3:1).

Peace

The ungodly world in which we live talks much of peace: peace in the Middle East, peace wherever there is fighting and war. No one enjoys bloodshed, killing, and strife; everyone would prefer peace. We may not forget, though, that the Bible has something to say about peace. True peace is one of the fruits of justification (Rom. 5:1).

The Bible tells us that there is no peace to the wicked (Isa. 57:21). They say, "Peace, peace; when there is no peace" (Jer. 6:14). They "are like the troubled sea, when it cannot rest, whose waters cast up mire and dirt" (Isa. 57:20). They do not even know the way of peace (Isa. 59:8).

All this is true because the only real peace is peace with God through Jesus Christ. He is the Prince of Peace (Isa. 9:6). His peace is the peace of being right with God, of knowing that God will not condemn; it is the peace of experiencing the forgiveness of sins through his sacrifice and the shedding of his blood on the cross.

True peace is a quietness of heart, soul, and conscience that comes from the knowledge that God is not angry with us and that Christ has taken away our sin, so that nothing anymore can separate us from the love of God: "And the work of righteousness shall be peace; and the effect of righteousness quietness and assurance forever" (Isa. 32:17).

This peace comes through faith in Christ as Justifier: "Therefore being justified by faith, we have peace with God through our Lord Jesus Christ" (Rom. 5:1). This belongs to those who walk in the way of obedience to all that God commands: "Wherefore, beloved...be diligent that ye may be found of him in peace, without spot, and blameless" (2 Pet. 3:14).

Without that true spiritual peace, nothing else matters. Peace among men is a sham if they are not at peace with God. Nor will they ever really be at peace with one another until they are at peace with God through Jesus Christ.

Politicians, negotiations, and cease-fires can never give true and lasting peace, for even if they should accomplish their aims, they have not changed the hearts of men. Until the grace of God in Jesus Christ comes to them, men will be "living in malice and envy, hateful, and hating one another" (Titus 3:3).

When there is no true peace with God, there cannot be a permanent end to strife and warfare in this world, and so the Christian puts no trust in the efforts, promises, and organizations of men, but looks for the coming of Christ, the end of this present world, and the new heaven and new earth described in Revelation 21. For the sake of the church, or even for the sake of his own family members, the Christian may pray for a temporary end to warfare and strife, but the peace he truly looks for is that which is beyond this world in the next.

This is the reason Jesus says to all who believe in him, "Peace I leave with you, my peace I give unto you: *not as the world giveth,* give I unto you" (John 14:27).

May God grant the true peace to you and me. May he give it to many!

Conversion

Conversion could very well be treated in connection with regeneration, for that is when conversion begins. Indeed, most Christians when they speak of conversion or ask, "When were you converted?" are referring to that *very first work* of God's grace in the hearts and lives of his people. Nevertheless, we prefer to deal with conversion in connection with sanctification and to emphasize that it is an ongoing, daily activity in the lives of Christians. We can see this when we remember that *conversion* means "turning."

The turning referred to is *from* sin (Ezek. 33:11) and *to* God (Luke 1:16). It must be *both*. There are those who turn from a specific sin, such as drunkenness, but do not turn to God. They are not converted. There are also those who claim to have turned to God but do not turn from their sins. They also are not converted.

Turning from sin involves both repentance (Acts 26:20) and a constant fight against sin, Satan, and the flesh (1 Cor. 9:26–27; Gal. 5:17)—what Scripture calls the *putting off* of the *old man* (Col. 3:9). The turning to God involves holiness of life (Acts 26:18)—what Scripture calls the *putting on* of the *new man* (Col. 3:10).

So many are mistaken here. They think the raising of a hand in a meeting or a "decision for Christ" is the evidence of conversion and even consider themselves or others "converted" on that basis. Without repentance and holiness, however, conversion is only a sham, and people remain far from the kingdom of heaven (Matt. 18:3).

The turning that takes place in conversion begins when God first reveals his sovereign grace in our lives. But it does not end with that. Every day of our lives we must be turning from our sins. As long as we sin, we must be repenting (1 John 1:8–9), and continually we must be "perfecting holiness in the fear of God" (2 Cor. 7:1).

This need for daily conversion must be emphasized. The important question is not really "When were you converted?" but "Are you *now* converted?" So-called "decisions for Christ" or experiences of many years ago mean nothing in the case of the person who is now living and walking in his old sins. So completely has this been forgotten that in some circles a new kind of Christian has been invented called a "carnal Christian," that is, someone who has made a profession of faith or had some conversion "experience" but still lives an unchanged and sinful life.

It does not matter that some cannot put a date and time to the beginning of their salvation. Not all are saved as Paul was (2 Tim. 3:15). If Christians are now by God's wonderful grace living converted lives—lives that have been *turned around* by the power of God's Holy Spirit—they are converted persons.

Let us not forget, either, that conversion is the work of the Holy Spirit. It does not depend on our decision or choice. As the prophet says,

"Turn *thou* me, and I shall be turned; for thou art the LORD my God" (Jer. 31:18).

Sanctification

Sanctification is one of the last steps in the order of salvation, but it certainly is not last in importance.

In sanctification the divine purpose of our salvation—the glory of God—begins to be fulfilled. Sanctification has to do with holiness, the word meaning "to make holy," and in their holy living God's people *begin* to show the glory of God and of his grace.

Sanctification, then, is the *lifelong* work of the Holy Spirit in the hearts and lives of believers by which they are made holy and delivered from the filthiness and power of sin, and in which they begin to live in obedience to God and to his Word. It begins with regeneration and ends with death and glorification.

In distinction from justification, sanctification is a work of Christ *in* us (justification is Christ's work *for* us), a lifelong work (justification is once only), a work in which we become active (in justification we are passive), and a work that removes the pollution of our sin (justification removes its guilt).

Being justified is like an immigrant becoming *legally* a citizen of his new country. Having become a citizen, however, he begins to learn the language, wear the clothing, eat the food, and adopt the customs of his new land—to live like a citizen of that country. Sanctification is similar. It is God's people learning to live the life of heaven.

Yet sanctification is all of grace. We learn nothing of ourselves but are "taught of God" in sanctification. Though we become active in holiness and good works, it is always God who works in us "both to will and to do of his good pleasure" (Phil. 2:13).

When we are sanctified, our salvation is not turned over to us so that we alone become responsible for it. In sanctification we do not suddenly begin to "cooperate" with God so that our salvation is no longer wholly of grace.

Though we do good works in sanctification, there is still no merit in these works (Eph. 2:8–10). Though we obey, we still have no reason to boast. Our holiness, too, is a gift of God, and all the glory and praise for our sanctification belongs to him.

Sanctification is not optional, although some seem to think so. They speak of "carnal Christians" and deny the lordship of Christ in the life of a Christian. They are wrong.

Sanctification is different from justification, but follows necessarily from it. When a person is found innocent of wrongdoing, he must be released from prison. Having been found innocent before God through our justification, we must in the justice of God be released from the prison of depravity and sin. In sanctification we are released.

Hebrews 12:14 shows us the impossibility of a Christian remaining unsanctified. *Without holiness* "no man shall see the Lord"! Let us not think, then, that holiness is optional or unimportant. It is that work of grace by which God is glorified in his people. As we read in Isaiah 43:21, "This people have I formed for myself; they *shall* show forth my praise." Grace guarantees it.

Holiness

The word *sanctification* means "being made holy." The meaning itself indicates that sanctification is not our own work, even though we become active in sanctification, but it is God's work in us. We are *made* holy.

This holiness, we have said, is not optional but vitally necessary. Without it no person can see God (Heb. 12:14). God is the Holy One (Isa. 40:25; Isa. 41:14), and no one can stand in his holy presence without being holy (Ps. 24:3 – 5).

But what is holiness?

The basic idea of the word *holiness* is that of "separation." To be holy is to be separate. Thus in the Old Testament, Israel was a holy people, *separate* from the other nations (Lev. 20:24 – 26). Among the Israelites themselves, the priests were "holiness to the Lord" (Ex. 28:36 – 38), because their whole life was *separated* for God's service in the temple (1 Chron. 23:13).

Today the church is a separate and holy nation and a nation of priests (1 Pet. 2:9). The members must therefore be holy (1 Pet. 1:15 – 16).

Holiness, however, always has two parts to it. It is both separation *from* something, and separation *unto* something. Both are important.

Believers are called first to be separate *from* wickedness and wicked persons (2 Cor. 6:14–18; Eph. 5:11–12). They cannot go out of the world (1 Cor. 5:9–11), but must nevertheless separate themselves as much as possible from the company, the fellowship, the deeds, and the life of the ungodly. Above all, they must keep themselves pure, "unspotted from the world" (James 1:27).

This separation between the church and the world, between believer and unbeliever, between light and darkness, is sometimes referred to as the "antithesis," described in 2 Corinthians 6:14–15.

That chapter also speaks of the fact that we are separated *unto* God (vv. 16–18). Without this, holiness is not complete. To be separated unto God is to be consecrated and dedicated to him, just as the priests were in the Old Testament. It is being set apart for God's service with our whole life: our time, our possessions, even our bodies.

This separation is not a part-time thing. To be holy, separated, and consecrated to God is not only for the Lord's day or for a few hours on the Lord's day. Also our whole life has been purchased by Christ, belongs to God, is consecrated to God, and must be lived in holiness.

To this we are *called*. Because God is holy (1 Pet. 1:15–16), because we are chosen and redeemed unto holiness (Eph. 1:4; 1 Pet. 1:18–19), and because God has sent us his Holy Spirit (1 Cor. 3:16–17), holiness is required of us. That call to holiness is heard repeatedly in Scripture. It is, as Willliam Law wrote, a *serious* call.[8]

Have you *heard* it?

Have you *obeyed* it?

The Antithesis

Occasionally some Reformed theologians will write of the "antithesis." In such cases they are referring to the *separation* and *opposition* between darkness and light, believer and unbeliever, church and world.

---

8. William Law, *A Serious Call to a Devout and Holy Life* (Grand Rapids, MI: William B. Eerdmans Publishing Company, 1966). Original first published in 1728.

This antithesis is the result of God's saving grace and is often referred to in Scripture, though the word itself is not used. The clearest passage that refers to the antithesis is 2 Corinthians 6:14–18. There the Word not only describes the antithesis, but it also tells us what it means in practice. In those verses the antithesis is described as the contrast between righteousness and unrighteousness, light and darkness, Christ and Belial, faith and unbelief, the temple of God and the temple of idols. In practice it means that we must "come out from among them, and be . . . separate" (v. 17).

This separation is spiritual. We are not called to come out of the world physically (1 Cor. 5:10). That is the mistake made by those who become monks or nuns, or who forbid marriage or the eating of certain foods. The antithesis does not mean that we separate ourselves physically from the world around us or from the things of this world.

It *does* mean that we have no fellowship with the *works* of the wicked (Eph. 5:11–12) and even that we do not make friends of the wicked or have fellowship with them (2 Cor. 6:17; James 4:4). We must be in their company since we must do our business and live our lives in the world (1 Cor. 5:9–11), but even then we must be separate by being holy.

Herein lies one of our objections to the teaching of common grace. The idea that there is a common grace of God to the wicked and reprobate makes a kind of common ground between God's people and the world. At least in some respects, therefore, believers can make common cause with the wicked, can keep fellowship with them, and can make friends of them. After all, they both have grace in common, so it is argued.

The Bible makes it very clear that keeping this separation from the wicked world is the safety and well-being of the church and of God's people. That was true already in the Old Testament. Deuteronomy 33:28 says, "Israel then shall dwell in safety *alone.*" In the New Testament it remains true. The promise of God—"I will receive you, And will be a Father unto you, and ye shall be my sons and daughters"—belongs to those who obey God's command "Come out from among them, and be ye separate" (2 Cor. 6:17–18). How much we need to hear that today!

Each of us must be separate. We must be separate for God's sake and for the sake of the church. If we are not separate, God will not be glorified through us, and the church will become like the world.

Preservation

Among the last steps in the order of salvation is preservation. The word *preservation* underscores that because of God's power and grace, believers cannot lose their salvation. God *preserves* his people (Ps. 37:28; Jer. 32:40; 1 Pet. 1:5). This word reminds us, therefore, that salvation is *all* of grace. That believers do not lose their salvation is not due to their obedience, their faithfulness, and their efforts, but solely to the grace of God that keeps and protects them from falling away.

What, then, does God preserve? He preserves the new life of regeneration that is in them as the seed of all their salvation (1 John 3:9). In preserving that, he also preserves their faith and their obedience, so that they continue to believe and to keep God's commandments, though imperfectly. To put it simply, God preserves his own work of grace in his people (Ps. 90:17; Ps. 138:8; Phil. 1:6).

God does *not* preserve the flesh and the works of the flesh! In the believer the flesh, its works, and its dominion are to be destroyed (Gal. 5:24). The believer must not want them to be preserved and must not try to preserve them.

We do well to remember that according to this doctrine, it is God's elect who are preserved. He preserves them because he has chosen them in Christ (Eph. 1:3–4, 11).

The elect are not preserved apart from faith, however. Faith is always the way of, though never the reason for, salvation. 1 Peter 1:5 teaches that the believer is "kept by the power of God *through faith* unto salvation."

From what, then, are believers preserved? They are *not* preserved from temptation, from weakness, or from falling into sin.

How important it is to remember this! Believers are not preserved from falling, but from falling away; not from temptation, but from being destroyed by temptation; not from sin, but from the sin unto death. Due entirely to their own weakness and sinfulness, believers can and do fall into temptation and sin. But Psalm 37:24 assures us, "Though he fall, he shall not be utterly cast down: for the LORD upholdeth him with his hand."

That believers can and do fall is demonstrated in Scripture by the examples of men like David and Peter. That they cannot fall away is demonstrated by their restoration. Indeed, in the case of Peter, the Lord gave assurance beforehand that Peter would not fall away: "And the Lord said, Simon, Simon, behold, Satan hath desired to have you, that he may sift you as wheat: But I have prayed for thee, that thy faith fail not: and when thou art converted, strengthen thy brethren" (Luke 22:31–32).

What a wonderful work of grace is preservation!

The Perseverance of the Saints

Perseverance of the saints is the usual name for the fifth of the Five Points of Calvinism. The name differs from the other four points by appearing to stress our calling and responsibility rather than God's work and the power of his grace. For that reason some prefer the name *preservation of the saints.* That name does stress God's sovereign grace.

Speaking of perseverance instead of preservation is not, however, a denial that our continuing in the way of salvation is "by grace alone." Without grace, there is no other way we could persevere.

Like the name *preservation*, perseverance teaches the wonderful truth that God's people, once saved, cannot and do not lose their salvation. They *persevere* in the way of salvation all the way to the end.

It also implies, however, that the way of salvation is full of difficulties and trials. Rather than being an easy way, it is the way of cross-bearing, of suffering for Christ's sake, of fighting against the devil, the world, and the flesh, and of enduring affliction. Yet God's people come safely through all these troubles and enter glory to be with Christ.

We use the name *perseverance* because of the objections of those who believe that God's people can lose their salvation. They say that the doctrine of preservation encourages worldliness and carelessness and destroys every motive for godliness.

Both the word *perseverance* and the word *saints* show that this is not so. God's people are *made* saints—holy ones—by the power of grace, and *in that way of holiness,* they continue on to heaven—not in the way of unholiness (Heb. 12:14). The way of salvation *is* the way of holiness, and there is no other way to glory. It is impossible that one who is purchased by the blood of Christ, renewed and regenerated by the Spirit of God and indwelt by the Spirit, should continue in the way of destruction (Rom. 6:1–2).

There are those who deny this, however. They suggest that a man can be saved and never show any change of life, but that he can continue to live in the same sinful way he did before he was saved. This is the teaching, for example, of those who say that one can have Jesus as Savior without having him as Lord, that is, without having one's whole life claimed by Christ and brought under his lordship.

For this reason we do not like the name "eternal security." The name itself is not bad, but those who use the name are very often those who teach, "Once saved, always saved," implying that it does not really matter how you live. It does matter and matters very much.

The perseverance of the saints is a great comfort. It assures not only that God's people will all be in glory with Christ in the life to come, but that they will be *holy* in this life. No believer can love his sins and want to keep them. He ought to hate them and desire to be fully delivered from them. The doctrine of perseverance of the saints teaches that he is and shall be delivered from sin.

Saints

We have been discussing the doctrine of the perseverance of the saints. Before we finish, something needs to be said about the reference to the *saints* in this doctrine. The word means "holy ones" and refers to the sanctification of God's people.

A proper understanding of the word *saints* is essential. If saints, as some suggest, are spiritually *self-made* people, or those who are holy by their own works and will, there is no certainty of perseverance. If saints make themselves holy, they can and also will make themselves unholy.

This is the teaching of "freewillism." It says that a person is saved by his own choice and that his sanctification and growth in grace also depend on him. He must then choose to make use of the grace that is available if he is to be holy. If this were actually the case, however, no one would ever be holy.

We believe that saints are made saints by grace, and that it is only by grace that they have any holiness at all. To put it another way, they are saints and faithful *in Christ Jesus* (Eph. 1:1; Phil. 1:1; Col. 1:1–2).

The holiness of the saints is not the result of their own freewill choice, but of God's sovereign election and choice of them. Thus we read in Ephesians 1:4: "According as he hath chosen us in him before the foundation of the world, that we should be holy and without blame before him." God's gracious election is the source of their holiness.

Moreover, the holiness of the saints is not obtained by their own works, but is purchased for them by the blood of Christ. Of this we read in Colossians 1:21–22: "And you, that were sometime alienated and enemies in your mind by wicked works, yet now hath he reconciled in the body of his flesh through death, *to present you holy* and unblameable and unreproveable in his sight." The shed blood of Christ is the ground of their holiness.

Nor is the holiness of saints dependent on themselves, as though God says, "I have provided all things for you; it is up to you to make use of them and be holy as I command." Saints become holy in their conduct and speech by the work of the Holy Spirit. Sanctification is the "sanctification of the Spirit" (1 Pet. 1:2). For this reason Scripture speaks of believers as those who are "called to be saints" (Rom. 1:7; 1 Cor. 1:2). It is the powerful Word of God's calling that brings them to holiness.

The Spirit does not begin the work of making saints and then leave it up to them to persevere in holiness to the end. Their continuing in holiness depends completely on the continued presence and power of the Holy Spirit. We do not learn to be saints by our own efforts. It is the grace of God that brings salvation, "teaching us that, denying ungodliness and worldly lusts, we should live soberly, righteously, and godly, in this present world" (Titus 2:11–12). The grace of the Holy Spirit is the power of holiness.

We must not forget that it is *only saints* who shall see the Lord (Heb. 12:14). How wonderful, then, to know that God gives us what is necessary to see him in glory!

Glorification

The last step in the order of salvation is glorification, which is the receiving of God's elect into heavenly glory. In our glorification God finishes the work of salvation that he began with regeneration. He not only delivers his people from all their suffering and from death, but delivers them, too, from all their sins.

A discussion of our glorification really belongs, therefore, to the doctrine of the last things. Nevertheless, though we have written in more detail of such matters as the intermediate state and the resurrection of the body in the last part of this book, it is necessary to say something about glorification here as well. It is in our glorification that God's great work is finished and that we are fully fitted for the glory of God in Jesus Christ our Savior.

There are three steps in our glorification. First, there is the gift of eternal life that we receive when we are regenerated. As a result of that gift, we are risen with Christ and sit at God's right hand (Eph. 2:5–6); our "conversation" (way of life) is in heaven (Phil. 3:20); and we have the new life of Christ in us (Gal. 2:20).

Second, there is the gift of eternal life that we receive when our souls, after death, enter immediately into conscious glory and blessedness in heaven (2 Cor. 5:1–8).

Third, there is the gift of eternal life that we receive when our bodies are raised and made like the glorious body of Christ, and when we enter into the new heavens and earth (Phil. 3:21).

It needs to be stressed, therefore, that we have the beginning of eternal glory *now,* even as we shall have it in the last day. That is one of the greatest motives for obedience that we have: we are already, as it were, partly in heaven. In Colossians 3:1–4 Paul speaks of this. Because we are risen with Christ and our life is hid with him in God, we must seek the things that are above and set our affection on them.

That we have the beginning of eternal life now is also the reason we sometimes long for heaven and long also to be delivered from this world and from the flesh. That, Paul says, is far better than remaining here (Phil. 1:21–24).

Our heavenly glory is described in Scripture in glowing terms and very often in pictures and types, because it includes things that eye has not seen, nor ear heard; neither has it entered into man's heart to understand (1 Cor. 2:9). It involves the things that God has prepared for those who love him.

While we ourselves shall be wonderfully changed and free from sin and its consequences, and while we shall receive all that God has promised, the real glory of heavenly life is that God and Christ are there. That is the blessedness, the joy, the glory, and the peace of heavenly life (Rev. 21:3, 7, 22–23; Rev. 22:3). For that, those who have the hope of being glorified purify themselves, are willing to lose the whole world, and do indeed forsake it for the things of the kingdom of heaven. They walk by faith and not by sight as they wait for that glory.

part 5

THE CHURCH AND THE SACRAMENTS

The Church

Scripture speaks so often of the church that the study of its teaching concerning the church is a separate part of the study of theology. Several New Testament books have the church as their main focus. Acts tells the story of the gathering of the New Testament church; 1 Corinthians speaks especially of God's faithfulness to his church (1:9); Ephesians has as its theme the church as the body of Christ (1:22–23; 5:30–32); Colossians emphasizes the glorious truth that Christ is the Head of the church (1:18; 2:10); 1 Timothy teaches us proper behavior in the church (3:15); and Titus promotes good order in the church (1:5).

The doctrine of the church ought not, then, to be neglected or overlooked. Yet there are few today who know what the Bible teaches concerning the church or realize why the church is so important.

The Greek word translated *church* means "called out." The name *church* in the highest and best sense refers to those who are saved and to them only. The name reminds us that the true members of the church are those who are "called . . . out of darkness into his marvellous light" (1 Pet. 2:9). It reminds us, too, that their place in the church is of grace. They are not members by their choice or works, but by God's *calling*.

That members of the church are called *out* refers not only to their salvation from sin (they are called *out of darkness*), but also to their spiritual separation from the world and its wickedness (2 Cor. 6:14–18). Implied in the name *church,* therefore, is the holiness and obedience of the church's members. A church whose members are not holy does not deserve the name *church.*

Holiness is essential to the very existence of the church. Unto holiness the members are called, chosen (Eph. 1:4), and redeemed (Col. 1:21–22). Church holiness is important because it has to do with God's purpose in the church. The reason for the church's existence is the glory of God (Eph. 1:6, 12). It is in the holiness of the church and its members that this purpose is reached. An unholy church, a church whose *members* are not holy, cannot and does not glorify God. In the holiness of the church, most of all, God's glory shines out.

It is to the shame and hurt of the church today that its members do not live as those who are *called out.* If the church itself is not any different from the world in its teaching, in the conduct of its members, and in its practices, its witness will be ineffective. The church's glory, and the

217

glory of its witness to this lost world, lies in its being called out, separate, and holy—different from the wicked world.

Pray, then, that all the members of Christ's church may be "holy and without blame before him . . . to the praise of the glory of his grace" (Eph. 1:4, 6). Only in that way will the witness and work of the church prosper.

Congregation and Body

In speaking of the church, the Bible does not always use the word *church* in the same way. It never uses the word to refer to the building in which a congregation meets, but it does use it to refer either to local congregations (1 Cor. 1:2; Rev. 2:1, 8, 12) or to the whole body of those who are chosen and saved in history (Eph. 1:23).

The distinction between the church as the *body of Christ,* and the church as the *local congregation,* can be made in various ways. Sometimes the church as local congregation is called the *church institute,* or the *visible church,* because it has a visible, institutional form in the world. Likewise, the body of the redeemed is sometimes called the *church organism,* or the *invisible church,* because it is alive in Christ (an "organism" being a living creature) and because it is spiritual and invisible (we cannot mark its boundaries).

The church as body includes only God's elect and redeemed people (1 Pet. 2:9), while the local congregations always contain hypocrites (Rev. 2:14–15; Rev. 3:17–18). The church as body includes those who have already died, those living today, and those who have been chosen in Christ but are not yet born or saved. The church as congregation includes only those who are on earth at a particular time in history.

This distinction between congregation and body is important. Although there are many congregations (Rev. 2 and 3), there is ever only *one* body of Christ (1 Cor. 12:12). That body cannot be harmed or destroyed by its enemies (Matt. 16:18), but particular congregations can be and often are (1 Cor. 1:11; Rev. 3:1, 16). A local congregation can even lose its place "among the candlesticks" as a church of Christ (Rev. 2:5). The distinction between the church in these two senses needs to be remembered so that we do not become confused.

In connection with church membership, the distinction between congregation and body is also significant. While *we* have an obligation to join ourselves to the visible church, that is, to a local congregation (Heb. 10:25), it is *God* who joins us to the body of Christ by election and the blood of Calvary (Col. 1:12–14).

Nevertheless, while these two uses of the word *church* can be distinguished, they do overlap. It is a part of the body of Christ that is found in the local congregations, and only *because* a part of his body is there can the local congregation even be called the church.

What we are saying is that the church in the truest sense of the word is *exclusively* the company and body of those who are saved. Certain congregations are rightly called "church" in Scripture because the redeemed *are* there, just as the Old Testament nation was called Israel because of the presence in it of the true Israel (Rom. 2:28–29; Rom. 9:6; Gal. 3:29).

Let us learn Scripture's teaching concerning the church so that we will love and honor the church, both as the body of Christ and in its institutional form.

The Names of the Church

There are many different names for the church in Scripture. These names are part of God's revelation to us concerning the church. Each of them tells us something important about it.

The name *church*, as we have seen, means "called out" and refers to the word and work of God by which he calls his people out of darkness into marvelous light and forms them into a peculiar (unique) people (1 Pet. 2:9). That the name *church* is most commonly used is not surprising. It shows us that the existence and blessedness of the church are the result of God's calling and sovereign grace.

That church is also called *the body of Christ* (1 Cor. 12:12–27). This name reminds us of the glory of Christ as the Head of the church, the church's living union with Christ, and the relationship of the members of the church to one another. In the body, Christians are members one of another, as well as of Christ.

This name *body of Christ* is used especially in Ephesians and Colossians, though with a slightly different emphasis in each epistle. In Ephesians the focus is on the church itself and on the glory that it has in Christ. In Colossians it is on Christ as the glorious Head of the church.

Scripture also compares the church to a *vine* (John 15:1–6) or a *tree* (Rom. 11:16–24). That the same comparisons are made in the Old Testament (Ps. 80:8; Isa. 5:1–7) shows that Israel and the church are one. The comparison also shows the close relationship and union between Christ and his church, as well as the church's complete dependence upon Christ. He is the vine; we are the branches.

Somewhat different is the name *temple of God* (1 Cor. 3:16–17; 2 Cor. 6:16; Eph. 2:20–21) or *house of God* (1 Tim. 3:15; Heb. 3:6; 1 Pet. 2:4–9). Note that not the building in which the church meets, but the *church itself,* the body of believers, is the house of God). When the church is compared to a building, such as a temple, it reminds us of its beauty, orderliness, and unity. Every member has his own place in that spiritual building. It also reminds us, as does the name *body,* of the diversity of the church in which each member is different and has a different place (1 Cor. 12), yet all members are one spiritual building belonging to God.

The main emphasis of the names *temple, house,* and *building* is on the blessed truth that the church is the place where God dwells with his people. He dwells with them under one roof as one family, through Christ their Head. There God and his people commune with one another, and thus he keeps covenant with them and blesses them forever.

Other Names for the Church

Scripture, as we have noticed, uses many different names and descriptions of the church to teach us what the church is and to help us love the church. The number of these names and descriptions shows how important the church is in God's eyes and ought to be in ours.

A whole list of names appears in Hebrews 12:22–24. In that passage the church is called *mount Sion, the city of the living God, the heavenly Jerusalem,* and *the general assembly and church of the firstborn, which are written in heaven.* The church is also the *holy nation* of the New Testament (1 Pet. 2:9).

From this we learn that Israel and the church are one. Israel is the church of the Old Testament, and the church is the Israel of the New Testament. The names used to describe the capital city of Israel, which God chose as his own and where he established his dwelling place in the temple (Ps. 68:16; Ps. 132:13–14), are the names also used in the New Testament for the church. This is true in Revelation 21 where an angel shows John *the city of God,* the *new Jerusalem,* and calls it *the bride, the Lamb's wife* (vv. 9–10ff.; compare with Eph. 5:32).

There is a kind of cumulative witness here. That the church is the vine (compare John 15:1–6 and Ps. 80:8ff.), the temple and house of God (Eph. 2:20–22; 1 Tim. 3:15), mount Sion [Zion], Jerusalem, and the city of the living God ought to leave us in no doubt that the church of the New Testament is everything that Israel was in the Old Testament.

Before we speak more of this, however, we wish to point out the significance of these names. The church described as a city, nation, or kingdom tells us that it is a spiritual commonwealth with a king, law, customs, and language all its own. The members of the church are citizens of a kingdom with all the rights and privileges of citizens. In that kingdom they are protected from their enemies and well governed by the King of kings.

The church was and is, however, a *spiritual* kingdom, nation, and city. Its walls are salvation, and its gates praise (Isa. 60:18). Its "keys" are the preaching of the gospel and the exercise of Christian discipline (Matt. 16:19; Matt. 18:15–20). The foundations of the church are apostolic and prophetic teaching: nothing less than the Word of God itself (Eph. 2:20–22; Rev. 21:14).

That the church is further described as the fortress mountain *Zion* serves to show us that under the rule of the church's King, it is invincibly strong (Ps. 48:12–14). How could it be otherwise with such walls and gates and foundations and keys? No wonder the gates of hell cannot prevail against it (Matt. 16:18).

This is seen only by faith, however. In the eyes of the world, the church is a small and despised remnant, a little flock (Luke 12:32), a cottage in a vineyard, a lodge in a garden of cucumbers, a besieged city (Isa. 1:8). Only by faith is it evident that the church is "comely as Jerusalem, terrible as an army with banners" (Song of Sol. 6:4, 10). Let us, then, by faith walk about Zion, tell its towers, mark well its bulwarks, and consider its palaces. It will always be evident that God is its God (Ps. 48:12–14).

The Church and Israel

We have pointed to the many names and descriptions used in Scripture that show that the church and Israel are identical. The church is mount Sion (Zion), the city of God, the heavenly and holy Jerusalem (Heb. 12:22–24; Rev. 21:9–10), the holy nation (1 Pet. 2:9), the vine (John 15:1–6; Ps. 80:8), and the bride of God (Eph. 5:31–32; Rev. 21:9–10). The church is everything that Israel was in the Old Testament.

This identity of church and Israel is further confirmed by the fact that Israel is called "the *church* in the wilderness" in Acts 7:38.

Along the same lines, the elect of God out of every nation are identified as the true Israel, the true Jews (Rom. 2:28–29; Rom. 9:8; Gal. 3:29; Phil. 3:3). Indeed, the prophecies of Scripture that seem to refer to national Israel are spiritualized and applied to the church in the New Testament (compare Hos. 1:10 with its fulfillment in Rom. 9:24–26, and Amos 9:11–15 with its fulfillment in Acts 15:13–17).

This is of critical importance as far as the doctrine of the church is concerned. Only in this light is the Old Testament, with its history, its warnings, and its promises, *for the church.* If the Old Testament Scriptures are concerned only with a people who are not identical with the church, then the Old Testament has *nothing* to say to us today. The Old Testament, then, can be only an object of curiosity to us.

Think about it. Those Christians who believe that Israel and the church are two different groups cannot do justice to the Old Testament in their preaching and teaching. The Old Testament has nothing to do with them, they say. But if Israel and the church are one and the same, the history of the Old Testament must be preached as the church's history, and its promises and warnings must be addressed to the church.

This unity of Israel and the church is also foundational to an understanding of baptism. It is the identity of covenants, promises, and of Israel and the church that lies at the root of the biblical teaching regarding infant baptism. To maintain "believer's baptism" rather than infant baptism, one *must* separate the Old and New Testaments, as well as their covenants and promises, and thereby differentiate between Israel and the church.

In all we have said, however, we must remember that in the truest sense of the word, only the elect are ever really called either *Israel* (Prince of God) or *church* (called out). The rest are not truly Israel or the church

(Rom. 2:28–29; Rom. 9:6–8). They have the name *Israel* or *church* only because they are outwardly identified with the people of God by birth or profession.

Natural birth does not make one a true Jew, nor a member of the church. As John the Baptist said, "God is able of these stones to raise up children unto Abraham" (Matt. 3:9). One must be born of the promise, born of God, to be a true Israelite. Of such true Israelites, both Jew and Gentile, God has raised up a spiritual seed of Abraham by the power of the promise. Are you that seed of Abraham?

Church and Kingdom

There is much talk today of the kingdom of Christ, and most of it is un-biblical. More and more we hear of a supposed kingdom that has its realization on this side of Christ's second coming and in this world. Yet that is the one thing Scripture does *not* teach about the kingdom. The kingdom of Christ is above all a *heavenly* kingdom (Matt. 26:29; John 6:15; John 18:36). It comes from heaven. It is heavenly and spiritual in nature (John 3:3, 5; Luke 17:20–21). Its realization also is heavenly (Rev. 12:10).

When we speak of the kingdom of Christ, we are speaking of the kingdom of his grace, where all things are ordered and ruled by his gracious, saving power. In one sense, of course, all things belong to the kingdom of Christ in that Christ rules sovereignly and by almighty power over all (Matt. 28:18; Phil. 2:9–11). Nevertheless, properly speaking, his kingdom is the place of his grace, and the place of grace that we call the kingdom is now the church of Christ. The kingdom is not something separate from and distinct from the church, but *is* the church. There and there alone grace rules. Grace does not even extend beyond the bounds of the church. There is no "common grace."

In the church, by grace, the citizens of Christ's kingdom are found. Into that kingdom they are gathered by God's grace and Spirit (Col. 1:13). In that kingdom they are kept by his gracious power, and as citizens of that kingdom they are translated into heaven and its glories, when the kingdom of Christ is fully realized. We pray for the coming of that kingdom in the Lord's prayer. To that kingdom belong the keys of which

Christ speaks in Matthew 16:19. That kingdom has for its walls salvation and for its gates praise, as Isaiah prophesied so long ago (Isa. 60:18).

That kingdom is present in this world, but as an outpost in enemy-held territory, so that in this world the kingdom always has the character of an army at war and a city besieged (Isa. 1:8; Matt. 16:18; Rev. 20:9). The church in this world is and remains the *church militant,* that is, the church at war.

Because the church is the kingdom of Christ, and because that kingdom is heavenly and spiritual, the church has no use for (may not use) the weapons of this world. Even if the church could obtain what some desire—world dominion—she would not advance the kingdom of Christ one whit. The kingdom is advanced when by the still, small word of the gospel, those who once were citizens of this world and servants of Satan are sweetly conquered and brought into the fellowship of Christ, obtaining citizenship with the saints and becoming part of the household of faith (Eph. 2:19). This is the victory of Christ's kingdom, a victory that is already won in the cross (Col. 2:15). No earthly power, not even the sinfulness of the kingdom's citizens, can resist that victory of the kingdom for a moment (Matt. 16:18).

Such is Christ's kingdom and so entirely spiritual is its nature that no one can even see it unless they are born again. To this kingdom, by grace and the gospel, belong all those who have been called and are not yet glorified. In this kingdom, through Christ, they are more than conquerors.

Are you a citizen of this great kingdom?

The Church Militant

Three distinct groups of people belong to the elect church of God, although in the end they shall all be gathered in one in Christ. There are, first of all, the elect on earth at any particular time in history (Eph. 1:10). They are referred to as the *church militant.*

Second, there are the elect who have fought the good fight, finished their course, and gone to glory. They are the *church triumphant* (2 Tim. 4:7–8; Rev. 6:10).

Last, there are those who belong to the church by election, but who are yet to be born and brought to repentance and faith. We call them the *church latent*, or *hidden* (2 Pet. 3:9).

The church on earth is rightly called the church militant, the fighting church. It is described in Scripture as an army (Song of Sol. 6:4, 10; Rev. 19:11–16). Its calling is warfare (2 Cor. 10:3–4; 1 Tim. 1:18; 2 Tim. 2:4). Its members are to put on the armor of God (Eph. 6:10–18). Christ is its Captain (Heb. 2:10; Rev. 19:11–16).

The term *militant* means that the church is not only *ready* to fight; it is always engaged in warfare. That is the church's whole calling and life (2 Tim. 2:4). The battle is not over until we leave this life and go to be with Christ in glory (vv. 7–8).

The church's warfare is not merely defensive. The church and its members are called to take the battle into the territory and camp of the enemy—to take the offensive. Surely this is what the Word means in 2 Corinthians 10:4–5: "(For the weapons of our warfare are not carnal, but mighty through God to the *pulling down* of strong holds;) *Casting down* imaginations, and every high thing that exalteth itself against the knowledge of God, and *bringing into captivity* every thought to the obedience of Christ." This passage also teaches that the battle is spiritual. The enemies (Eph. 6:12), the weapons (vv. 13–17), and the warfare itself are all spiritual, but this does not make the struggle any less real or difficult.

The enemies are Satan, the world, and our own sinful flesh—sin and temptation in all their guises and wherever they are found, even in ourselves. Against such enemies, the battle cannot be fought with political, social, economic, or military might. It is fought by faith and the Word of God (Eph. 6:13–17; 1 John 5:4).

It is a battle for the minds and souls of men, a battle against false ideas and heresies as well as against wickedness and temptation (2 Cor. 10:4–5; James 4:7). It is a battle against everything unfriendly to God and to the knowledge of God.

In that battle, however, we do not fight *for* the victory. We fight *in* the victory as those who already have it through the suffering, death, resurrection, and ascension of our Lord. We are more than conquerors through him who loved us (Rom. 8:37). But we must fight. We are not here to enjoy ourselves, but to be soldiers (2 Tim. 2:3–4).

Are you fighting, or playing?

The Church Triumphant

Church triumphant is the name given to that part of the church now resting from its labors in glory. Those who belong to the church triumphant have fought the good fight of faith, have finished their course, and have received a crown of righteousness from the Lord (2 Tim. 4:7–8).

That we speak of the church *triumphant* should not suggest to us that the church on earth is *not* triumphant in the battle of faith. Even those who are still fighting the battle, suffering and struggling here, are more than conquerors through him who loved them (Rom. 8:37). *Christ has triumphed gloriously over his enemies*—death, sin, and Satan—and totally defeated them (Luke 10:17–18; Eph. 4:8; Col. 2:15). We *are* victorious in Christ.

That needs emphasis today. Christ is not *waiting* to be crowned King of kings. He has been crowned with glory and honor at God's right hand (Heb. 2:9), and he rules in the midst of his enemies (Ps. 110:2). Even while the battle is still being fought, we already have the victory with him and fight a defeated enemy. All that remains are what are called, in military terms, the "mopping up operations." The kingdom is won. It must only be delivered up to the Father (1 Cor. 15:24).

Christ's victory prevails even while wicked men grow worse and worse and the whole world lies in darkness. The wicked are so completely defeated that Christ not only continues to rule over them, but by his sovereign rule also uses them for his own purpose.

We refer to the saints in glory as the church triumphant because they have entered into the *enjoyment* of the victory. While the saints on earth continue the struggle, they rest from their labors (Rev. 14:13) and "go no more out" (Rev. 3:12). While the earthly warriors must still wear the armor of faith, the saints in heaven have put it aside and are clothed in white (v. 5). They no longer see the faces of their enemies, but behold the face of the Lamb (Rev. 22:4). Their tears are wiped away, and there is for them no more death or sorrow or crying or pain (Rev. 21:4).

It is good for us to think of the church triumphant in heaven. Their glory is a testimony that the victory is ours also. Before long we shall be where they are, and we shall rest with them. What a great day that will be! And while we wait, they pray in heaven for God's vengeance upon our enemies, a prayer that God surely hears (Rev. 6:9–11).

Only in two respects is the triumph of the saints in heaven still incomplete. First, their bodies are not yet raised, so that they do not enjoy heavenly glory with both soul and glorified body. Second, the rest of the church is not yet glorified, and as verses 9 – 11 suggest, their glory is not complete without us. The whole body of Christ must be gathered in one for the glory of God the Father, and until it is, the church triumphant must wait as we do.

In the sure hope of that coming day—sure by God's decree, by Christ's blood and rule, and by the sovereign work of the Spirit—the church militant struggles and waits and prays while the church triumphant rests and waits and prays. Soon we shall be together.

The Church Unborn

Those glorified in heaven and those saved and still living here on earth are not the only ones who belong to the body of Jesus Christ, the church invisible. There are also those who have not yet been born and saved, but who have been chosen by God. They, too, belong to the church by election and by the shedding of Christ's blood on the cross, though not yet by regeneration and faith.

Christ spoke often of those the Father gave him who had not yet been saved (John 6:37, 39; John 10:16, 29; John 17:2). They had been given to him before the foundation of the world (John 17:6; Eph. 1:4), and it is for them he prays (John 17:9) and dies (vv. 13, 19). Their salvation and place in his church, therefore, are guaranteed.

It is for these persons that Christ delays his coming. Before he can come again in the will of God, all of them must be born and saved. This is what we read in 2 Peter 3:9. Most take the words *not willing that any should perish* as referring to a desire on God's part for the salvation of every person without exception, but the verse has nothing to do with such a supposed will of God for the salvation of every individual.

The ninth verse clearly speaks of *us*. Christ is long-suffering (merciful) to "us-ward." His mercy means that he is not willing that any of us should perish, but that all of us should come to repentance. The word *us* is clearly inferred in the last two phrases of the verse as well. What is so striking is that the *us* referred to includes those who have not yet come to repentance. They are part of us—part of those who "have obtained like precious faith . . . through the righteousness of God and our Saviour Jesus Christ" (2 Pet 1:1), who have been given "all things that pertain unto life and godliness" as well as "exceeding great and precious promises" (vv. 3–4).

We understand that these people have all these blessings only as chosen in Christ and purchased by him, not as those who themselves now enjoy these blessings through repentance and faith. Nevertheless, election and the blood of Christ are so sure that they can be said to have these things with us and to be part of us.

Indeed, it is along these lines that the verse *must* be understood. To think that the verse speaks of a desire of God for the salvation of every person is to make nonsense of the verse. Christ's promised coming (2 Pet. 3:4, 10) cannot take place until *all* have come to repentance (v. 9). For that, God in his mercy is waiting.

But if God is waiting for the salvation of all without exception, then Christ will *never* come. All men without exception never have and never will come to repentance. There have always been, and always will be, those who perish.

Rather, the coming of Christ is tied to the salvation of the whole of the elect church—the bringing of those "other sheep." When all of them have been brought to repentance by the grace of God, we can be sure that Christ will come.

To that end the church in heaven prays (Rev. 6:10–11), and the church on earth joins with them (Rev. 22:20), asking for the salvation of all whom God has chosen, but who are still in darkness and unbelief.

The Election of the Church

In election God has not only chosen individuals but chosen the church and each elect individual to a place in that church and in the body of Christ (Ps. 132:13 compared with Heb. 12:22; 1 Pet. 2:9). What a glorious truth this is!

Election is not arbitrary and random, but purposeful, something very evident in the election of the church. The biblical picture of the church as a building or a house is very useful here. As a builder chooses his materials, so God has chosen each person to fit into a place in that spiritual building and in the body of Christ (Eph. 2:20 – 22; 1 Pet. 2:5).

No more than a builder would attempt to build a house without first designing it, does God build his church. It is the will of God, not the will of men, that determines who shall have a place in that house and what place he shall have. Even as the stones and timbers of a building cannot determine what place they will have in the building, men cannot by their own choice determine what place they shall have in God's house.

God does not go out and gather the materials for his house as he happens to find them. Rather, having carefully planned his spiritual house, he from eternity "orders in" the materials from which he will build that house in the same way that a builder does. In predetermining all the circumstances of a person's life, God in election determines how each person will be shaped and formed to fit the exact place he has prepared for him (Jer. 1:5).

Likewise, because that house must be built firm and sure, to last for all ages, God has also chosen Christ as its Foundation and Cornerstone (1 Pet. 2:6). All the house is formed and fitted to Christ.

When all the elect have been gathered and glorified, that spiritual house will be the dwelling place of God himself (Eph. 2:22). All its glory and beauty will be of him. He will be not only the designer and builder of the house, but the chief inhabitant as well.

There is more. This election of the church both commands and guarantees the *unity* of the church (John 10:16; Eph. 1:9–10). The elect are all chosen *in him*, that is, in Christ, and that makes them one in him (v. 4). That is the reason Paul does not tell us in Ephesians 4:3 to *have* unity, but to *keep* it. The unity is implicit in our being chosen in Christ, and then gathered in him.

Election also guarantees the holiness of the church (Eph. 1:4). We are chosen not because we *are* holy, but that we *might be* holy. That holiness is necessary because the church is to be the dwelling place of God. God by his Spirit will not dwell in the midst of filth and unholiness. To use the figure of a building once more, we could say that election, the plan, guarantees the beauty of the building.

The great work of gathering and building the church is not finished. Its final glories belong to those things that are still unseen. What we see now is not what the church will be. When the church is fully built, it will show forth the praises of him who calls the elect out of darkness into marvelous light, and it will stand as an eternal monument to his power, wisdom, and grace.

The Holiness of the Church

When we speak of the holiness of the church, we are speaking of one of its *attributes*. The other attributes are oneness, catholicity, and apostolicity.

The holiness of the church is the holiness it has as the body of Christ in union with Christ. The church's holiness is Christ's own holiness, and the church's holiness is *only* in Christ. The church has no holiness of its own (1 Cor. 1:2; 1 Cor. 3:16–17; 1 Pet. 2:9).

This holiness belongs to the church in principle; that is, holiness belongs to the church and to every elect member of the body as something purchased by Christ's death. It will be and is given to every member of the body as Christ brings each one into union with himself through faith and sanctifies him.

We see the holiness of the church in several ways. Remembering that holiness means "separateness," we see the holiness of the church in the separation of the visible church from the world. It is a separate kingdom with a different King, different laws and customs, and a different hope (1 Pet. 2:9).

Indeed, holiness is the boundary of the church in the world. The church has no political boundaries and no boundaries of race or language. Holiness is the line that divides the church from the world. Therefore, those who will not be holy must be put out of the visible church and kept out.

Holiness is also the cause of the continued conflict in which the church is involved. Always the church opposes what is unholy, first in its own members themselves. It condemns those within the church who are hypocrites and carnal, and it witnesses against the wickedness of this sin-cursed world.

If the church and its members are striving to be holy, there will always be conflict between the church and the world (John 15:18–20).

The church has no holiness of its own. Its holiness is God's own holiness shining in the church (1 Pet. 1:15–16). This is what the ungodly hate and oppose (John 3:19; Rom. 8:7).

That holiness of God appears in the church through the holiness of the church's members. They are "saints" because by grace they are given God's holiness and called to be holy as he is holy. Holiness becomes evident in their separation from the wicked and from wickedness (2 Cor. 6:14–7:1).

That is not to say there is no sin in believers or in the visible church. In fact, there is much carnality in the church and much sin in its members. For this we grieve (Ps. 51:3; Ps. 119:53, 136). But that is why the holiness of the church must be a matter of faith, not of sight. We *believe* that the church *is* holy, even the church in this world.

If we go only by what we see, we will surely despair of the church, for we will see much sin in its members. *Believing* that it is a holy communion of saints, we can be sure that it will be presented to Christ "a glorious church, not having spot, or wrinkle, or any such thing" (Eph. 5:27).

Let us, then, in practice and in prayer, as members of the church, follow after holiness, without which no man shall see the Lord (Heb. 12:14).

The Catholicity of the Church

When the Apostles' Creed refers to the "holy *catholic* church," it is not referring to Roman Catholicism. Rome claims to be the holy catholic church but is, in fact, neither holy, nor catholic, nor the church of Jesus Christ, but the false church.

The word *catholic* means "universal" and is a proper description of the true church of Christ. We ought not abandon the word to Romanism.

That the church is universal is clear from many passages of Scripture. Revelation describes the catholic church in chapter 7 verse 9. There we read of a multitude that no man could number, of all nations, kindreds, people, and tongues, standing before God's throne.

The catholicity of the church means not only that people from every nation are gathered into the church by the power of God's sovereign grace, but also that God gathers his church *through all ages*. Its catholicity, therefore, assures us that we shall be with Abraham, Isaac, and Jacob in God's heavenly kingdom (Matt. 8:11). It allows believers now living to be referred to in Revelation 6:11 as the fellow servants and brethren of the martyrs.

Lastly, the catholicity of the church means that all *kinds* of people belong to the church. Rich and poor, great and small, young and old, master and servant, male and female. The church has room for them all.

This is what the Word is thinking of in 1 Timothy 2 when it commands us to pray for *all* men (vv. 1–2). The word *all* does not mean "all without exception." It would be impossible to pray for all in that sense anyway. Rather, the word refers to "all kinds [of men]" as the reference to rulers shows. We are to pray for all kinds of men, because God wills to save all kinds, and Christ has died for all kinds (vv. 4–6).

James has this same aspect of the catholicity of the church in mind when he blames Christians for showing favor to the rich and for despising the poor (2:1–9). We do similarly when we despise other Christians for their outward condition.

Properly interpreted, Galatians 3:28 speaks of catholicity in this sense. It says, "There is neither Jew nor Greek, there is neither bond nor free, there is neither male nor female: for ye are all one in Christ Jesus." This verse is not denying the headship of the man over the woman or differences of gifts given to Christians. Instead it is saying that all men and women, Jew and Gentile, bond and free, are equal as Christians because they are all in Christ Jesus. They are all Abraham's spiritual children.

The idea that one language is better suited to express the Christian faith than another, or that people of some races do not make very good Christians, denies the catholicity of the church. So does the notion that one country or people represent in some special sense the kingdom of God, as dispensationalism and British Israelitism teach.

Let there be, therefore, no prejudice or bigotry in the church of Christ and no rejection of others because of their skin color, language, nationality, or customs. These things make no difference at all.

Believing in the catholicity of the church, we confess that "the same Lord...is rich unto all that call upon him" (Rom. 10:12–13).

The Apostolic Church

Though the Apostles' Creed does not refer to an "apostolic" church, some early church creeds did, such as the Nicene Creed, which says, "I believe one holy catholic and *apostolic* church." What is meant by this?

The church of Rome considers itself apostolic because it claims that the popes are the successors of the apostles and that there is an unbroken line of succession. None of these claims, of course, are true.

Some Protestant churches claim to be apostolic because they believe they have returned to apostolic practice or doctrine. While this may be true, it is not what is meant in the Nicene Creed.

Both in the Nicene Creed and in Reformed theology, the reference is to Ephesians 2:20, which describes the church as "built upon the foundation of the *apostles* and prophets." Obviously and closely related is Matthew 16:18, where Jesus says, "Upon this rock I will build my church; and the gates of hell shall not prevail against it."

The church of Rome takes this rock to be Peter himself, and the popes as the successors of Peter because of the similarity of the name "Peter" (whose name is *Petros* in Greek) and the word "rock" (*petra* in Greek). The grammar of the text forbids this, however. These are actually two different words in Greek, the word *petros,* referring to an isolated rock or small stone, and the word *petra,* referring to a cliff, mountain, or mountain chain. In fact, Jesus is not saying that he is going to build his church on Peter himself (he was not great enough to be the foundation of the church), but that he would build his church upon Peter's confession that Jesus is the Christ, the Son of God (Matt. 16:16). This is a firm and indestructible foundation.

In that light, Ephesians 2:20 must also be interpreted as referring to apostolic (and prophetic) teaching and doctrine, in other words, to the inspired Scriptures of the Old and New Testaments. They are the church's foundation.

Built upon the teaching and doctrine of the apostles, the church is built upon Christ. He, then, is the chief Cornerstone "in whom all the building fitly framed together groweth unto an holy temple in the Lord" (v. 21).

The implication is, of course, that all the doctrine and teaching of the church concerns Christ. "Search the scriptures," Jesus says. "They are they which testify of me" (John 5:39). Speaking for all the apostles, Paul

233

says, "For I determined not to know any thing among you, save Jesus Christ, and him crucified" (1 Cor. 2:2).

A church that is truly apostolic, therefore, is truly the church of Christ. No wonder, then, that when the church is built on such a foundation, even the gates of hell cannot overcome it (Matt. 16:18).

Few churches today are truly apostolic. Most of them have little or none of the teaching of the apostles and prophets, so they are vulnerable to the assaults of the forces of hell. May God help and save his church and build it once again on a firm foundation.

The Unity of the Church

We have spoken of the church's holiness, its catholicity, and its apostolicity. There is another characteristic or attribute of the church, and that is its unity.

When we speak of the church's unity, we mean that there is essentially only *one* church and body of Jesus Christ. Christ does not have more than one body.

This unity of the church is not easily seen because of the multitude of different denominations, congregations, and churches that exist. To some extent this variety is due to the sinfulness and weakness of the church and its members; to some extent it is not.

Geographical differences and differences of language make it impossible to have complete unity in the visible church. Those differences will be removed only in the new heavens and the new earth when there is "no more sea" (Rev. 21:1). In heaven, no distances, and no differences of language or anything else, will separate believers from one another.

On this earth, however, the sins of the church and its members make institutional unity difficult, even where it is possible. Differences of doctrine and practice, all of which are the result of a sinful failure to understand and obey the Word of God, also separate believers from one another.

Because sin destroys church unity and keeps believers apart, Christians ought always to be doing all in their power to overcome these differences by studying the Word and by speaking to one another of what they believe. They ought not be tolerant of division. Even where ecclesiastical unity proves impossible, they ought nevertheless to keep fellowship with other Christians as much as possible. They ought not to reject them or speak as though there are no Christians besides those in their own group.

Believers may not, however, seek unity at the expense of the truth. They are to buy the truth and sell it not (Prov. 23:23). That is where ecumenism goes wrong. It sells the truth for a mess of ecclesiastical pottage that is without value and does not produce true unity.

Seeking and praying for unity, the saints should not forget that this unity is *in diversity*. The unity of the church does not mean that every believer must be exactly alike. Nor does it mean that every congregation and church must be a carbon copy of the others.

Paul makes this clear in 1 Corinthians 12. Not only is there a diversity of members and gifts, but every member is necessary, something we all too often forget. Only thus is the church the *body* of Jesus Christ.

Nevertheless, until sin is destroyed, there will be divisions. Because of this, the unity of the church is now largely a matter of faith. Christians *believe,* as the Nicene Creed reminds us, "*one* holy catholic and apostolic church."

Believers must, therefore, with regard to the unity of the church, walk by faith, not by sight (2 Cor. 5:7). How important this is! Faith will keep them from abandoning the visible church when they see its faults and sins and the divisions within it.

Nor is that faith vain. When Christ returns, he will "gather together in one all things in Christ" (Eph. 1:10) and destroy sin. Then even the possibility of disunity will be gone.

The Church in the Old and New Testaments

One very important aspect of the church's unity is its unity *in the Old and New Testaments,* which means that Israel is the *church* of the Old Testament, and that the church of the New Testament is the true *Israel* of God. Few seem to see this, yet the Bible is clear on the matter.

That Israel *is* the church and the church *is* Israel lies at the root of a defense of infant baptism (one church, and therefore one covenant and one sign of the covenant). Likewise, this understanding is essential in avoiding the errors of dispensationalism, the teaching that Israel and the church are two entirely different entities and have two different futures.

Acts 7:38 shows us clearly that Israel and the church are one. There Israel is called "the church in the wilderness," and the usual New Testament word for the church is used.

Philippians 3:3 is further proof. There Paul, speaking to a *Gentile* church, says, "For *we are the circumcision,* which worship God in the spirit, and rejoice in Christ Jesus, and have no confidence in the flesh" (see also Rom. 3:28–29; Gal. 3:29). All who worship God in spirit and love our Lord Jesus are the true Jews, God's Israel.

As far as the Bible is concerned, being a real Jew has nothing to do with physical descent from Abraham, that is, with one's genealogy and natural birth. As far as that goes, the Bible says, "God is able of these stones to raise up children unto Abraham" (Luke 3:8).

A real Jew, according to Scripture, is one who is born by the power of the promise (Rom. 9:8); one who has the same justifying faith as Abraham (Gal. 3:8–9); one who, like Abraham, belongs to Christ (v. 29); and one who is circumcised in heart (Rom. 3:29). The rest are not counted as Jews (Rom. 2:28) and have nothing to do with the promises (Acts 2:39).

The unity of Israel and the church is also clear from Hosea 1:10–11 and its quotation in Romans 9:24–26, and from Amos 9:11–15 and its quotation in Acts 15:13–17. In the Hosea passage the Word of God makes reference to the ten tribes [that had deserted Judah and Benjamin] and to their future restoration. Romans 9:24–26 shows us that this prophecy is fulfilled in the gathering of the New Testament church.

In Amos 9:11–15 we read again of the restoration of the nation of Israel to its own land and of the rebuilding of the temple. Acts 15, however, makes clear that this is fulfilled in the gathering of the *Gentiles* into the New Testament *church.* The rebuilding of the tabernacle of David, which was fallen down and ruined (v. 16), refers to God's visiting the Gentiles "to take out of them a people for his name" (v. 14).

It is only when we see these truths that we will begin to realize that the

Old Testament as well as the New is written for *us* as New Testament Christians. Its promises, even its threats, are not for some foreign people with whom we have nothing to do, but are for us and for our children. This makes quite a difference in the reading of the Old Testament. Then we no longer read with a veil over our eyes, but with understanding and profit.

The Offices in the Church

After he ascended into heaven, our Lord instituted various offices in the church (Eph. 4:11). He instituted these offices so that those who serve in them might represent him and serve his church in their offices. Though he remains the only Head and King of the church, these offices are necessary for the well-being of the church.

There has been much controversy about the number and nature of these offices. Without entering into that controversy, we believe that the offices that remain in the church are three: elder, deacon, and minister.

We say these offices "remain" because there have been other, temporary offices, such as apostle, prophet, and evangelist. These offices, which involved bringing the *inspired and infallible* Word of God to its hearers (Acts 21:10–11; Heb. 2:3–4; 2 Pet. 3:15–16), are no longer necessary since we now have the completed Scriptures (2 Pet. 1:19–21).

It is clear that it is only the offices of ruling elder, deacon, and minister that remain, since these are the only offices mentioned in the later epistles of Paul—1 Timothy and Titus especially—where he is giving instruction to the successors of the apostles. This is further confirmed by the fact that these epistles have to do with proper behavior in the church (1 Tim. 3:15) and with setting things in order in the church (Titus 1:5).

We are not concerned to argue the point that both the ministers and ruling elders are identified as elders in the New Testament. The fact of the matter is that these offices have distinct duties and are viewed as separate offices in the New Testament (1 Tim. 3 and 4).

What does concern us is that the three offices are neglected and forgotten in the church today. Few churches have all three offices, and where the offices are present, one often finds deacons doing the work of elders or vice versa, or ministers doing the work of all three. Likewise, in many cases the offices have become nothing more than honorary positions, and those who are chosen to them are chosen on the basis not of spiritual qualifications, but of prominence or wealth.

This can only be to the detriment of the church. Indeed, insofar as the offices are representative of Christ, their absence in the church means that in some ways Christ himself is not present among the people of God, as he ought to be.

We believe that these offices are aspects of Christ's threefold office of Prophet, Priest, and King. This is very evident in the offices of ruling elder and minister. It is hard not to see that those two are extensions of Christ's kingly and prophetic offices. The office of deacon, properly understood, is an extension of Christ's priestly office, or at least of some aspects of that office.

If it is true that church offices reflect Christ's offices, they are most important to the church and may not be neglected as they often are today. It is our hope and prayer that they may be restored to their proper place and function.

The Office of Elder

Scripture uses two different words for elder. One word, translated "elder" (Acts 14:23; Acts 15:2, 4, 6ff.; 1 Tim. 5:1, 17, 19; Titus 1:5; James 5:14; 1 Pet. 5:1,) is the Greek word *presbyter* and means "older person." The other word, translated "bishop" or "overseer" (Acts 20:28; Phil. 1:1; 1 Tim. 3:1–2; Titus 1:7), refers to a person who has authority and rule over others.

That these two words refer to the same office is clear from Scripture. In Acts 20 Paul calls the *elders* of the church of Ephesus "overseers" (v. 28), elsewhere translated "bishops" (1 Tim. 3:1, 2). In Titus 1:5–7 Paul uses both "elder" and "bishop" to apply to the same persons. This is contrary to Roman Catholicism and Episcopalianism, both of which teach that the office of bishop is a different and higher office than the other offices.

Scripture does make a distinction between *ruling* elders (1 Tim. 3:4–5; 1 Tim. 5:17) and *teaching* elders (1 Pet. 5:1). This does not, however, put one office above another. As these passages show, there is not even an absolute distinction between these offices. Ruling elders also must be able to teach (1 Tim. 3:2), and teaching elders, "who labour in the word and doctrine," also rule (1 Tim. 5:17).

The difference, therefore, is more a difference of function than anything else. *Teaching* elders labor *especially,* though not exclusively, in word and doctrine in contrast to the other elders. Ephesians 4:11 also refers to those elders as pastors and teachers.

It is the office of ruling elder that we are concerned with, and we must make several points about it. These points are important if the office of elder is to be a blessing and not a curse in God's church.

First, there must be a plurality of elders. Scripture never speaks of one elder ruling alone, whether he is a minister or otherwise. Rule by one is tyranny and does not harmonize with the Word of God in Proverbs 11:14, Proverbs 15:22, and Proverbs 24:6.

Second, the elders are servants of God's people (Matt. 23:11; 1 Cor. 9:19; 2 Cor. 4:5). This is especially clear from Colossians 4:17, where Paul tells the church to admonish its minister to take heed to and fulfill his ministry. That elders see themselves as servants avoids tyranny and lording in the church.

Third, that the elders rule means that they rule all aspects of the church's life, including the preaching and the conduct of the other officers and of the ministers (Acts 20:28 – 31). It is the duty of all the elders to keep from the church "hirelings" and "wolves." *No one* is a law unto himself in the church.

Fourth, the ruling authority that elders have in the church is given them by Christ (Acts 20:28), belongs to Christ (Matt. 28:18), and must be exercised in obedience to him (1 Pet. 5:4). In practice, that means that their authority must be the Word of God in Scripture. They must rule with it, bring it to the members, admonish by it, and teach it alone, rather than their own notions.

Such elders will be a blessing in Christ's church.

The Office of Deacon

The office of deacon is the most neglected office in the church of Jesus Christ. Many churches do not even have deacons, or if they do, the deacons rarely perform their biblical function.

In most churches that have deacons, the deacons do the work of elders, ruling the church. In other cases they merely take care of the financial affairs of the church, something for which ordination and office are not necessary.

To understand the office of deacon, it is necessary to examine Acts 6, where the story of the first deacons is told. The word translated "deacon" in Scripture is simply the Greek word for "servant," and Scripture uses it to describe anyone who serves in *any* capacity in the church or among believers (John 12:26; Rom. 16:1). Nevertheless, Acts 6 makes it clear that some are "servants" in a special sense.

Acts 6 teaches us, first, that the office of these special servants, the office of deacon, is an *office* to which one must be *ordained* (vv. 3, 6; see also Phil. 1:1 and 1 Tim. 3:10, 13). This implies that the office is more than a matter of keeping the church's books. It also implies that certain *spiritual* qualifications are necessary (Acts 6:3; see also 1 Tim. 3:8–13).

Acts 6:3 suggests, and 1 Timothy 3:8–13 confirms it, that deacons, like elders and ministers, should be *men*. This follows from the fact that it is an ordained office involving the exercise of *authority* in the church, though not the same ruling authority that the elders have. Churches that have women as deacons are as much in disobedience to God's Word as those that have women elders and preachers.

We also learn from Acts 6, which tells about the Grecian widows, about the office and function of the deacons. Their business involves especially the care of those who are in need. That this involves more than the care of widows and waiting on tables, however, is clear from Acts 4:35. There we see that the "business" that the apostles turned over to the deacons involved collecting for, and distributing to, all who were in need.

We would emphasize, too, that in doing this work as ordained officers of the church called by Christ himself, the deacons perform more than mere charity. It must follow that having been ordained in Christ's service to this work, the deacons are responsible for helping in Christ's name and for his sake: "It is very beneficial that they do not only administer relief to the poor and indigent with external gifts, but also with comfortable words from Scripture."[1]

---

1. Form of Ordination of Elders and Deacons, in *The Confessions and the Church Order of the Protestant Reformed Churches* (Grandville, MI: Protestant Reformed Churces in America, 2005), 292.

In doing this, the deacons are fulfilling a certain priestly function in the church. Like the Old Testament priests, theirs is an office of mercy in that they receive the gifts that are brought and "offer" them in the service of Christ and his people.

We believe that they must follow the rule of Galatians 6:10 in their work, so that their office is first and especially for the church. When their office is restored in the church, the words of Psalm 37:25 will be true: "Yet have I not seen the righteous forsaken, nor his seed begging bread."

The Office of Pastor and Teacher

The office of pastor and teacher (Eph. 4:11) is the third permanent office in the church. That it is an office requiring ordination is seen in 1 Timothy 4:14 and Romans 10:15. The primary task of those holding this office is laboring "in the word and doctrine" (1 Tim. 5:17), that is, the preaching of the gospel.

As 1 Timothy 5:17 shows, those who labor in the word and doctrine are elders along with those who rule in the church. Indeed, this verse shows us that the ministers of the gospel also rule, just as the ruling elders are also pastors (Acts 20:28). Scripture makes no absolute separation between the two offices of ruling elder and minister.

The primary task of the elders who labor in "the word and doctrine" is the preaching of the gospel. This is shown in 2 Timothy 4:2 and many other passages. This office, as Ephesians 4:11 reminds us, is a *teaching* office. The business of the preacher, therefore, is not to entertain. His business is not even primarily to "evangelize," in the usual sense of that word. His work is teaching.

We need to stress this. Many preachers of the gospel seem to have forgotten it. Whatever they are doing, they are doing precious little teaching. Often the members of the congregation sit under their preaching for years and learn next to nothing. That is not always the fault of the preacher, of course, but more often than not, it is.

Not only does the preacher have the calling to teach the older members of the congregation, but also the children (John 21:15). The preacher ought, then, to give regular instruction to the children of the church, teaching them both Bible history and Bible doctrine, and not us-ing silly and useless "children's sermons," where nothing of consequence is taught or learned.

The preacher even has the calling to instruct young men and to pre-pare them for the ministry of the Word (2 Tim. 2:2). In harmony with this, Reformed churches have always appointed ministers of the gospel to this work. In this, as in all else, a preacher is also a pastor, a shepherd of God's people with the great responsibility of caring for them (Ezek. 34:1–6).

As part of his calling to teach, the preacher also has the responsibil-ity to read and study (1 Tim. 4:13) and to give heed to doctrine, that is, to learn and know it (v. 16). These duties are often neglected by those who hold this office. For this reason it is preferable that those who hold the office have opportunity to "give heed to doctrine" and to receive training and instruction before they take up their responsibilities. How this is done is not as important as *that* it be done.

The congregation, too, has a responsibility in all this. Like the church in Colosse, they must say to their preacher, "Take heed to the ministry which thou hast received in the Lord, that thou fulfil it" (Col. 4:17). The congregation *must* say this. They must say it often, and especially when the minister is not giving heed to his biblical responsibilities.

This office of pastor or teacher is not meant to be an easy job for those who hold it, but it is appointed by God for the salvation of his peo-ple. Woe to those shepherds who do not feed the flock (Ezek. 34:2)!

Church Government

One thing that has often divided the church of Jesus Christ is the whole matter of church government, particularly the question of indepen-dency versus denominationalism. It is with some trepidation, therefore, that we approach this subject.

We do believe that independentism is not only wrong, but deadly as far as the existence of the church is concerned. We see it as a most sig-nificant reason for the decline of the church in many places.

Independentism leaves both the members and officers of the church without recourse or help when problems arise. It therefore ignores the Word of God in Proverbs 24:6 and similar passages. It does not follow the pattern of Acts 15, and it fails to promote unity on any broader basis than the local church.

Nevertheless, faults are found on the other side also. All too often the church is run "from the top down" by committees and boards for which there is no biblical warrant, so that neither the local church nor its members have any "say" in the church. Nor, in that case, are the church's leaders answerable to the members (or anyone) for their conduct.

This, in Presbyterian and Reformed denominations, is hierarchism, a kind of popery in which assemblies and committees have power in the church that only Christ should have. This, too, we abominate.

We believe the Bible gives us an answer that avoids the problems on both sides. That answer is, first, that in the work Christ has given them to do, congregations *must* join together for mutual help and supervision (Acts 15). This is necessary to "keep the unity of the Spirit" (Eph. 4:3).

Second, the "autonomy" (self-rule) of the local church must be maintained. It is to the church, not to church assemblies or committees, that the work of preaching the gospel, administering the sacraments, and exercising Christian discipline belongs (Acts 13:1–4; 1 Cor. 5:4–5). The authority Christ has given for these things resides in the local church. The church is not, therefore, run from the top down. This means, too, that the assemblies must be carefully limited in their functions. As in Acts 15, they must be for mutual help and advice. When these assemblies make biblical decisions on such matters as come to them, these decisions must be heeded (vv. 23–29), not because some higher authority has decreed it, but because the *churches themselves together* have decided it in harmony with God's Word.

Third, in the local church the offices must function according to the pattern laid down in Scripture, and all the officers of the church must be answerable to the church itself, that is, to the body of believers. With all the authority Christ has given them, they are not lords over the church, but servants of it (2 Cor. 4:5; Col. 4:17).

These are the first steps in seeing to it that things are done decently and in good order in the church of Jesus Christ. Such good order is necessary for the safety and well-being of the church.

The True Church

What is the true church of Jesus Christ, and where is it to be found? That is a difficult but important question, a question that must be asked if we are to become members of the visible church. Very often it is a question that is not so easy to answer.

What makes this question the more difficult is the possibility that a church that was once the church of Christ becomes the false church. Christ warns the church of Ephesus about this possibility in Revelation 2:5.

That the church of Ephesus was in danger of becoming the false church is evident from Christ's threat to remove its "candlestick." Those candlesticks were pictures of the true church, burning with the oil of the Spirit (Zech. 4:1–6; Heb. 1:9) and existing as a light in the world (Matt. 5:14). The church of Ephesus was in danger of losing both the Spirit and his light. That the church there was threatened with the removal of its candlestick from its place meant that it would no longer be Christ's. He would no longer walk in it (Rev. 1:12–13). In the same manner Christ threatens to spit the church of Laodicea out of his mouth (Rev. 3:16).

What is so frightening in the case of these two churches is that Christ threatens them with judgment for losing their first love (Rev. 2:4) and for lukewarmness and carnal security (Rev. 3:16–17). No doubt there are many churches today that are in danger of coming under the same judgments and for the same reasons.

The true church of Christ, therefore, is the church that keeps its first love (Rev. 2:4), does what Christ commands (v. 5), is faithful (v. 10), repents of its sins (v. 16), holds fast to what it has (v. 25), is watchful (Rev. 3:3), sees to it that its members do not defile their garments (v. 4), keeps Christ's word, and does not deny his name (v. 8). There are not many such today.

It is evident from these passages that not all churches are equally pure. The churches that Christ addresses in Revelation 2 and 3 range from those against which he has no complaint to those threatened with destruction. Nevertheless, they are all still addressed as *churches,* as is also the church of Corinth with all its problems.

We should keep this in mind, too, because it means that in searching for the true church, we should not be looking for a *perfect* church.

As long as there is sin in the world and in God's people, a perfect church cannot be found.

No church or denomination can claim, as Rome does and as some Protestant churches also do, to be the *only* true church of Christ. There is a wide range of churches, more or less pure and true, that represent, at least to some degree, the church of Jesus Christ. If we forget that there are imperfections in the church on earth, we may decide to join *no* church, but that would be contrary to Hebrews 10:24–25, which says, "And let us consider one another to provoke unto love and to good works: Not forsaking the assembling of ourselves together, as the manner of some is; but exhorting one another: and so much the more, as ye see the day approaching."

Nevertheless, Christ's words to the churches in Revelation 2 and 3 make it clear that both in seeking church membership and in fulfilling the responsibilities of church membership, we must seek purity, truth, and faithfulness for his sake.

The Marks of the True Church

That the true church of Christ *can* be found in the world is evident from Christ's promise: "I will build my church; and the gates of hell shall not prevail against it" (Matt. 16:18). But how and where do we find that true church in order that we may join ourselves to it in obedience to Hebrews 10:25?

The question of membership is urgent in light of the fact that the true church is not represented by just one church or denomination, as we have shown. With the abundance of different churches and denominations available today, which one are we to join? The answer is that we are to join ourselves to the church that is most faithful to Christ, and therefore purest—though never perfectly pure—in doctrine, life, and practice.

Thus we speak of the *marks of the true church*. These are marks that indicate the extent to which a church is true to Christ and to his Word. Insofar as a church has these marks, it is part of the true church of Christ. Any so-called church that lacks these marks has become the false church, a "synagogue of Satan" (Rev. 2:9).

There is some debate about the number and nature of these "marks."

The Belgic Confession of Faith mentions the pure preaching of the Word, the administration of the sacraments according to Christ's command, and the faithful carrying out of Christian discipline in the church[2] (Matt. 16:18–19; Matt. 28:19–20; 1 Cor. 11:23–34). Some would add to the third mark, or substitute for it, biblical worship.

It is evident, however, that all these add up to one mark: that *everything* in the church is done in obedience to Christ. As the Belgic Confession says, the true church is where "all things are managed according to the pure Word of God, all things contrary thereto rejected, and Jesus Christ acknowledged as the only Head of the church."[3]

Whether we speak of one or several marks, certain things are marks of the true church because they are marks of the *presence of Christ* in the church. That is what matters. If Christ is not present (Rev. 1:12–13; Rev. 2:5), everything the church does is in vain, and membership is pointless. It cannot even be called the *church* if Christ is not there.

We must remember this in bringing up our children. If the marks of Christ's presence are hardly to be found in a particular church, what hope have we there for our children? Only Christ, by his presence, is able to save them and show them the way.

That the marks of the true church show the presence of Christ is especially evident in connection with the preaching of the gospel. Properly carried out, the preaching is *Christ himself speaking in the church* (John 10:27; 1 Cor. 1:23–24; Eph. 2:17). Pure biblical preaching is proof, therefore, of Christ's presence. The same is true of the sacraments and discipline.

That these are marks of *Christ's* presence must be emphasized. We do not join the church because of the members, because of their godly conduct or friendliness, as important as those things are. We join the church in order to follow Christ, the only Savior and Bishop of our souls.

The Gospel

The church's great calling—really the church's *only* calling—is to preach

---

2. Belgic Confession, Article 29.
3. Ibid.

the gospel. This is certainly the intent of the "great commission" in Matthew 28:19. Few people seem to know anymore what the gospel is, however.

The word *gospel* means literally "good news," or in the words of the angel who announced Christ's birth, "glad tidings." Indeed, the content of the gospel is the best news that has ever been heard in this sin-filled world. It is good news because it speaks of salvation by God's free and sovereign grace.

Yet there are many who change the message of the gospel so that it is no longer *good* news. By their errors the gospel becomes no better news than what we read in the daily newspapers. This is especially true of those who pervert the gospel by making salvation depend on man's own works. Salvation by works is bad tidings, since the Bible assures us that all our works are evil (Ps. 14:1) and our righteousnesses as filthy rags (Isa. 64:6).

The gospel is no longer good news when it is suggested, either in the message itself or in the way that message is presented, that salvation depends on the will, choice, and decision of the sinner. That is horrible news to changeable, indecisive, unwilling, disobedient creatures such as we are (John 5:40; John 6:44; John 8:44).

Equally disturbing news, often published as the gospel, is the teaching that Christ died for everyone and that God loves and wants to save everyone without exception. The teaching that Christ died for everyone is hardly good news if some for whom Christ supposedly died end up in hell. The teaching that God loves and wants to save everyone is also not a glad tiding when it speaks of a God who is not able to do, or who does not do, what he wants. If some for whom Christ died go to hell, this would destroy all our confidence in Christ. If God wishes to save everyone but cannot do so, this would destroy all our confidence in God.

Also wrong is the practice of avoiding certain truths as being inappropriate for the preaching of the gospel. There are several problems with this practice. *All* Scripture is gospel. There is no difference between teaching the truths of Scripture and preaching the gospel. Matthew 28:19, "Go ye therefore, and *teach* all nations," shows us this, as does the example of the apostles in Acts chapters 2, 7, 13, and 17, where Bible history, doctrine, poetry, and prophecy are all preached as gospel and where every doctrine from the sovereignty of God over the wicked to the doctrine of creation and providence is included. *Any* truth of Scripture is good news to God's people, because it speaks of the God of their salvation.

No less disturbing is the practice of reducing the gospel to a few truths, usually preached over and over again at an evening evangelistic service, hung on a different text each week, and addressed to the unsaved who may or may not be present.

Directing a sermon only to the unsaved is not biblical. All God's people need to hear *all* the truths of Scripture. As long as they are in this world, believers need to be called to repentance and faith as much as the unsaved. They must be comforted by Scripture's promises, admonished by its warnings, and instructed by its precious truths. May God restore such preaching in the churches.

Preaching

What is preaching? Is it just another form of teaching, the only difference being that the Bible is taught? If it is just another form of teaching, why does Scripture so strongly emphasize its importance? In fact, preaching is something unique.

To understand why preaching is of vital importance, we must understand what it is and how it is unique. The Bible tells us a great deal about preaching, especially in the Greek words that the New Testament uses for "preaching."

One word tells us what the *content* of preaching is. That word is really the word from which comes our English word *evangelize,* meaning "to bring good news." The other word, the one on which we will focus, shows us what preaching itself is all about. Translated, the word means "to be a messenger." The reference, though, is not to just any messenger, but to the kind once called a "herald." A herald was a messenger commissioned, usually by a king or great ruler, to bring a specific message to the people *in the words of the king himself.* A herald was not allowed to add anything to, to leave anything out of, or to "interpret" the message. He simply had to say, "Thus says the king!" He was, then, very similar to an ambassador (2 Cor. 5:20; Eph. 6:20).

Applied to preaching, this word *herald* teaches us that anyone who preaches must be *commissioned,* or sent, by the King of kings, Christ Jesus. No one has any right to appoint himself a preacher or to take up the work on his own. Even Christ did not do this (Heb. 5:5). If a person sets himself up as a preacher, his message has no official weight, and no one is obliged to hear it.

An illustration may help here. As a private citizen, I may have some knowledge of what my government's plans are, and visiting a foreign country, I might take it upon myself to inform that government of my own country's plans. Even if my information is correct in every particular, what I say has no authority, and no one is obliged to pay any attention to it. Only if an ambassador or some other official representative of my government brings the message is the foreign government obliged to listen.

Thus Scripture tells us that those who preach must be *sent* (Rom. 10:15). If they are not sent, no one need give any heed at all to what they say. This sending is done *by the Holy Spirit through the church* by means of ordination or the laying on of hands, as Acts shows so clearly in the case of the apostle Paul himself (Acts 13:1–3).

This implies, too, that the minister is accountable not only to God, but to the church or churches that send him (Acts 14:27). Calling always means accountability. Even as Christ uses the church to send a minister, so he also uses the church to call the minister to account with regard to the message he brings.

For these reasons we believe in an ordained ministry, and we do not believe that "lay preaching" is biblical. Men who are sent by no one and accountable to no one are not true ambassadors or heralds of Christ.

Christ and the Preaching

The most important thing that the Bible says about preaching is that in it God's people hear the voice of Christ himself. In John 10:27 Jesus tells us that we must and do hear his voice.

That we hear his voice in the *preaching* is clear from other passages as well (Rom. 1:16–17; Rom. 10:13–14; 1 Cor. 1:18, 23–24; Eph. 2:17). Notice, for example, in Ephesians 2:17, that it is *Christ* who comes and preaches peace, to both Jews and Gentiles. Even in the Old Testament it was the Spirit of *Christ* who spoke through the prophets (1 Pet. 1:10–11).

This is of the utmost importance. If Christ does not speak through the preaching, no one will ever be saved by the preaching of the gospel. No *man*'s voice can convict sinners and lead them to repentance. Only Christ's voice can do that. No one has power to convert sinners and bring them to God but Christ (John 10:27).

Because Christ speaks through the preaching and causes his voice to be heard, the gospel is "the power of God unto salvation" (Rom. 1:16). Indeed, the gospel is "*Christ* the power of God, and the wisdom of God" (1 Cor. 1:23–24).

That Christ speaks through the gospel also explains that the gospel always has a two-part effect. It saves, but it also hardens. It is a savor of life, but also of death (2 Cor. 2:14–16). No one can come so near to Christ as to hear his voice and be neutral. He will either by the grace of God love that voice and desire to hear it always, or he will hate its very sound and shut his ears and heart to it (Isa. 6:9–10).

When people stumble through unbelief, therefore, they stumble over Christ. *He* is the stone of stumbling and rock of offense, not the preacher, at least not if the gospel is preached properly.

In order for Christ to be heard through gospel preaching, however, several things must be true. First, *only the Scriptures* must be preached. They, and they alone, are Christ's Word to his people. Anecdotes, jokes, entertainment, and the preacher's own thoughts, however valuable they may be, are of no use in preaching. The *Word alone* must be preached.

Second, the preaching must be *expository*. That is another way of saying that it is the *Word* that must be preached. In our day so much preaching is *not* expository. Some nice thoughts are hung on a text of Scripture, but Scripture itself is never explained, nor the chosen passage expounded.

Third, the preacher, as we said earlier, must be *sent* (Rom. 10:15), that is, authorized and ordained by Christ's church (Acts 13:1–4. Note that the sending by the church is equated with the sending of the Holy Spirit in verse 4). If the preacher is *not* sent, neither he nor his audience have any guarantee that Christ will use him and speak through him. What use is preaching then?

May God grant that Christ's voice be heard once again in the churches.

The Necessity of Christian Discipline

Biblical church discipline is almost completely missing in the church today. We rarely hear of anyone's being excommunicated from the church, except for gross sin, and people are not always disciplined even for that. People who live unchristian lives are allowed to remain in the church as members. Unbelievers serve in church offices. Ministers are allowed to preach anything and everything, no matter how unbiblical it may be. Sin, unbelief, backsliding, and disobedience are rarely even rebuked.

Especially is this true of many things that are counted "little" sins, but are especially destructive when allowed to remain unrebuked and unchecked in the church. It would be an unusual thing for sins such as speaking evil of others and gossiping to be rebuked, or for sins such as envy, hatred, or strife to be named as sin, yet they are destructive both of the church and of the service of God (Prov. 26:17–28; Matt. 5:21–24). They are the little foxes that spoil the vineyard (Song of Sol. 2:15).

The result of this lack of discipline is that sin in all its ruinous power flourishes and grows in the church, so that eventually the church is ruined. As the Word reminds us when speaking of sin in the church of Corinth, "A little leaven leaveneth the whole lump" (1 Cor. 5:6). Even the lack of first love, though everything else was in place, brought on the church of Ephesus the threat of having its candlestick removed (Rev. 2:1–7).

Christian discipline reaches its conclusion in censure and excommunication. In spite of the fact that such action is not pleasant, it is of the utmost importance for the safety and well-being of the church, and so Scripture speaks of it often (Matt. 18:15–17; 1 Cor. 5:1–13; 2 Thess. 3:14–15; 1 Tim. 1:19–20; Rev. 2:2).

In Scripture, excommunication is described in terms of delivering a person to Satan (1 Cor. 5:5; 1 Tim. 1:20) and of excluding him or her from fellowship (Matt. 18:17; 2 Thess. 3:14), especially from the fellowship of the Lord's supper (1 Cor. 5:11, 13). In some cases at least, it involves an actual trial of those who have sinned (Rev. 2:2).

Christian discipline involves such extreme measures that this is probably the chief reason it is seldom carried out. Nevertheless, it is vital not only for the well-being of the church, but for the salvation of the sinner. Having described discipline in the strongest possible terms, 1 Corinthians 5:5 insists that discipline's main purpose is "the destruction of the flesh" and the salvation of the spirit in the day of the Lord Jesus (see also 2 Thess. 3:14). One of the Reformed confessions, therefore, refers to excommunication as "the last remedy."[4]

Discipline does not, however, mean just excommunication. It involves *watchfulness and rebuke* on the part of *all* the members. Matthew 18 teaches that the church as a whole is not even brought into the matter unless the sinner, when confronted with his sin, refuses to repent. We are convinced that there would be little need for formal discipline and exclusion from the church if the members faithfully fulfilled these responsibilities.

The Way of Christian Discipline

Because Christian discipline is such a serious thing, careful rules are laid down for it in the Word, especially in Matthew 18. These rules are essential.

For one thing, as we have noticed, discipline ordinarily begins with *private admonition.* When someone has sinned against us or offended us, we are required to go to him and point out his sin to him, not *first* to bring the matter to the church.

Several aspects of this private discipline require our attention. First, when dealing with sin privately, it is the sinner himself who must be told, *not everyone else.* Telling everyone else the sins of others is itself the sin of talebearing or gossiping and is a deadly evil in the church (Prov. 26:20–26). This is the reason Jesus says in Matthew 18:15, "Tell him his fault *between thee and him alone.*"

Second, it is the *person sinned against* who has the primary obligation to go to the one who has sinned (v. 15). All too often in our pride and anger we wait for the person who has sinned to come to us, and the result is that we are not reconciled to him.

Third, rebuking of sin must be done with humility and love. In Matthew 18 Jesus calls our sinning fellow saints "brothers." In 2 Thessalonians 3:15 we are told that even one who has been excommunicated

---

4. Form for Excommunication, in *Confessions and Church Order,* 276.

must still be admonished "as a brother." Too often our failure to gain a brother is due to the *way* in which we point out his sins.

Only if the sinner will not receive admonition and repent is the matter brought to the attention of others, but then *not* in the way of talebearing. The sinner must be approached in the presence of witnesses (Matt. 18:16; Num. 35:30), who also have the obligation, if they are convinced he has sinned, to admonish him (Matt. 18:17).

The matter is brought to the church, functioning through its ordained elders, only if the sinner continues unrepentant. Then, eventually, he is excommunicated, both for the sin he committed and for his refusal to repent. This excommunication, as the very word suggests, involves his being barred from the Lord's table, and finally from membership and fellowship in the church.

It is good to notice, too, that Scripture speaks of *admonitions*, not a single admonition. Love demands that every opportunity must be given for repentance. In admonishing, as much as possible, the sinner must be spared, especially if he repents (2 Cor. 2:5 – 8). Thus Scripture says love covers sin, not to hide it so that it is not dealt with, but to spare the sinner unnecessary shame and reproach, if possible (James 5:19–20).

In a few cases, however, Scripture indicates that sin must be immediately and publicly rebuked. Thus did Paul deal with Peter (Gal. 2:11–14), probably because of Peter's prominent position in the church. Two cases are given in 1 Timothy 5:20: where the person has sinned before all, that is, sinned publicly; and where the person is a leader in the church (Paul is speaking here especially of elders).

In these ways, sins will be dealt with in the church and will not destroy it. Our holy God will not then be mocked, but glorified in the church, and sinners will be saved.

The Sacraments

Having spoken of preaching and discipline, we come now to the difficult subject of the sacraments. On the one hand, it is troubling that the sacraments, appointed by Christ as marks of church unity, are a principal cause of divisions in the church. On the other hand, almost everything a church believes comes to focus in the sacraments, so it is not surprising that they mark the divisions between churches and between Christians. We speak of the sacraments not to promote divisions, but with the hope and prayer that there may be unity in the truth.

What are the sacraments? The word *sacrament* comes from a Latin word meaning "oath," and though it is not found in Scripture, we use it because each sacrament is a visible, tangible (touchable) promise or oath from Christ to his church.

The word *sacrament* is used to refer to certain rites specially given by Christ to his church to confirm his promises to the church. These rites are to be used in the church until Christ returns (Matt. 28:19–20; 1 Cor. 11:26).

These rites or ceremonies are symbols or signs. This is evident from the fact that Jesus calls the bread of the Lord's supper "my body" and the cup "the new testament in my blood" (Luke 22:20). Since the bread and cup cannot be these things literally, as we hope to show, they must be *signs* of Christ's body and blood.

We see this same thing in baptism. Scripture calls by the same name both water baptism and the washing away of sins by Christ's blood. Both sign and spiritual reality have the same name: *baptism* (compare Acts 2:41 and 1 Pet. 3:21).

These symbols and signs are given to help our faith (Judges 6:36–40; Luke 1:18–20; Luke 2:12). They help our faith in two ways: by picturing invisible, spiritual realities; and by pointing to Christ as the complete Savior. We need them because our faith is often weak, and we must believe without seeing (John 20:29; 2 Cor. 5:7).

Trusting that there is continuity between circumcision and baptism, and between the passover and the Lord's supper, we see the sacraments also as *seals* (Rom. 4:11). Indeed, if they are signs, they must also be seals, for signs always confirm or seal something.

As seals, the sacraments function not only by picturing spiritual realities to believers and teaching us certain things, but also by *strengthening and confirming our faith*. The sacraments strengthen our faith by assuring us in baptism that as truly as water washes our bodies, so the blood of Christ washes our souls, and in the Lord's supper that as truly as bread and wine nourish and refresh us, so Christ is daily the food and drink and life of our souls.

The sacraments, then, are a wonderful and remarkable testimony to the goodness and mercy of God, who does not spurn us, but supports us in our weakness. For that reason the sacraments are necessary, and our use of them is an evidence of our trust in God.

Two Sacraments

Why are there two sacraments and only two? That question needs answering because of the errors of Romanism with its seven sacraments, and because of the tendency of some Protestant groups to exalt such things as foot washing, snake handling, and other rites to a place in the church where they are equal to the sacraments.

How do we know that something is a sacrament? The answer is that it must be a *symbolic ritual* commanded by Christ himself and confirmed by the command or practice of the apostles. This we refer to as the "institution" of the sacraments. This rules out foot washing, which, though done by Christ, is neither commanded by him as a church rite, nor confirmed by either the command or example of the apostles.

It is plain that the sacraments added by Rome do not meet these criteria any more than foot washing. Confirmation of children, penance, and religious orders are not symbolic of anything, and such practices as last rites ("extreme unction") and religious orders are not commanded by Christ or by the apostles. Nor is marriage, though symbolic, required by Christ or the apostles as a church sacrament (1 Cor. 7:1, 6–8, 25–27, 32–34).

All this, however, does not answer the question, Why two sacraments? and more particularly, Why these two—baptism and the Lord's supper? These questions must be answered so that we may the more profitably make use of the sacraments.

The reason there are only two sacraments is found in the sacraments themselves. Together they symbolize the *whole* of our Christian life. Baptism symbolizes our *entering into* God's covenant and salvation and *the way* we enter. The Lord's supper symbolizes our life *within* that covenant as we enjoy and live out the salvation that Christ has freely given us. There is no need or place, therefore, for other sacraments, because there is nothing else to symbolize.

The wonderful thing about the sacraments is that in picturing these two aspects of our Christian life, they give a united testimony to Christ. Together they say that everything we have is of him, through him, by him, and in him—that without him we are nothing and have nothing. Together they say what Peter says in Acts 4:12: "Neither is there salvation in any other; for there is none other name given under heaven among men, whereby we must be saved." Their testimony is that of Paul in Ephesians 1:3: that we have "*all* spiritual blessings" *in Christ.*

The sacraments speak of the fact that Christ's death and blood are central. Baptism reminds us that by his blood and sacrifice we enter into the Christian life. The Lord's supper adds that by Christ's blood and sacrifice, we live and move and have our spiritual being, strength, and nourishment when once we have entered into God's fellowship. Christ's sacrifice is everything to us.

What wonderful gifts God has given us in the sacraments! Let us not use them carelessly or faithlessly.

The Symbolism of Baptism

We begin our study of baptism with some trepidation, knowing the differences that exist among Christians over this important matter. Nevertheless, though we have no wish to offend those who are of a Baptist persuasion, we believe the testimony of Scripture is clear. We ask only that they hear what we have to say.

The first matter, then, is the *symbolism* of baptism. We do not believe that the water of baptism itself has any efficacy or power, as Romanism, Anglicanism, and Lutheranism teach. Its value lies in the fact that it is a *symbol.*

All would agree, we are sure, that the water of baptism symbolizes the blood of Christ, and that the application of the water (we leave aside for the moment the matter of *how* it is applied) represents the washing away of sins by Christ's precious blood.

In other words, baptism represents the application of salvation in justification (the removal of the guilt of our sins) and in sanctification (the removal of the filth and pollution of our sins). Baptism represents, therefore, the forgiveness of our sins as we receive that forgiveness in our justification and through faith, as well as the work of God by which we are made holy in regeneration and sanctification.

Insofar as baptism represents the application of salvation—the washing away of our sins in justification and sanctification—the water represents not only the blood of Christ, but also the *Spirit* of Christ. He is the one in whom and by whom we are washed (baptized), in both the remission and cleansing away of sin.

This is the reason Scripture describes the gift of the Spirit as a baptism (Matt. 3:11; Acts 1:5; Acts 11:16; 1 Cor. 12:13). It is a baptism, but not for any other reason than that the Spirit has an important function in the cleansing of sin. He is the one who applies to us the blood of Christ, for both our justification and our sanctification, and since he does this by giving himself to us, we can be said to be baptized not only *in the blood* but also *in* or *with the Spirit* when we are saved.

This has many important consequences. For one thing, it is the answer to the error of Pentecostalism, which teaches that the baptism in the Spirit is something additional and subsequent to salvation. Baptism in or with the Spirit is nothing other than salvation. This is clear from Scripture (Acts 2:38–39; Rom. 5:1–5; Rom. 8:9; 1 Cor. 12:13 compared with John 7:37–39; Gal. 3:2; Eph. 1:13–14).

All this has consequences also for the *mode* of baptism. If the water of baptism represents *both* the blood and the Spirit of Christ, it must be noted that Scripture invariably describes the application of both in terms of pouring or sprinkling. This is a point we will explain under the heading "The Mode of Baptism." The point here is that baptism beautifully symbolizes the washing away and removal of sins *by the blood and Spirit of Jesus Christ* and thus it shows how we enter God's covenant: by grace alone and by Christ alone.

The Sign and the Reality of Baptism

It is paramount, when speaking of baptism, to realize that the New Testament uses the word *baptism* in two different ways. Failure to recognize this often leads to misunderstanding and error.

Sometimes when the New Testament uses the word *baptism,* it is referring to the sacrament or rite: what we might call *water baptism* (Matt. 3:7; Matt. 28:19; Acts 2:38, 41; 1 Cor. 10:2). Water baptism is really not baptism, properly speaking, but the *sign of* baptism, a symbol pointing to an invisible, spiritual reality.

In distinction from the symbol or sign, the *reality of baptism* is the washing away of sins by the blood and Spirit of Jesus Christ. That is the reality of which water baptism is only a picture. Speaking of baptism in this spiritual sense, it is entirely proper to say that baptism saves us (1 Pet. 3:21).

Many passages in the New Testament speak of this spiritual saving reality and not of the sign of water baptism. The most notable of these are Romans 6:3–6, 1 Corinthians 12:13, Galatians 3:27, Ephesians 4:5, Colossians 2:12, and all those passages that speak of being baptized in or with the Holy Spirit.

None of these passages speak of water baptism. Unless we realize this, we will fall into all sorts of errors and come to very wrong conclusions, as *water* saves (1 Pet. 3:21) or *water* brings us into fellowship and communion with Christ (1 Cor. 12:13).

The difference between sign and reality is evident in the fact that not all who are baptized with water receive the *reality* of baptism. Nor do all who remain unbaptized with water thereby forfeit the spiritual reality of baptism by which we are saved.

Nevertheless, the two are related. The one is the sign or picture of the other, and that may not be forgotten. A sign that read "Chicago" but pointed to Houston would only mislead and deceive. The sign must always point to the reality if it is to be of help to us. Thus the sign must match the reality, and the reality must match the sign.

For example, the question of the mode of *water* baptism can to some extent be answered by examining the mode of *spiritual* baptism. If we ask, "How are we baptized by the blood and Spirit of Christ?" the answer of Scripture is, "by sprinkling or pouring." It would be strange, not to say misleading, if sign and reality did not match at that point.

By the same token, the reality must also match the sign. It would not do at all to have the *eating* of bread and *drinking* of wine, though they also represent the death of Christ, as symbols of the *cleansing* of sin by Christ's sacrifice. The sign must suggest cleansing, too.

Indeed, Christ has given us the sign to help us understand and believe the reality. I may say, "Can anything really wash away *my* sin— wash it *all* away? That is too much to believe. My sins are too great and too many." Then the sign of baptism says, "As truly as water washes away the filth of the body, so does the blood of Christ truly wash away sin," and so it encourages my faith in Christ and his sacrifice.

The Meaning of Baptism

It has often been claimed that the New Testament word *baptism* means only "to immerse" or "to submerse." Without entering here into the whole question of the mode of baptism, a little word study will show that this is not the case.

Such study will show that there are a number of passages in the New Testament in which the word *baptism* cannot and does not have the meaning "immerse/submerse." We plead, therefore, with those who believe otherwise to hear our side of the matter and not to blindly charge us with following human traditions in not practicing baptism by immersion. Baptism does not mean "immersion" in any of the following Scriptures.

Mark 10:38–39: "But Jesus said unto them, Ye know not what ye ask: can ye drink of the cup that I drink of? and be baptized with the baptism that I am baptized with?" This speaks of baptism, but to understand baptism as immersion in this passage is meaningless. Jesus is referring, of course, to his suffering and death in these verses (see also Luke 12:50). To say that he was to be immersed in suffering or death is not the point.

1 Corinthians 10:2: "And were all baptized unto Moses in the cloud and in the sea." This verse speaks of the Israelites being baptized into Moses. They were *not* baptized in the cloud or sea, but literally, in the Greek, "into" Moses himself "by" the cloud and sea. Can the verse possibly be saying that they were immersed in Moses? The word *baptism*, then, must mean something else.

1 Corinthians 1:13: "Is Christ divided? was Paul crucified for you? or were ye baptized in the name of Paul?" Here Paul uses similar lan-

guage to 1 Corinthians 10:2, and Jesus himself speaks similarly in Matthew 28:19. What could it possibly mean to be *immersed* in the *name* of the Father, Son, and Holy Spirit, or in any other name?

1 Corinthians 12:13: "For by one Spirit are we all baptized into one body, whether we be Jews or Gentiles, whether we be bond or free; and have been all made to drink into one Spirit." Can the Word of God be saying that we are *immersed* in one body? It is difficult to see how that could be the proper meaning. Indeed, the Word itself here speaks not of immersion, but of drinking!

Verses that speak of baptism in or with the Holy Spirit do not refer to an immersion, but to the outpouring, shedding forth, or sprinkling of the Spirit (Acts 1:5; Acts 2:17–18). We are not immersed in the Holy Spirit.

What, then, does the word *baptism* mean? It means "to bring two things into the closest contact, so that the condition of the one is changed by the other." The word says nothing about *how* this contact comes about: whether by sprinkling, pouring, immersion, or any other mode.

Therefore, to be baptized into Moses, as 1 Corinthians 10:2 puts it, meant that Israel was brought into contact with him as the God-appointed and typical mediator. In that way their condition was changed from slavery to freedom. That Christ was baptized with death does not mean he was immersed in it, but that he was brought into the closest possible contact with it so that his condition was changed from being counted guilty before God for our sakes, to being justified on our behalf.

When Romans 6:1–6 says that we are baptized into Christ's death and resurrection, it is not saying that somehow we are immersed in those events (whatever that would mean). It refers to the fact that we through faith are brought into contact with his death and resurrection in such a way that our condition is wholly and forever changed. That is the meaning and the reality of baptism for believers.

The Mode of Baptism

In speaking of the mode of baptism, we do not wish to antagonize anyone or to promote division within the church of Christ. It is our deepest desire to see unity in these matters, especially with those who are otherwise agreed with us.

We often hear, though, that there is no biblical basis for sprinkling infants and that such a practice is simply a carry-over from Roman Catholicism. Indeed, there are a number of anti-Calvinist books on the market that simply assume that if a church baptizes infants, it must also be wrong on other matters as well.

As far as the mode of baptism is concerned, we believe not only that there is a sound, biblical basis for the practice of sprinkling, but that it is the *only* mode of baptism recognized by Scripture. Let us look at the matter more closely.

As to the charge that sprinkling is simply a carry-over from Romanism, we would point out that this is no argument at all. If everything Rome teaches that is found in Protestantism must be discarded, even the doctrine of the Trinity must go! Moreover, the Romish liturgy for the baptism of children says in its instructions for the persons performing the baptism, "He *immerses* the child or *pours water on it.*" Rome, too, immerses. The so-called argument about Romanism can therefore be set aside.

As to the biblical ground for sprinkling or pouring, the evidence, it seems to us, is unmistakable. We would point to the following facts.

All the ceremonial baptisms of the Old Testament were by sprinkling or pouring. That these are real baptisms is clear from Hebrews 9:10, where the New Testament word *baptisms* is used, but translated in the King James (Authorized) Version as "washings" (see also vv. 13, 19, 21).

The baptism of the Holy Spirit, symbolized by water baptism, is always described in Scripture in terms of sprinkling or pouring (Isa. 44:3; Ezek. 36:25; Joel 2:28–29; Mal. 3:10; Acts 2:17, 18; Acts 10:44–45).

Likewise, the application to us of the blood of Christ, symbolized by the water of baptism, is always described in Scripture as being by sprinkling (Isa. 52:15; Heb. 10:22; Heb. 12:24; 1 Pet. 1:2).

The great typical baptisms of the Old Testament, called baptisms in the New Testament (1 Cor. 10:2; 1 Pet. 3:20–21), were not by immersion. In fact, the only ones who were *immersed* in these typical baptisms were Pharaoh and his armies, and the ungodly world of Noah's day. Thus, too, the wicked shall be immersed in the lake of fire. Immersion is a picture, we believe, of judgment, not of salvation.

The Baptisms of the Ethiopian Eunuch and of Jesus

Continuing our study of the mode of baptism, we wish to look at the baptisms of the Ethiopian eunuch (Acts 8) and Jesus (Matt. 3; Mark 1). These are usually taken to be the clearest examples in Scripture of baptism by immersion.

The baptism of the eunuch. It is usually assumed that the words "down into the water" and "up out of the water" in Acts 8:38–39 describe the *baptism* of the eunuch and that he must have been immersed. There are two problems with this view.

One problem is the prepositions used—"into" (*eis* in Greek) and "out of" (*ek*) do not imply immersion at all. They do not necessarily even imply that anyone was in the water. The word *into* in the New Testament is translated in many different ways, including: "at" (20 times), "in" (131), "into" (571), "to" (282), "toward" (32), and "unto" (208). This can be checked with a good concordance. The words *out of* are also translated variously: "from" (182 times), "up from" (2), and "out of" (131). Substituting these different translations in the two verses will immediately show what a difference this makes. The point is that these two words are not describing the baptism at all, but what took place immediately before and after baptism.

The two prepositions used in Acts 8 obviously cannot be describing the baptism since they are applied both to the eunuch and to Philip. If they are describing an immersion baptism, then Philip also baptized himself by immersion. He also "went down into" and "came up out of" the water. Either the words describe the baptism by immersion of both—Philip baptizing himself as well as the eunuch—or they do not describe the baptism at all.

Finally, and more importantly, the baptism of Jesus, when looked at in the light of Scripture, cannot have been by immersion. Let us look at some facts about Jesus' baptism given in Matthew 3 and Mark 1.

In Mark 1 the same Greek words are used as in Acts 8. In Matthew 3:16 a different preposition is used, the Greek word *apo*. This word is translated "from" 372 times and "out of" only 27 times.

There is a further consideration in the story of Jesus' baptism. It may not be overlooked that he was baptized at thirty years of age (Luke 3:23), by a priest (John the Baptist was a priest like his father, Zacharias, Luke 1:5, 13), and with water. At the time of his baptism,

Jesus said of all these things, "Thus it becometh us to fulfil all righteousness" (Matt. 3:15).

That Jesus fulfilled "all righteousness" by his baptism can only refer to his fulfilling the righteous demands of the law. What law? It was the law for the consecration of a priest. A priest was not consecrated until he was thirty years old (Num. 4:3, 47). At that time he was consecrated by another priest (Ex. 29:9; Num. 25:13), and he was consecrated by *sprinkling* with water (Num. 8:6–7).

In fulfilling the law, therefore, Christ could not have been baptized in any other way than by sprinkling, or else he would have been breaking the law, not fulfilling it. Christ's baptism is not proof, therefore, that immersion is the proper mode of baptism, but exactly the opposite. We plead with those who believe otherwise to consider this carefully.

Infant Baptism in the New Testament

One common objection to the practice of infant baptism is that there are no New Testament Scriptures that speak of infants being baptized. This is simply not true. There are, in fact, two of them.

One is 1 Corinthians 10:2, which we have looked at already in another connection: "And were all baptized unto Moses in the cloud and in the sea." The passage of the Israelites through the Red Sea is described as a baptism—a baptism that clearly included infants (Ex. 10:9; Ex. 12:37). Indeed, it would be difficult to deny that there were children among the Israelites at this time, for more than two million Israelites went out of Egypt (Ex. 12:37–38).

The point is that the Red Sea crossing is a baptism by the New Testament definition and use of that word. The New Testament word *baptism* is used to describe this event in 1 Corinthians 10:2. The Baptist objection that this happened in the Old Testament cannot change that. The use of the word *baptism* in this verse shows that the New Testament word does not always mean "immersion," as we have proved earlier. The Israelites were not immersed in the Red Sea.

Moreover, that the Red Sea crossing happened in the Old Testament actually underlines the important point that baptism is *not* something new in the New Testament. There were many baptisms in the Old Testament, as Hebrews 9:10 clearly shows: "Which stood only in meats and drinks, and divers washings, and carnal ordinances, imposed on them until the time of reformation." The word *washings* is actually the word *baptisms.* And that they were real baptisms is evident from the New Testament references to them as such. One of these baptisms is described in verse 19 as being applied to "all the people," and we know from Scripture that this included children (Ex. 20:12).

The Baptist objection that these were *typical* baptisms does not change anything. *All* water baptisms are symbolic and picture something. In fact, those of the Old Testament as well as those of the New symbolize *exactly the same thing:* the washing away of sins by the blood and Spirit of Jesus Christ (1 Cor. 10:2; especially Heb. 9:13–14, 22; and 1 Pet. 3:21).

These verses are significant because they show that the Old Testament baptisms had exactly the same meaning as those of the New Testament. They both signified purification and remission of sins by the shedding of blood (Heb. 10:22–23). To be baptized in the Old Testament had exactly the same significance as in the New, the only difference being that in the Old Testament it looked ahead; since the death of Jesus, it looks back.

Hence, there is no fundamental difference between the two testaments, even in the matter of baptism. To think otherwise is to go in the direction of dispensationalism and to separate the Old Testament from the New.

Baptism was not something new and unheard of to the Israelites when John began baptizing at the River Jordan. The thought of infant baptism in the Old Testament should be no surprise to us, either. There is but one people of God, one covenant, one way of salvation, and one sign of the covenant, in both the Old and New Testaments.

Family Baptism

We prefer to describe baptism as "family" or "household" baptism rather than as "infant" baptism. There are several reasons for this.

First, no one baptizes only infants. Those who are converted later in life and have never before been baptized are baptized as adults, even in churches that baptize infants.

Second, family or household baptism is the kind of baptism Scripture describes when speaking of those who ought to be baptized.

Third, "family baptism" serves as a reminder of how and why such passages as Acts 16 are proof for the practice of baptizing infants as well as adults.

It is quite clear that Scripture speaks of family baptism. In Acts 16 the households both of Lydia and of the Philippian jailer were baptized by Paul (vv. 15, 33). Paul speaks in 1 Corinthians 1:16 of having baptized the household of Stephanas. We read in Acts 10:48 of the baptism of the household of Cornelius by Peter. This, then, is the New Testament pattern for baptism.

These passages, therefore, are used to support the practice of baptizing the *children* of believers. It is true, of course, that we do not know if there were small children in any of these households, but it is unlikely that there were no infants at all among these four families. Nevertheless, if family or household baptism is the pattern laid down in Scripture, it is impossible to practice such without baptizing infants, since most households do include them.

We would add that if "believer's baptism" only is the rule of Scripture, which the Baptists teach, family or household baptism becomes an impossibility. Even if it so happens that different members of the same family are converted and baptized at the same time in a Baptist church, they still are not baptized as members of a household or family, but as individuals, each as a result of his own profession of faith.

The baptism of households and families follows from the belief in God's family covenant: that he sovereignly, graciously, and unchangeably promises salvation to families and households, promising to be the God of believers and their children (Gen. 17:7; Acts 2:39).

The practice does not, however, mean it is presumed that every member of a household is necessarily saved. But baptism even of those who profess faith as adults can never be a guarantee, either. *Never* does baptism prove or say that the person baptized is certainly saved.

The practice of baptizing families or households, following the clear example of Scripture itself, is a memorial to the fact that God himself is a family—Father, Son, and Holy Spirit—and that he magnifies his grace and reveals himself in sending salvation to families. He is, indeed, the God of families (Ps. 107:41).

Baptism and Entrance into the Kingdom

A passage often used by those who practice infant baptism as proof of what they believe is Mark 10:13–16, which describes Jesus' blessing of little children. Those who hold to so-called "believer's baptism" find the use of this passage baffling, since it does not speak of baptism at all.

Mark 10 is, nevertheless, a proof text that *can* be used to support infant baptism. This is true for several reasons, but we must notice from the outset that these children were in fact *infants* (Luke 18:15).

First, the infants in this passage were received by Jesus, who also took them in his arms and blessed them. To be received into Jesus' arms and blessed is nothing less than salvation itself. That these infants were saved by Jesus is evident from verses 14 and 15, where he speaks of them receiving the kingdom.

Of that salvation and reception of the kingdom, baptism is a *picture* or *sign,* which shows us how we enter the kingdom. The argument, then, is this: If these infants can receive the *reality* to which baptism points, why cannot they receive the *sign*? To put it differently, if they can receive the greater thing, why not the lesser? We believe that since they can and do receive the reality, they *ought* also to receive the sign. Salvation is promised to them as well as to adults in the covenant of grace.

Second, Jesus tells us in verse 15 that no one receives the kingdom except in the way an infant receives it, that is, passively, without knowledge and by the power of grace alone. To receive the kingdom as a little child, therefore, is to receive it without works—without any effort on our part. That is the only way an infant *can* receive the kingdom.

In truth, this is the only way *anyone* can receive the kingdom. Initially, when salvation first comes, we are neither seeking it nor desiring it. We are, after all, dead in trespasses and sins, and it is only when God graciously *gives* us salvation and the kingdom by regenerating us that we also begin to seek and know what he has done. Jesus therefore tells us that there is only one way to receive the kingdom—as a little child. If we have not received it in that way, we have not received it at all.

Therein lies another reason for baptizing infants. We do not say that every baptized infant is necessarily saved, but we see in the baptism of every infant a picture of how salvation is possible for an infant according to the promise of God's covenant, namely, by the power of sovereign grace.

Indeed, in every baptized infant we have a picture of how any and every one of us has been saved—not by his willing or effort, but by the almighty power of sovereign grace, which came to him when he was neither looking or seeking for it. God gives us new life and birth.

The purpose, then, of infant baptism is to show *how* we are saved, not to prove the salvation of the infant who is baptized (water baptism alone can *never* do that). Baptism shows the only way of salvation and reminds us that God promises to save infants of believers by the same sovereign grace that saved their parents. How sad that many do not have or see that testimony in the baptism of helpless infants.

Baptism and Circumcision

One of the arguments for family or infant baptism is the correspondence between circumcision and baptism. This is not so easy to see, since the outward signs appear to be so entirely different from one another.

It must be pointed out, however, that what we refer to as circumcision and baptism are only the *signs;* and as far as the meaning of these signs is concerned, they are *exactly* the same. The *reality* of circumcision is exactly the same as the *reality* of baptism.

The real circumcision and the real baptism are salvation itself, that is, the removal of sin by the sacrifice of Christ on the cross. In the case of circumcision, this is clear from Deuteronomy 30:6 and Colossians 2:11, and in the case of baptism from Romans 6:1–6 and 1 Peter 3:21. The signs are exactly the same as far as the spiritual reality is concerned, and though the signs themselves may appear to be very different, they symbolize the *same* spiritual truth.

To say that the two are completely different is to fall into the error of dispensationalism and to say that there are *two different ways of salvation,* one way in the Old Testament and another in the New. Most Baptists try to avoid this by insisting, in spite of Deuteronomy 30:6 and Colossians 2:11, that circumcision in the Old Testament was *not* a sign of salvation, but only some sort of mark to identify the members of the nation of Israel.

This Paul rejects in Romans 2:28, where he insists that outward circumcision is not the real thing at all, and that to be a Jew outwardly is nothing; the only circumcision that matters is that of the *heart,* and the only Jew is he who is one *inwardly.* All those who wish to maintain that there is something special about being a natural descendant of Abraham ought to read this verse.

Why, then, is there a difference between the outward signs of circumcision and baptism? This can be seen in light of the chief difference between the Old Testament and the New. In the Old Testament all those things that pointed ahead to Christ involved the shedding of blood (Heb. 9:22), but once the blood of Christ was shed, there could be no more shedding of blood (Heb. 10:12), not even in circumcision.

This is the *only* real difference between the signs of circumcision and baptism. In meaning and reality they are exactly the same. Scripture itself identifies them in Colossians 2:11–12. Perhaps because this is one long sentence in two verses, we are inclined to miss the point Paul is making. He says there that to be circumcised *is* to be baptized. This is one of the main points of Colossians 2. Speaking to Gentile believers, Paul tells them that they have *all* things in Christ (vv. 10–11), *including circumcision!* They lack nothing at all in Christ, in whom dwells the fulness of the Godhead bodily (v. 9).

The fact that circumcision and baptism not only have the same meaning, but are also the same as far as their *spiritual realities* are concerned, is the reason that their outward signs must be administered (under the one everlasting covenant of God) to the people of God, including infants, in both the Old and the New Testaments.

Unbelievers and the Covenant

One objection of the Baptists to infant baptism is that some are baptized who are not saved and never will be saved. They constantly remind those who practice infant baptism that in baptizing infants, they baptize those who have not repented and professed faith. To Baptists this seems wholly arbitrary.

In answer to this objection, we would point out that it is *impossible,* in either Baptist or Reformed churches, to baptize *only* saved persons. Because the secrets of the heart are unknown to us, even Baptist churches can baptize those who only make a *profession* of faith and repentance.

When we have pointed this out to various Baptist friends and acquaintances, their response has usually been, "But we baptize *fewer* unsaved persons than you do." The truth is that if a Baptist baptizes even *one* unsaved person, he is no longer practicing "believer's baptism," but something that might be called "professor's baptism."

More to the point, however, is that in Scripture both circumcision and baptism are deliberately applied to unbelievers. Abraham circumcised Ishmael after being told that Ishmael had no part in the covenant (Gen. 17:18–19), and Isaac circumcised Esau after being told that Esau was reprobate (Gen. 25:23–24).

The Baptist argues at this point that circumcision was only a mark of national identity. This simply is not true, however, in light of what Scripture says about circumcision. It was always a sign of "putting off the body of the sins of the flesh by the circumcision [death] of Christ" (Col. 2:11; see also Deut. 10:16; Deut. 30:6; Jer. 4:4).

The same is true of baptism. The baptism in the Red Sea (identified as a baptism in 1 Cor. 10:1, 2) was applied by God to many with whom he was "not well pleased" and who subsequently were destroyed by Satan (vv. 5–10). Ham, too, was "baptized" (1 Pet. 3:20–21) with the rest of Noah's family.

The only question, then, is this: "Why is God pleased to have the sign of the covenant and of salvation, in both the Old Testament and the New, applied to unsaved as well as to saved persons?" Whether they are adults or children really makes no difference. Even the Baptist must answer this question.

The answer to the question lies in the eternal purpose of God. Only someone who firmly believes that God has eternally ordained all things, including the salvation of some and not of others, can give a clear and unequivocal answer to it.

The answer must be that circumcision in the Old Testament and baptism in the New, like the preaching of the gospel, are a power and a testimony both for salvation *and for hardening and condemnation,* and they do this according to the purpose of God (2 Cor. 2:14–16). We baptize infants as well as adults, therefore, understanding that God will use it for the salvation of some and for the condemnation of others, according to his own purpose, as in the case of Ishmael or Esau or Ham.

Faith and Baptism

We now wish to deal with the important Baptist argument that faith must *necessarily* precede baptism. Thus Baptists speak of baptism as "believer's baptism."

The first thing that must be said is that the Baptist position is an impossibility. As we have pointed out, Baptists can, at best, baptize only those who make a *profession* of faith. Because no one can know the heart, there is no way of ensuring that all baptized persons are indeed believers.

The usual Baptist response is that they baptize far fewer unbelievers than do those who practice family or infant baptism. This, of course, is beyond proof, but if a Baptist church baptizes even one hypocrite or unbeliever, it is no longer practicing "believer's baptism."

That, however, is not the main point. The words of Jesus in Mark 16:16 state, "He that believeth and is baptized shall be saved; but he that believeth not shall be damned." This verse needs to be explained, especially as its words are the command and warrant for the New Testament church to be baptizing.

First, the verse does not say (though every Baptist reads it that way), "He that believeth and *then* is baptized shall be saved." It only says that both faith and baptism are necessary for salvation.

Second, just because faith and baptism are *listed* in that order does not mean that they must necessarily *happen* in that order. In 2 Peter 1:10 calling is listed before election, but calling does not come before election, as every Calvinist knows.

The order in Mark 16:16 is simply the order of importance. Faith is listed before baptism because it is far more important. We see this in the last part of the verse where baptism is not even mentioned again, though faith is.

If the order in Mark 16:16 is the temporal order, or the order in which things must actually take place, then the order is faith, baptism, *salvation:* "He that believeth and is baptized shall be *saved.*" No one wants that order!

In addition to that, there are passages in the New Testament suggesting that at least in some cases, faith did *not* precede baptism. Acts 19:4 tells us of John's baptism and how John told the people *when he baptized them* that they should believe on him who was coming after him. He did *not* baptize them because they had *already* believed on Christ.

With respect to verse 4, the Baptist has two options. He can say that John's baptism was not true New Testament baptism, though more than half the references to baptism in the New Testament *are* to John's baptism (and then no conclusions at all can be drawn from it for New Testament practice), or he can admit that faith need not always precede baptism.

Repentance and Baptism

Another argument of the Baptists for so-called "believer's baptism" is that not only faith, but also repentance, must precede baptism. To some extent we have answered this argument, but there are some things that still need to be pointed out.

Let us look first at Mark 1:4, which speaks of the baptism of repentance: "John did baptize in the wilderness, and preach the *baptism of repentance* for the remission of sins." Many conclude from this verse that repentance must precede baptism.

This is by no means evident, however. The word *of* could mean "the baptism that has its source in repentance" and could be suggesting that baptism ought to *follow* repentance. The words *of repentance* might also mean that baptism and repentance belong to one another, without saying anything about the order in which they occur.

We believe that the phrase says nothing about the order in which the two occur, but rather means that repentance and baptism always belong together—that baptism demands repentance (either prior to baptism, or following it, or both).

If there is any order between baptism and repentance, Scripture teaches that baptism is *followed* by repentance. Matthew 3:11, a parallel passage, shows this. There we read of a baptism *unto* (literally "into") repentance, where the word *unto* has the idea of "motion toward something." The idea is that baptism is administered with a view to repentance *following*, or even as a kind of call to repentance.

In suggesting that baptism looks forward to and not back to repentance, Matthew 3:11 identifies an important difference between the Baptist and Reformed views of baptism. The Baptist view is that baptism is a sign or mark of *what we have done* in repenting and believing. The Reformed position is that baptism is the sign or mark of *what God has done* in regenerating us. It does not mark our response to grace, but the work of grace itself.

Baptism, in the very nature of the rite, is a picture of the washing away of sins by the blood of Jesus. This is what God does in saving us, and he does it *first*. He does it when we are yet incapable of responding to his gracious work. Repentance follows.

If we understand this, infant baptism will not seem something strange, but fitting. After all, there is no one of us, saved as an adult or as an infant, who does not enter the kingdom of heaven *as* an infant, that is, by a work of pure grace that precedes all activity and response on his part. That work of grace is what infant baptism marks and commemorates.

Discipling and Baptizing the Nations

Matthew 28:19 is the command of Christ authorizing baptism in the New Testament church: "Go ye therefore, and teach all nations, baptizing them in the name of the Father, and of the Son, and of the Holy Ghost." It also establishes baptism as a universal and not simply a Jewish rite.

There are two things we wish to point out about this important verse. Rather than being proof against infant baptism, this verse is just the opposite—very strong proof for it. Baptists argue that Jesus commands us first to teach (disciple) the nations and then to baptize. Infants, they say, are not old enough to be taught or discipled and therefore cannot be baptized. This, however, misses several important points.

First, as we have already shown in connection with Mark 16:16, the word *then* is not in the verse. Jesus does *not* say, "Teach all nations and *then* baptize them." If he had, the Baptists would be correct in teaching believers-only baptism.

Second, the verse speaks of nations, not individuals. In the very nature of the case, therefore, these two activities of discipling and baptizing must be going on simultaneously. One cannot wait until the whole nation is taught before starting to baptize, or there would be no baptism.

The grammar of the text is against the Baptistic view. The text must be understood literally as saying, "Teach all nations *when* baptizing them," or "Teach all nations *after* baptizing them." It cannot mean, "Teach all nations *before* baptizing them." The passage, in fact, says *nothing* about the order in which teaching and baptizing take place.

Furthermore, nations include children. It is impossible to disciple and baptize nations without also discipling and baptizing the children who belong to that nation.

Nor may it be forgotten that Matthew 28:19 is a fulfillment of Isaiah 52:15: "So shall he sprinkle many nations." In Matthew we must always look for the Old Testament prophecies that are fulfilled, for that is one of the great themes of this Gospel. Matthew always shows Jesus as the fulfillment of the Old Testament (see chapters 1 and 2 especially). The most obvious choice for prophecy fulfilled in this case is Isaiah 52:15.

This sprinkling of the nations in the Isaiah verse follows upon Christ's work in suffering and dying for sin. In the way of having his visage "marred more than any man" (v. 14), he sprinkles many nations. This we see happening in the New Testament in obedience to the command of Christ in Matthew 28:19.

And not only does Isaiah 52:14 identify the baptizing of the nations with sprinkling, but throughout the book the prophet speaks of these nations being gathered for this sprinkling *with their children*. When they come to Christ for sprinkling and salvation, they bring their sons and daughters and even their nursing children with them (Isa. 49:22; Isa. 60:4). This promised sprinkling of the nations, fulfilled in the saving work of the Lord Jesus Christ, is pictured and remembered in baptism. Not in imitation of Roman Catholicism or by mere tradition, but in obedience to God's Word, the Reformed practice infant baptism.

The Lord's Supper

Under the heading "Two Sacraments," we have said that the difference between the two sacraments lies in the fact that baptism pictures our entrance into the covenant and fellowship of God, while the Lord's supper pictures our life in that covenant once we have entered. The two together, therefore, picture the whole of our Christian life and show that it is by grace alone.

The unique testimony of the two sacraments is that Christ and his sacrifice are *everything*. The water of baptism shows that we enter the covenant of God by the death and blood of Christ, while the Lord's supper says that once we have entered into the covenant and kingdom of God, the same death and body and blood of Christ are our life, nourishment, and strength.

The Lord's supper symbolizes what it means to live in the covenant of God. It pictures us sitting down at the table of the Lord as members of his family and speaks of how God, our Father, cares for us and provides for all our needs. Indeed, the Lord's supper, as we shall see, not only pictures these things, but is also a means by which we enjoy that fellowship and that care.

The symbolism of the Lord's supper has a number of different elements, all of them emphasizing God's fellowship and provision as well as what it means to live in the covenant of God.

First, there is the *table* itself. This element is sufficiently important so that the sacrament is even called "the Lord's table" (1 Cor. 10:21). The table symbolizes our place in the family of God and the fact that the Lord loves us as a Father and supplies all that we need.

Second, there is *the bread and wine.* Broken and poured out, they symbolize the broken body and shed blood of Christ as our daily spiritual food and drink, our nourishment and refreshment, and the means by which our spiritual life is fed and supported, grows and develops, and is preserved unto eternal life. Let us take note of that. The sacrifice of Christ is not only payment for our sins and the way in which we are restored to God's favor and fellowship, but it is also our daily strength and nourishment and help until we leave this life and enter our eternal home. The Lord's supper says that Christ is all, and in all.

Third is *the eating and drinking.* This pictures our faith and shows us the importance and necessity of faith. Food and drink are of no benefit without our eating and drinking. The broken body and shed blood of Christ are of no benefit to us without faith. There is not, as Roman Catholicism teaches, any automatic blessing in eating and drinking the bread and wine of the Lord's supper. The Belgic Confession, one of the Reformed creeds, calls faith "the hand and mouth of our soul."[5] Thus the eating and drinking in the Lord's supper remind us that just as we take and eat our

---

5. Belgic Confession, Article 35.

daily bread and so receive it into our bodies, so by faith we really do receive Christ, who by faith dwells in us and is our strength and life.

What a beautiful picture!

The Presence of Christ in the Lord's Supper

It is to be regretted that the Lord's supper, which symbolizes the unity of the family of God, is the subject of so much division and debate among the churches. Nevertheless, the issues involved are not unimportant.

The major question, of course, has to do with whether and how Christ is present in and at the Lord's supper. Our views on this matter have a great deal to do with how we use the supper: superstitiously or believingly, carelessly or carefully.

The different views are as follows.

The view of *Roman Catholicism,* called *transubstantiation,* teaches that the bread and wine of the Lord's supper are "changed into" the body and blood of Christ when blessed by the priest. This view sets faith aside, for all one needs to do to receive Christ is to eat the bread and drink the wine. It also lays the groundwork for the doctrine of the mass, for when the bread, which is supposedly no longer bread but body, is broken, then Christ's sacrifice is repeated all over again. *Mass* even means "sacrifice."

The view of the *Lutherans* teaches that the physical body and blood of Christ are present *with* the bread and wine. This view, called *consubstantiation,* is open to the same criticism as the view of Roman Catholicism, although it does not include the doctrine of the mass. Both teach a *physical* presence of Christ.

The view of most *evangelicals* today was reputedly also the view of the sixteenth-century Swiss reformer Ulrich Zwingli. It is that Christ is not present in any fashion in the Lord's supper, but that the supper is just a *memorial* or *remembrance* of the death of Christ. While clearly avoiding the errors of Romanism and Lutheranism, this view nevertheless is not biblical, as we shall see, and it does not explain why the Lord's supper must be used with such care. If the supper is just a remembrance, there is no need for self-examination and no fear of "damnation" (1 Cor. 11:29).

The *Reformed view* of the Lord's supper is that Christ is *really pres-*

ent, but *spiritually,* not *physically.* He is, in other words, present to the faith of God's people and has fellowship with them and feeds them with himself through faith. He uses the bread and wine to direct their faith toward him.

This Reformed view is clearly taught in 1 Corinthians 11:29, which speaks of "discerning the Lord's body" in the Lord's supper, and is also implied in Jesus' own words at the institution of the Lord's supper: "This is my body." Only because Christ is present in the supper can a person eat or drink judgment to himself when eating or drinking without proper self-examination. Only because Christ is present can there be any blessing in the supper. The Reformed view, which is also biblical, gives so much more meaning and profit to the Lord's supper. Then in the sacrament we meet with and enjoy Christ in all his fullness, as our Savior and Redeemer. Let us so use it.

Bread and Wine in the Lord's Supper

One question we might ask in connection with the Lord's supper is, "Why are there two elements (bread and wine) in this sacrament when there is only one (water) in the sacrament of baptism?" This is quite a significant question as far as the meaning of the Lord's supper is concerned.

If we study Scripture, we will find that bread symbolizes the basic necessities of life. For this reason we commonly refer to bread as "the staff of life" and pray for our "daily bread" in the Lord's prayer, thereby praying for all our earthly needs. The bread of the Lord's supper, therefore, pictures the sacrifice of Christ as the absolute necessity for our spiritual life. No more than we can live without "daily bread" can we live without Christ, the bread of life.

But why wine?

Wine in Scripture symbolizes luxury, abundance, fatness, prosperity, joy and gladness, and feasting (Deut. 28:51; Ps. 104:15; Isa. 55:1; Joel 3:18). It represents that which is above and beyond the necessities of life, that which makes life more than mere existence, that which gives gladness and rejoicing.

The wine of the Lord's supper, therefore, symbolizes that Christ is not only the basic necessity of our spiritual life but the fatness and prosperity and joy of it as well. Or, to put it differently, the wine reminds us that God in Christ gives us what we *need,* but besides that, always gives us "exceeding abundantly above all that we ask or think" (Eph. 3:20). God is indeed rich in mercy and full of lovingkindness to his people.

These two elements of the Lord's supper, taken together, remind us once again that Christ is everything. The principal testimony of the Lord's supper is that Christ is the Alpha and the Omega of our salvation; that we have nothing without him, and with him we have everything; and that he and he alone is worth desiring, seeking, loving, and serving.

May we, enjoying God's gift of the Lord's supper, seek him with undivided hearts and enjoy him in all his fullness, not trusting in ourselves or seeking anything besides him, but feeding on his fullness and being refreshed by his grace, enjoying a taste of what we shall have when finally we leave this life and go to be with him in the home he has prepared for us in Father's house.

Self-examination and the Lord's Supper

Scripture commands diligent self-examination in connection with the Lord's supper (1 Cor. 11:28–29): "But let a man examine himself, and so let him eat of that bread and drink of that cup. For he that eateth and drinketh unworthily, eateth and drinketh damnation to himself, not discerning the Lord's body." Since this is our duty not only when the Lord's supper is administered, but always (Lam. 3:40; 2 Cor. 13:5), we ought to know what self-examination is all about.

Let us notice, first, that we are speaking about *self-*examination. It is not the lives of *others* we are called to examine, but our own. Examination of others leads to self-righteousness. Examination of self leads to true repentance and faith in God. Examination of others is usually our way of *avoiding* self-examination.

Second, self-examination is examination *of* self, but not *by* self. If we judge ourselves, we will not be judged (1 Cor. 11:31). God himself and his Word must be the examiners (1 Chron. 28:9; Ps. 26:2; Ps. 44:21). Our prayer must be that of Psalm 139:23–24: "Search me, O God, and know my heart: try me, and know my thoughts: And see if there be any wicked way in me, and lead me in the way everlasting." Self-examination is submission to God's examination of us.

Third, the purpose of self-examination is *not* to see if we *are* saved or *have* faith. That would be an impossibility. Those who do not have faith cannot conduct self-examination, and those who have it must not doubt or encourage doubt in themselves by questioning their salvation. Doubt is sin. Rather, the purpose of self-examination is to determine whether we are *in* the faith (2 Cor. 13:5), that is, living in all godliness and honesty and walking by faith before God.

With that in mind, self-examination involves the scrutiny of three things: our own sinfulness, God's work of grace in us and for us, and our calling to live in obedience and holy gratitude to him. We look at our own sinfulness to learn again the depth of our own depravity and to make sure that our own hearts have not deceived us—that we are not concealing our sins (Prov. 28:13)—and so that we may the more hate and forsake our sins and flee to the cross. We examine God's work of grace in us so that we may be the more convinced that it is by grace alone that we live and move and have our spiritual being, that we may be the more thankful for all that God has done for us, and that we may the more depend on grace alone. We examine our calling so that we may be persuaded of it, strive the more earnestly to fulfill it, and so go on in God's way. We are, then, called to examine the whole of our Christian life, conduct, and experience in the light of God's Word.

Where our life and experience do not match the pattern set for us in God's Word, we are required to repent, flee to Christ, and pray for grace. Then self-examination becomes self-reformation and is abundantly fruitful for God's glory and for our growth in grace and knowledge.

part 6

THE RETURN OF CHRIST AND THE LAST THINGS

The Last Days

Scripture speaks often of the last day or days and of the last time (Gen. 49:1; Isa. 2:2; Micah 4:1; John 6:39; Acts 2:17; 2 Tim. 3:1; Heb. 1:2; James 5:3; 1 Pet. 1:5; 1 John 2:18; Jude 18). It also speaks of the end of the world or the end of the age (Matt. 13:39–40; 1 Cor. 15:24; 1 Pet. 4:7; Rev. 2:26).

When are these last days—this last time? Are these near, or far in the future? Do they have any relevance for us today? What does it mean that the world will "end"? These are questions that must be answered.

Scripture is clear that the *whole New Testament age* is the last time, the end. We see this in 1 Corinthians 10:11, where Paul enforces his teaching by telling the Corinthian believers and us that the ends of the world *are come* upon us. Likewise, Hebrews 9:26 says that it was *in the end of the world* that Christ came to put away sin by the sacrifice of himself (see also Heb. 1:2; 1 Pet. 1:5, 20; 1 Pet. 4:7; 1 John 2:18).

While it is not unbiblical to refer to the second coming of Christ and the great judgment as the "end" of the world (Mark 13:7) and to the days immediately preceding his coming as "the last days" (2 Tim. 3:1), this is not a special and separate age, but part of the New Testament age. The age in which we live, this "day," this time, is the *last*. There is nothing to follow but the new creation, the new heavens and earth.

If today is already the end of the age, it is difficult for us to believe that the world may still last many thousands of years before the Lord returns, as some suggest. Will the end be longer than the beginning, longer than all the history that has preceded it? That would be a strange end indeed.

Scripture views this whole age as the last time and as the end because of the promise that Christ shall come *quickly* and because it is the time in which God will "finish" his work and "cut it short in righteousness" (Rom. 9:28). The two are related. That Christ comes quickly is not to be measured so much in number of years; rather, God is finishing his work and will send Christ as soon as that work is fully accomplished.

The truth that the whole of the present age is the end of time is of enormous practical significance. It means that we are all living in the end and will experience to some degree the events of the end (Matt. 24:34); that we must all live in expectation of the end and not as though it is far in the future, without any immediate relevance for us (1 Cor. 10:11); and that our hope must be in that which is to come and not in this world and the things of this world. They are already coming to their end.

What a frightening yet wonderful thing it is to know that we live in the last days. We stand always, as it were, within sight both of the final judgment and of the coming of our Savior. Ministers preach *knowing* the terror of the Lord. We all live as pilgrims and strangers, knowing that our journey must soon be finished and that soon we shall have our first sight of the eternal city. We acknowledge that we live in perilous times. We know the end is upon us, yet we are not afraid, for we see our redemption drawing nigh.

Different Comings of Christ

We have explained that the whole New Testament age is the *last* time, according to Scripture. The last day or last time—the end—is not only something future, but something present, something with which each of us must reckon, no matter when he lives.

The coming of Christ must be understood in light of this fact. It is, of course, *the* great event of history through which all things are brought to their appointed end. It is not only something future, but something present as well.

Christ's coming is described in Scripture as *one event,* including his birth in Bethlehem, his return for judgment, and all that happens in between. This is why the prophets in the Old Testament seemed to mix events that to us are separated by thousands of years of history. They saw it all as one event, and they were not wrong.

Both from the viewpoint of God's purpose and from the viewpoint of eternity itself (2 Pet. 3:8), Christ's coming is one event that finishes history, accomplishes God's sovereign purpose, and ushers in the eternal and heavenly kingdom of God (Dan. 9:24). This is what the Old Testament prophets saw, under the inspiration of the Spirit.

The truth that this is all actually one event means that Christ is *already* coming. That is the way Scripture speaks. Though it also speaks of his coming as a future event, looking ahead to his personal and bodily return, it more often speaks in the *present* tense to show that he *is* coming throughout all history. He is on the way, and his personal appearance at the very end is only the final stage of something that began in Bethlehem.

Scripture, therefore, speaks not only of Christ's birth as part of his "coming," but it also speaks of various other events as part of the "coming" of Christ. There are especially three of these events.

Christ comes through the Spirit (John 14:16–18). Because the outpouring of the Spirit is part of the coming of Christ, even the apostle Peter in his Pentecost sermon does not make a clear distinction between the Spirit's outpouring and those things that we connect with the very end of the world: blood and fire, smoke and darkness (Acts 2:16–21).

Christ comes for believers at death. He himself comes, though not personally and bodily. He assures us of this in John 14:2–3: "In my Father's house are many mansions: if it were not so, I would have told you. I go to prepare a place for you. And if I go and prepare a place for you, I will come again, and receive you unto myself; that where I am, there ye may be also." That, of course, is our comfort in dying. Even if Christ does not come personally and visibly in our lifetimes, yet we hear his voice in the gospel and follow him (John 10:27). We believe, too, that Christ comes to us by his Spirit, the Comforter, and that when we die, he comes and receives us unto himself (John 14:3) so that we will see him and enjoy him forever.

Christ comes through the preaching of the gospel. That Christ himself speaks through the gospel is evident (John 10:27; Eph. 2:17). Through the gospel, therefore, he comes and is present. This is the point in Matthew 28:19–20. In the preaching of the gospel, we must reckon with Christ's coming.

All this means that the coming of Christ is not only a future event with no immediate bearing on us, but also something present with which we must *always* reckon. Indeed, in one or another of these senses, Christ comes every day and will certainly come in our own lifetimes when he comes to take us to himself.

Christ's Return

We have said that the coming of Christ has many different aspects, including his coming through his birth, through the gift of the Spirit, through the preaching of the gospel, and through our death. All these, we have shown, are but different aspects of the *one* coming of Christ for judgment and for salvation.

That is not to say, however, that we cannot speak in a special sense of Christ's coming at the very end of the world and refer to it as his *second* or *final* coming. This final coming will be one of the great events of history, like his birth and crucifixion, because it brings about the end of history and of all things as we now know them.

In several ways this coming is unique, and it is the focus of all our hopes.

Christ's final coming will be *personal* (Matt. 24:30; 1 Thess. 4:16). Instead of coming through the Spirit or through preachers as his representatives, Christ himself will return. Every eye shall see *him* (Rev. 1:7), and in him all the fullness of the Godhead will be revealed *bodily* (Col. 2:9). As the personal representative of God, Christ will judge the world in righteousness (Acts 17:31) and receive his people into eternal glory. This personal coming is the focus of our hope, for it is *him* we long to see.

Christ's final coming will be *visible* (Acts 1:11). Indeed, at his final coming *every eye* shall see him, even those who pierced him (Rev. 1:7). Thus Scripture refers to his final coming as a *revelation* or an *appearance* of Christ (2 Thess. 1:7; 1 Tim. 6:14; 1 Pet. 1:7). Jesus must be visible to us, for we can have no confidence to stand before God without him. He must be visible to the world as the one whom they crucified and slew. Thus Scripture refers to this final appearance as Christ's *second* coming (Heb. 9:28), not because there are not other aspects to his coming, but because it is only in Bethlehem as a babe and at the end of the world that he "comes" personally and visibly.

Finally, Christ's coming at the end of all things will be *with power and glory* (Matt. 24:30; Matt. 25:31). His second coming is different from his first, for at his first he came in the form of a servant and in the likeness of sinful flesh (Rom. 8:3; Phil. 2:7). Then he shall come in the glory of his Father (Matt. 16:27). His power and glory at the end of all things will be the terror of the ungodly (Rev. 1:7; Rev. 6:15–17) and the delight and desire of his own (Rev. 1:3; Rev. 22:20).

The day and hour of Christ's return (and the month and year also) are unknown to us. Nor would it be good for us to know, for then we either would become careless and worldly or would lose hope. Not knowing, we watch and pray, are sober, and continue in holiness and godliness (Matt. 24:42–51; 1 Thess. 5:1–8; 2 Pet. 3:10–12). Yet we believe that Christ *shall* come, for he has promised. And even if he does not come personally and visibly in our lifetimes, we expect that we shall hear his voice in the gospel and follow him (John 10:27); that he will come to us by his Spirit, the Comforter; and that when we die, he will come and receive us unto himself (John 14:3).

One Final Coming of Christ

There are those who believe in more than one personal and visible coming of the Lord Jesus Christ before the end of the world. Both premillennialism and dispensationalism teach *multiple* comings of Christ, contrary to the clear testimony of Scripture. We shall be explaining these views in more detail later.

Premillennialism teaches a coming of Christ *prior to* the establishment of his millennial kingdom, that is, some thousand years *before* the end of the world; thus the name *pre*-millennialism (*before* the thousand years). This coming is referred to as "the rapture." That premillennial coming is said to be followed one thousand years later by another personal and visible coming of Christ for judgment, in which Christ will create the new heavens and earth.

Dispensationalism not only believes in a rapture, but holds as well to a *third* personal and visible coming of Christ, called "the revelation." This coming, according to its proponents, is "with his saints." Dispensationalists use as proof texts 1 Thessalonians 3:13 and Jude 14, and they say the revelation follows the rapture by several years. According to this teaching, Christ, at the time of the revelation, will establish a kingdom in Jerusalem with the Jews.

We believe that Scripture teaches only *one* personal and visible coming of Christ after his incarnation and before the end of the world. The passages that are supposed to prove a premillennial "rapture" and a dispensational "revelation" do not speak of anything but the coming of Christ at the very end of the world.

Jude 14 and 15, a passage that speaks of a coming of Christ *with his saints,* in fact is speaking of the coming of Christ for judgment at the very end of the world. We read there that "the Lord cometh with ten thousands of his saints, *To execute judgment upon all.*" That this judgment is the final judgment of all creatures is clear from Jude 6 and 7, which speak both of "the judgment of the great day" and of the destruction of Sodom and Gomorrha by fire, which is a picture of the final judgment (see also 2 Peter 2:6).

The other passage that speaks of Christ's coming with his saints (1 Thess. 3:13), and the main Scripture reference used for the rapture (1 Thess. 4:15–18), are also very clearly speaking of the end of all things. The coming of the Lord, as described in these passages, is accompanied by the sound of a trumpet, elsewhere referred to as "the last trump" (1 Cor. 15:52). It is not followed by a thousand years of history, other trumpets, and other ends.

So, too, 1 Thessalonians 3 and 4, speaking of the coming of the Lord, make it clear that this is followed by the eternal glory of the saints with Christ: "and so shall we ever be with the Lord" (1 Thess. 4:17; see also Rev. 21:3; Rev. 22:4). Christ's coming in 1 Thessalonians 3 and 4 is *not* followed by a thousand years of rule on earth and only after that by the life of heaven.

Finally, there are a number of passages that link the rapture with the final judgment, and not with events one thousand years prior to the final judgment. We refer especially to Luke 17:28–37. Note the references to Sodom, and compare this passage both with Jude 7, which makes it clear that Sodom is a type of the *final* judgment, that is, of "eternal fire," and with Matthew 24:37–41.

Only *one* coming—for judgment and for salvation. May it be soon!

The Signs of Christ's Coming

Scripture says that Christ's coming is always accompanied by *signs.* So it was with his coming in the flesh (Luke 1:18–20, 41–45; Luke 2:12). So it will be with his return (Matt. 24:3, 30; Luke 21:11, 25). These signs are important and must be rightly understood.

The signs fall into several different categories. There are signs in creation (Matt. 24:7, 29), in history (vv. 6–7), and in the church (vv. 10–16). Some are only "the beginning of sorrows" (vv. 5–8); others speak more clearly of the end (vv. 14–16); and some actually accompany the visible coming of Christ (vv. 29–31).

There are several things we wish to emphasize about these signs in connection with the wonderful biblical truth that Jesus *is* coming. Remember, Scripture speaks of his coming as something *already happening*. He is already on the way.

That Christ *is* coming means that all the signs of his coming are not like the signs along the highway, which simply make an announcement or point to something in the distance. These signs of Christ's coming are like the sound of a train's whistle and the humming of the rails. Such sounds are *part of* the train's coming and are *caused by* the coming of the train.

We might, therefore, describe these signs of the coming of Christ as the sound of his footsteps as he approaches. Just as the sound of a person's footsteps is heard the more loudly and clearly the closer he comes, so these signs of Christ's coming are seen and heard the more clearly as his final appearance approaches.

This, we believe, is the meaning of the progression in the book of Revelation. The seals, trumpets, and vials affect, progressively, *one-fourth* of the earth (Rev. 6:8), then *one-third* of the earth (Rev. 8:7–12; Rev. 9:18), and finally the *whole* earth (Rev. 16:3–4, 17). In other words, the seals, trumpets, and vials mentioned in Revelation picture the *same* signs and judgments, but these signs and judgments increase in intensity and are seen more clearly as history progresses and Christ approaches.

However, there is a sense in which these signs are more than just the sound of Christ's footsteps. The truth is that these signs are caused by the coming of Christ, just as the coming of the train causes the sound of its whistle and its wheels to be heard. These signs are caused by the coming of Christ because he rules all of history and creation, as well as the church.

As the sovereign King and Lord of all, Christ is the one who brings all things to pass and causes all things to happen in heaven and on earth (Matt. 28:18). That is the comfort of believers, for they know that nothing happens by chance or apart from his will.

We might think, then, of those signs as the evidences of Christ's hand and work in creation and in history. They are signs that he is not working at random, but day by day bringing all things to their appointed end.

What a different perspective that puts on all that happens to us and around us. Instead of being afraid and despairing, we hope and wait, for all things speak of his power and coming. In the midst of wars, disasters, and apostasy, while men's hearts are failing them for fear and while the powers of heaven are shaken, we can look up and lift our heads, for our redemption draws nigh (Luke 21:25–28).

The Rapture

The word *rapture* is not in Scripture, but it can be used without objection to describe the sudden, visible appearing of Christ in the heavens when his saints will be caught up in the clouds to meet the Lord in the air. Of this the Word of God speaks in 1 Thessalonians 4:15–17. We reject as unbiblical, however, the teaching that this rapture is secret, that it takes place prior to the final great tribulation so that God's people do not go through the tribulation, and that it comes one thousand years before the end of the world (a *premillennial* rapture). These ideas have no support in 1 Thessalonians 4, nor in the rest of Scripture.

The rapture is not secret. The events described in Thessalonians are anything but secret. We read of a shout, of the voice of the archangel, and of the trump of God. It could safely be said that this will be one of the noisiest and least secret events in all history.

Other passages that speak of the event give the same testimony. Matthew 24:30–31 is describing the same thing as 1 Thessalonians 4. Both mention angels, a trumpet, and the gathering of the elect to Christ. Matthew 24:30–31 adds that the tribes of the earth will mourn when they see the Son of man. There is nothing at all secret about that.

1 Corinthians 15:51–52 undoubtedly is describing the same thing as 1 Thessalonians 4:15–17: that there will be two groups of saints who will be raptured—those who have died already and those who have not. The latter are described in Corinthians as those who are "not asleep" and in Thessalonians as those who are alive and remain to the coming of Christ. The Corinthians verses, too, describe an event that is public and not secret.

These same passages make it crystal clear that the rapture takes place at the end of all things and after the final tribulation. Matthew 24:29 says,

"Immediately after the tribulation of those days…" And when we read of the tribes of the earth mourning, that mourning has reference to Christ's second coming for judgment at the end of the world, as is evident from a comparison of the Matthew passage with Revelation 1:7 and Revelation 6:12–17.

Matthew 24:37–41 and Luke 17:26–37 likewise describe this rapture as something that takes place just before the last judgment. The taking and leaving of people described in these passages is compared to the days of Sodom and the days of Noah; in other words, those who are left, are left for a judgment exactly like that of Sodom and Gomorrha (see also Jude 7) and of the world in Noah's day (2 Pet. 3:3–7).

Furthermore, 1 Thessalonians 4 speaks of the resurrection of our bodies, something that Scripture everywhere says shall take place at the last day (John 6:39–40, 44–54; John 11:24). Surely the last day is not followed by 365,000 other days. So, too, we are specifically told in John 12:48 that the last day is also the judgment day.

We look, therefore, not for a secret rapture one thousand years before the end and prior to the great tribulation, but for a public rapture of saints at the end of all things, the result of which shall be our continued presence in glory with the Lord (1 Thess. 4:17).

Jesus' Sudden and Unexpected Coming

If the rapture will be a loud and public event, why do we read of Christ's coming as sudden and unexpected (1 Thess. 5:1–9)? He comes, Scripture says, as "a thief in the night" (Matt. 24:43; 2 Pet. 3:10; Rev. 3:3; Rev. 16:15).

The truth is that Christ comes as an unexpected thief *only in relation to the ungodly and unbelieving.* This is made abundantly clear in 1 Thessalonians 5:1–9. There Paul speaks of the ungodly as "they" and "them" in distinction from "ye" and "you." He tells the believers in Thessalonica that inescapable *destruction* shall come upon "them" (v. 3) and adds, "But *ye*, brethren, are not in darkness, that that day should overtake *you* as a thief" (v. 4).

The wicked are not expecting the final judgment and the coming of Christ. Though many of them have heard that he is coming and know that God will judge the world, they hold this truth in unrighteousness (Rom. 1:18). They are the scoffers of whom Peter speaks (2 Pet. 3:1–8). Because God does not pour out his wrath on them immediately, they conclude he will not judge them at all. Nor do they recognize the judgments he *does* send on them now (AIDS, earthquakes, famines, and wars).

Such people are also found in the church. There they are represented by the five foolish virgins of Matthew 25:1–13. When the bridegroom comes, they are sound asleep and without oil for their lamps; they are therefore *excluded* from the wedding feast. They belong to the church and have the name of believers (*virgins*), but are in fact hypocrites and unbelievers.

God's people, represented in the parable by the five wise virgins, are *not* taken completely unawares (further proof that the rapture is not secret). Though always imperfectly, they are watching and waiting for the coming of Christ, believing that Christ shall certainly come as he has promised. To be taken unawares by the coming of Christ is to be taken in unbelief. The people of God are not in the darkness of unbelief and sin, as 1 Thessalonians 5:4 reminds us. Nevertheless, even the believers do not know the day or hour of Christ's coming (Matt. 24:36, 42; Matt. 25:13; Mark 13:32). To them also Christ says, "In such an hour as ye think not the Son of man cometh" (Matt. 24:44).

For this reason we have the urgent calling to watch and wait and pray. Matthew 25:13 speaks of that calling. So does 1 Thessalonians 5: "Therefore let us not sleep, as do others; but let us watch and be sober . . . Let us, who are of the day, be sober, putting on the breastplate of faith and love; and for an helmet, the hope of salvation" (vv. 6, 8).

This warning is needed. The five wise virgins are also sleeping when the bridegroom comes (Matt. 25:5). They have oil (the biblical symbol of the Spirit of God) in their lamps, but they themselves are slumbering. It is with this in mind that Jesus says in another place, "When the Son of man cometh, shall he find faith on the earth?" (Luke 18:8). This is said in connection with a call to fervent, frequent prayer.

That we need this warning should be evident from the fact that we are often careless and live as though Christ will never come. Indeed, the thought of Christ's coming—*right now*—more often than not would fill us with dismay. Let us, then, watch and pray that we enter *not* into temptation.

Jesus' Quick Coming

What does Christ mean when he says, "Behold, I come *quickly*" (Rev. 22:7, 12, 20)? This question is especially urgent when we remember that it is more than two thousand years since Christ made this promise.

The ungodly and scoffers see this long time as evidence that he will never come (2 Pet. 3:3–4). Nevertheless, believing him to be the Son of God who cannot lie, we continue to watch and pray for his coming. Yet, lest we grow discouraged, it is good to examine what he meant when he spoke of his coming quickly.

There is a sense, as we have seen, in which Christ comes quickly in that he is *always* coming: through judgments, through the preaching of the gospel, through the work and presence of the Holy Spirit, and personally, for every man, through death. In all these different ways his reward is with him, and he gives to every man according to his work (Rev. 20:12; Rev. 22:12).

Nevertheless, as Revelation 22 makes so very clear, Christ is referring especially to his final, personal, and visible coming when he speaks of coming quickly. In that respect, too, he keeps his promise to us.

That promise of a quick coming means, first of all, that he will not tarry or linger one moment longer than necessary in order to bring his people to himself. The very moment all is ready, he will come in all the glory of his Father to make all things new.

The timetable for this event must be looked at in the light of God's purpose. God has sovereignly foreordained all things, including the time of Christ's coming. In harmony with that, he has also foreordained that all things should reach their appointed end at the very same time. At that moment in history, God's purpose with his elect will be finished, and the last of them will be gathered in (2 Pet. 3:9). His purpose with the ungodly and unbelieving will also be finished then. At the same time the elect have all been saved, then also the ungodly and unbelieving will have filled up the measure of their wickedness and will be ripe for God's judgment (Gen. 15:16; Ps. 75:8; Rev. 14:10, 15–20).

At that moment, too, Christ will come. He will not come a moment sooner, for that would be too soon, but neither will he come a moment later. Even in this, it is his meat and drink to do the *will* of his heavenly Father.

Christ also comes quickly in this respect: he comes at the *end* of history, and the history of the world is not long, especially in comparison to God's everlasting years. The ungodly speak of billions of years past and future, but we know that a few thousand years are all that belong to the history of this world.

Finally, Christ comes quickly in the sense that he comes too soon for the wicked to accomplish *all* their evil designs. Always throughout history their work has been interrupted and their purposes defeated by God's coming in judgment, and this will be true also at the end.

May his coming never be too soon for us!

The Wonder of Christ's Coming

We should never forget that the coming of Christ at the end of the world is a wonder and a miracle—the last this world shall ever see. It is a work of God, wonderful in our eyes and something that transcends our understanding. In fact, all that belongs to the end of the world is a wonderwork of God, a miracle.

The signs of Christ's coming, the resurrection of the dead, the catching up of the saints to be with Christ, the destruction of the old earth and heavens by fire, the final judgment, and the glorification of believers: all belong to those things that are wholly unexplainable in terms of what is natural and earthly. They all belong to the realm of the supernatural and are therefore received only by faith.

There are various Scripture passages that make plain that this is true also of the coming of Christ. For one thing, Revelation 1:7 testifies that "every eye shall see him, and they also which pierced him" (see also Matt. 24:27, 30). Not only does this indicate that the general resurrection will have already taken place when Christ returns, but it shows that the coming of Christ is a miraculous work of God.

How every eye shall see him when he appears is impossible to say, but we have no doubt that the Word of God speaks truly. Indeed, every eye *must* see him, for he comes as the revelation of God, for both salvation and judgment. Every creature, living and dead, will be judged—saved or damned—in relation to *him*.

Another passage that reveals the coming of Christ to be a miraculous and wonderful work of God Almighty is 2 Thessalonians 2:8, which says that the man of sin, "that Wicked," will be destroyed by the very brightness of the coming of Christ. Again, it is difficult to know exactly how we are to understand this, but it reminds us of that his coming is no natural event.

Christ's coming is our hope, because although we, too, must stand before the judgment seat and give an account of our works, Christ will be there with us at the judgment. He will be our Judge. Even the thought of the judgment, then, cannot destroy the wonderful hope we have in him. Our salvation in and through the judgment is part of his saving work.

It is for this coming, therefore, that we wait and watch and hope. Our whole life as believers can be described from this point of view: it all has as its goal and purpose the appearing of Jesus Christ. Nothing else should matter to us so much as that.

What this all adds up to is that the coming of Christ is *part of the miracle and wonder of salvation.* From the beginning of history, God has revealed himself as the only Savior in that he does for us what is utterly beyond the power or the imagination of man. He saves us by the miracle of grace in Jesus Christ. The return of Christ is the final revelation of that great miracle of grace and mercy.

The Millennium

Scripture's testimony concerning the coming of Christ raises the question, "When and how will he come?" It is in answering this question that the subject comes up of the "millennium" of Revelation 20. The different millennial views—premillennialism, postmillennialism, and amillennialism—all have to do with the *time* and *manner* of Christ's coming.

From one point of view, it is to be regretted that the millennium, something mentioned only a few times in Scripture and in one chapter of Revelation, a difficult and symbolic book, should have become such a matter of debate and disagreement among Christians. Nevertheless, the difference between these millennial views is important and not to be dismissed as of no account. The time and manner of Christ's coming *do* matter.

The different views of the millennium raise questions about the nature of Christ's kingdom—whether it is earthly or heavenly, present or future, Jewish or Christian. And these questions, too, are weighty ones. We are called to seek the kingdom and pray for its coming, and we must know what it is we seek if we are to fulfill our calling.

We will not, therefore, dismiss the subject of the millennium as unessential, but will attempt to explain the different views and to show from Scripture what ought to be believed. We do this not to increase divisions among Christians or to offend those who hold different views, but to show *what* the Word teaches and *why*.

The term *millennium* means "one thousand years," and it refers to the thousand years mentioned six times in Revelation 20. During that thousand years, according to God's Word, Satan is bound, and those who have part in the first resurrection live and reign with Christ. At the end of that period—whatever period of time it may describe—Satan is loosed for "a little season," and the nations are deceived by him and gathered to battle against the beloved city. God then intervenes and judgment follows. These elements are clear from Revelation 20. What it all means, however, has been the subject of much controversy.

Some believe this happens in the future, including the thousand years itself (premillennialism); others believe that it has already begun, and that we are already in the period described as a thousand years (amillennialism). Still others teach that while it may have begun, its principal fulfillment is still future and will be seen only when a period of unprecedented peace, blessing, and prosperity is experienced by the church (postmillennialism).

Premillennialists believe that the next coming of Christ is prior to (*pre-*) a future millennium, and they teach that there is more than one future coming of Christ. *Postmillennialists* teach that Christ's coming is after (*post-*) the millennium and will take place only once. Like the postmillennialists, the *amillennialists* believe that the coming of Christ, which happens only once, will occur after the millennium. They differ from both the pre- and postmillennialists, however, in not seeing the millennium as a literal one-thousand-year period at all (*a-* is a prefix meaning "not" or "without"). Instead, amillennialists see the thousand years as a symbolic number that stands for the entire gospel age, starting with Christ's death.

Premillennialism and Dispensationalism Compared

Strictly speaking, premillennialism and dispensationalism belong to the same school in that they both teach that the personal and visible coming of Christ will be prior to a future thousand-year reign of Christ. There are a number of similarities in their views. Both teach a literal thousand-year (millennial) kingdom. Both teach that this millennium and kingdom are future. Both teach that the millennial kingdom of Christ is earthly, centered in the city of Jerusalem, and that there Christ will reign on earth personally and visibly. Both teach that the promises of God to Abraham and to the Jewish nation regarding the land have a future, literal, earthly fulfillment to that nation. Both believe that "Israel" in Scripture always and only refers to the physical descendants of Abraham: the Jews. And both teach more than one resurrection and more than one judgment.

There are, nevertheless, important differences between premillennialism and dispensationalism. Dispensationalism teaches two comings of Christ prior to the millennium (one thousand years before the end of history), namely, the rapture and the revelation (Christ's coming *for* his saints and *with* them). Dispensationalism also teaches a *secret, any-moment rapture* that will occur *prior to the great tribulation,* which means the church will not pass through the tribulation but will be with Christ.

Dispensationalism teaches that the New Testament church is a "parenthesis" in history, and that the Jewish nation alone constitutes the people and kingdom of God. Similarly, the view of the dispensationalists is that the millennial kingdom of Christ will be an exclusively *Jewish* kingdom; that is, the Jews and they alone are the kingdom people. Along with all of this, dispensationalism teaches that the Holy Spirit will be absent from the earth during the time between the rapture and the revelation, the two stages of Christ's premillennial coming.

To add to all the confusion, the older dispensationalism of the notes in the *Scofield Study Bible*[1] teaches different ways of salvation for Jews and Gentiles, denying that salvation in the Old Testament was only by the blood and sacrifice of Jesus Christ and through faith in him. In contrast, *historic premillennialism* rightly teaches that the rapture and revelation are *one* event, not *two*. Historic premillennialism also denies a

---

1. Scofield and Rikkers, eds., *Scofield Study Bible.*

secret, any-moment rapture and insists that the church *shall* pass through the great tribulation of the last days. Over against dispensationalism, historic premillennialism also teaches that the church *has* a part and place in Christ's kingdom and is not a "parenthesis" in history between God's past and future dealings with the Jews. Finally, historic premillennialism knew nothing of the heretical teaching of the dispensational *Scofield Study Bible* notes, which say that there are different ways of salvation in the different dispensations, and which teach the strange and unbiblical notion that the omnipresent Holy Spirit will be withdrawn from the earth for a period of time.

We believe that while historic premillennialism is free of many of the false teachings of dispensationalism, it does not go far enough. As we hope to explain, premillennialism of both the older or newer variety is unbiblical.

Premillennialism's Errors

Premillennialism, sometimes called "chiliasm," is the teaching that the personal, visible return of Christ will take place one thousand years before the end of the world. It says that apostasy and wickedness will increase and result in the final revelation of the antichrist. At that time will begin a period of severe persecution described in Matthew 24:21 as "the great tribulation." This reign of antichrist and period of persecution will end with the coming of Christ, who will raise his saints, change the bodies of those who are still living, judge them, remove the curse from the earth, and establish in Jerusalem a kingdom that will last one thousand years.

That kingdom, premillennialism says, will be the result of a mass conversion of the Jews, who will be restored to their own land. They, along with the Gentile Christians, will make up the kingdom of Christ, centered in Jerusalem, although the Jews will have the priority. That kingdom will be characterized by righteousness, peace, and prosperity here on this earth and will last exactly one thousand years. At the end of this period of Christ's earthly rule, the rest of the dead will be raised, and the last judgment and the creation of the new heavens and earth will follow.

Some of these views of premillennialism are very strange. For one thing, the citizens of the millennial kingdom are supposed to be a mixture of those who have been raised and glorified and those who are still in their present earthly bodies, which is contradicted by 1 Corinthians 15:50. For another thing, the kingdom, supposedly, will be on an earth from which the curse will have been removed, but that is not yet completely delivered from sin, sickness, and death. On that earth the resurrected saints will live along with those who are still subject to sin and death.

There are, however, more important objections to this teaching.

First, Scripture contradicts the premillennial teaching that the coming of Christ precedes the end of the world by one thousand years, teaching rather that it is simultaneous with the end of this present world (1 Cor. 15:23–24), the creation of the new heavens and earth (2 Pet. 3:9–10), the resurrection of *all* the dead (Rev. 20:12–13), and the last judgment (Matt. 24:37–41; Luke 17:28–37; Jude 6–7, 14–15).

Second, Scripture does not teach more than one resurrection and judgment (John 5:25–29), nor a resurrection and judgment that precede the end of the world by one thousand years (John 6:39–40, 44–45; John 11:24; 1 Cor. 15:51–52. Note the emphasis on "last" in 1 Cor. 15:52.)

Third, Scripture teaches the very opposite of an earthly kingdom; it insists that the kingdom is heavenly (John 18:36; Heb. 12:22–23).

Fourth, Scripture teaches that Christ's kingdom is everlasting, not one thousand years in length (Dan. 4:34; Dan. 7:27; 2 Pet. 1:11).

Fifth, Scripture does not teach that the Jews are *only* the *physical* descendants of Abraham. Instead, it tells us that all believers—Jews and Gentiles alike—are the true Jews, the true Israel of God (Rom. 2:28–29; Gal. 3:29; Phil. 3:3). Israel is the *church*, and the church is Israel. So, too, the kingdom is the church, and the church is the kingdom.

For these reasons especially, we reject premillennial teaching.

Dispensationalism's Errors

Dispensationalism, once known as Darbyism after John Nelson Darby (1800–1882), the originator of both dispensationalism and brethrenism, is the most serious of all errors regarding the millennium. It is not only a certain teaching about the millennium and the future, but also a whole erroneous theological system.

The name *dispensationalism* comes from the theory's division of history into different "dispensations," in each of which God has a different covenant relation with men that ends with their failure to meet God's requirements. We are now, according to Darby's classic dispensationalism, in the "church age," or dispensation of grace, with only one more age to come, the dispensation of the kingdom.

Some of dispensationalism's errors that we have already dealt with are its teaching regarding a secret, premillennial, pretribulation rapture and its teaching regarding multiple comings of Christ.

Other teachings of dispensationalism that we will explain later are its belief in multiple resurrections and judgments and its literalist interpretation of Scripture, especially Revelation 20.

A few of the more flagrant errors of dispensationalism have to do with its wrong use of Scripture.

First, dispensationalism has a faulty method of interpreting Scripture. The result of this method is that the whole Old Testament and some of the New Testament are applied to the Jews and are said to have no application to New Testament Christians, except perhaps as an object of curiosity. The notes of the *Scofield Study Bible* teach, for example, that the Sermon on the Mount is not Christian but Jewish. Over against this, Scripture teaches that *all Scripture* is profitable (and applicable) to New Testament Christians (John 10:35; 2 Tim. 3:16–17). Because dispensationalism denies this, it has been accused of *wrongly* dividing the Word of truth, even though it claims the opposite.

Second, dispensationalism follows a strict literalism, which, as one writer points out, is really the literalism of the Pharisees, who would not and could not see that Christ is a *spiritual* King, and so they crucified him. This strict (though inconsistently applied) literalism and its opposition to what dispensationalists call "spiritualizing" are also contrary to Scripture (1 Cor. 2:12–15). In many passages Scripture itself "spiritualizes" the things of the Old Testament, notably 1 Peter 2:5–9 and the whole book of Hebrews. We would point out that while Scripture must be interpreted carefully and soberly, there are things that *cannot* be taken literally, such as the white stone of Revelation 2:17.

It is dispensationalism's opposition to spiritualizing that leads to its denial of the heavenly and spiritual kingdom of Christ. It is dispensationalism's erroneous view of Scripture that is the root of all its errors.

Further Errors of Dispensationalism

We have pointed out what we believe to be the principal errors of dispensationalism. Other errors are as follows.

Dispensationalism's separation of Israel and the church. One of the fundamentals of dispensationalism is that Israel is Israel, and the church is the church, and never may the two be confused. This is contrary to Scripture's teaching that Old Testament "Israel," both nationally and spiritually, *is* the church (Rom. 2:28–29). In Acts 7:38 Israel is called "the church in the wilderness." In Hebrews 12:22–24 Jerusalem and Zion are identified with the church (see also Gal. 3:29 and Phil. 3:3). In Revelation 21:9–10 the bride, the Lamb's wife, is identified with the holy Jerusalem.

The separation in dispensationalism between Christ's work on behalf of the Jews and his work on behalf of the church. Dispensationalism teaches that Christ is King of Israel but Head of the church. The notes of the *Scofield Study Bible* even teach that the Old Testament people were saved in other ways than by faith in Christ's atoning work and that God has more than one plan of salvation. This is contrary to Scripture's clear teaching that Christ is the same Savior, in both the Old and New Testaments (Gal. 3:28–29; 1 Tim. 2:5–6; Heb. 11:6).

Dispensationalism's exclusion of Old Testament saints from the "body" and "bride" of Christ. This follows, of course, from the separation that it makes between Israel and the church, and between Christ's relation to Israel as King, and to the church as Head. It is also contrary to Scripture, which includes Old Testament saints in "the household of faith" and numbers them in the body and bride of Christ (Eph. 2:11–18, especially v. 16, which says that Jew and Gentile are reconciled "in one body"; Rev. 21:9–10, where "the bride, the Lamb's wife" is identified with the holy Jerusalem).

The teaching of dispensationalism that the Holy Spirit is gone from the earth during the seven-year period between the rapture and the revelation. During this period the Jews are supposed to be saved and brought to faith in Christ without the sovereign and gracious operations of the Holy Spirit. This, too, is contrary to the teaching of Scripture that faith is the gift of God through the Holy Spirit, and it is contrary as well to the scriptural teaching that regeneration, or the new birth, which is essential for salvation, is the unique work of the Spirit (John 3:3–8; Eph. 2:8).

Dispensationalism's teaching regarding the so-called "mystery" church. Classic dispensationalism teaches that the history of the church in the New Testament is a "parenthesis" and that the church itself is a mystery never spoken of in the Old Testament. This contradicts the teaching of Scripture, which not only prophesies the church, but actually views true Israel as the church and the church as Israel. In Acts 15:13ff. James applies an Old Testament prophecy concerning Israel to the establishment of New Testament Gentile churches (compare this with Acts 7:38). Likewise, the church is not viewed in Scripture as a "parenthesis," but as the goal and purpose of all God's work in history. It is "the fulness of him that filleth all in all" (Eph. 1:22–23), the "glorious church" that he presents to himself by all his saving work (Eph. 5:25–27).

For all these reasons dispensationalism must be rejected.

Postmillennialism

Postmillennialism we have defined as the view that while the millennium may have begun, its principal fulfillment is still future and will be seen only when a period of unprecedented peace, blessing, and prosperity is experienced by the gospel and the church. There are different kinds of postmillennialism, each with its own interpretation of the millennium.

There is, first of all, the older postmillennialism of many of the Puritans and of some modern writers, which expects a great future work of God among the Jews that will lead to the conversion of many, even a majority of them. Some, along the same lines, expect a great end-time revival in the church prior to the coming of Christ, when the gospel will once again bear fruit as it did in the times of the apostles and at the time of the great Protestant Reformation of the sixteenth century.

A more radical postmillennialism has arisen in more recent times that is a part of what is sometimes referred to as Christian Reconstructionism or "dominion theology." This postmillennialism expects not only a glorious future for the church, but also teaches that the whole of society and human life shall someday come under the dominion of Christians, and that this "christianized" society will be the fulfillment of the scriptural promises concerning the kingdom of Christ.

This more recent form of postmillennialism expects that the principal realization of the kingdom of Christ will be *in this present world,* and that it will come about by the preaching of the gospel and the growth of the church as well as by Christian "action" and involvement in the different areas of life. Most who are of this conviction would insist that it is essential for Christians to be involved in, and eventually "take over," the various areas of society and so claim them for Christ, thus, as they say, crowning Christ *King* in every area of life.

The majority who hold these views are also "preterists" (the Greek word *preterite* means "past"). They believe that Matthew 24:1–35 and most of the book of Revelation are already fulfilled or past—that the events described were fulfilled in the destruction of Jerusalem by the Roman armies in AD 70. Most of them say that the biblical prophecies concerning antichrist and the great tribulation are already finished. Their rosy view of the church's and society's future precludes any belief in an end-time tribulation and revelation of antichrist.

These same people are almost always theonomists (*theonomy* means "God's law"). They believe that the law of God, including the Old Testament civil laws, will be the basis for this future christianized society, a kingdom of Christ here on earth. Not the gospel but the law will be the main force in this kingdom, for while all will not be converted, they will all be brought under the law of God and the "dominion" of the law.

While we do not agree with the older postmillennialism of the Puritans and its modern counterpart, we have many more problems with this modern radical postmillennialism. We consider it to be an error as serious as that of dispensationalism.

Postmillennialism's Errors

We have compared an older postmillennialism with a more recent postmillennialism, the latter an integral part of the Christian Reconstructionist movement. This type of postmillennialism is very different from the older postmillennialism of the Puritans and far more dangerous.

First, this type of postmillennialism devalues the preaching of the gospel. Action in politics and economics is at least as important as the gospel for the coming of the kingdom, according to its adherents. For them, the victory of the kingdom is not so much in the salvation of men through the gospel as in Christians' taking dominion over the whole of society.

Second, this postmillennialism devalues and trivializes the church. Believing that the kingdom is something beyond and greater than the church, it does not view the church as the chief object, next to Christ himself, of the Christian's affection. This is refuted, however, by Psalm 122:6 and Ephesians 1:17–23. Nor is the gathering and preservation of the church the main goal of the Christian's life and work in the postmillennial view, contrary to Psalm 122:9 and Ephesians 1:17–23. For many, the church is only a training ground for Christian involvement in politics, economics, and other areas of social life.

This trivializing of the church leads to a great disinterest in matters of church government, worship, and doctrine as well as a kind of ecumenicalism—a willingness to join with those whose teaching may be unbiblical. After all, the main thing is not the church but the kingdom, according to them.

Those who hold to this form of postmillennialism, therefore, often accuse the church of failing in its calling from early on in its history, for though the church has faithfully preached the gospel and sought the salvation of sinners, it has not taken dominion over all of society. In this, they say, the church has failed miserably.

Third, this type of postmillennialism undermines a faithful Christian witness. With its emphasis on the necessity of political action and involvement in various areas of social endeavor, it undervalues the witness of the ordinary Christian as he lives his life honestly and faithfully in his own God-given place. The most important thing is not being a good witness, even while digging ditches, in order to be used by God for the salvation of others, but to be taking over society.

Fourth, the proponents of this postmillennial view represent in many cases a new type of legalism with its emphasis on the law. Those who expect the kingdom to be realized by the bringing of all men under the dominion of law really think that the law will do what the gospel fails to do. They forget the weakness of the law as described in Romans 8:3: "For what the law could not do, in that it was weak through the flesh, God sending his own Son in the likeness of human flesh, and for sin, condemned sin in the flesh."

Finally, postmillennialism of this sort, with its emphasis on a millennial kingdom that will have its primary realization in *this* world, tends to become a religion that "minds earthly things," something that Paul warns us about in Philippians 3:19: "Whose end is destruction, whose God is their belly, and whose glory is in their shame, who mind earthly things." Thus one finds among its adherents denials of the resurrection of the body, of heaven as a real place and the final home of believers, and even of the ascension of Christ to heaven, which is, of course, the guarantee of all the believer's heavenly hopes.

Amillennialism

The word *amillennial* means literally "no millennium." Strictly speaking, it is not the case that amillennialism teaches *no millennium at all.* The truth is that amillennialism does not believe in a *literal, future* millennium.

Amillennialism teaches that the millennium of Revelation 20 is the *whole New Testament age* from the first coming of Christ to the end of the world. The thousand years of Revelation 20 is, therefore, understood symbolically rather than literally.

This teaching is based, first, on the fact that numbers in Scripture, including the number one thousand, are often symbolic rather than literal. A good example is Psalm 50:10, where Scripture certainly does not mean literally and only "*a thousand* hills" but *all* hills.

Since the binding of Satan is one of the chief features of this thousand-year period (Rev. 20:1–3), amillennialism teaches that Satan is bound throughout the New Testament age. He is not completely bound, but bound only "that he should deceive the nations no more" (Rev. 20:3). He is bound, in other words, so that he cannot prevent the gospel from being preached and having its fruit in the conversion of the Gentile nations.

That Satan was bound *at the time of Christ's first coming* is clear from Matthew 12:29. There, in an obvious reference to Satan, Jesus uses the same Greek word for binding as does Revelation 20:2. He tells the Pharisees that "the strong man [Satan]" must be bound. In the context of this statement, Jesus is speaking of the coming of the kingdom through the gathering of the Gentiles by the preaching of the gospel (Matt. 12:14–

21, 28 – 30). Matthew 12:29 interprets Revelation 20:2 and shows that the result of Satan's binding is the success of the gospel among the nations in the New Testament.

Amillennialism, therefore, does not look for a millennium yet to come, but believes that we are in the middle of the millennium now, and that when the millennium is finished, the end of the world will have arrived. This New Testament age is the last age of the world.

Amillennialists do not expect a rapture one thousand years before the end, nor a coming of Christ one thousand years before the end, nor do they expect that the great tribulation will take place one thousand years before the end of the world. Rather, they teach that all these events will take place *at the end* and will be followed by the eternal state.

Amillennialism, then, teaches that the "trump" of 1 Corinthians 15:51–52 is the *last,* and that following the rapture (1 Thess. 4:16–17), the elect will ever be with the Lord in heavenly glory. Likewise, in amillennial teaching the great tribulation of Matthew 24:29 is *immediately* followed by the trumpet that announces Christ's coming in the actual appearing of Christ on the clouds and the gathering of his elect.

Amillennialism does not teach a period of unprecedented peace and prosperity for the church before the end, but takes seriously the biblical truth that the great tribulation of the church shall precede the end of all things—that in those last days "perilous times shall come" (2 Tim. 3:1), times in which "evil men . . . shall wax worse and worse" (v. 13).

Because of this, some accuse amillennialism of pessimism. It is not pessimistic, though. Amillennialists believe that Christ rules, and that with sovereign power he causes all things to work together, even these grievous things, for the good of his own.

Literalism and Revelation 20

As we have seen, amillennialism does not take the thousand years of Revelation 20 literally, but understands it as a symbolic reference to the complete New Testament age. The symbolism is found in the fact that 1000 is $10 \times 10 \times 10$, where 10 is understood to represent completeness. It is this non-literal understanding of the thousand years that we wish to defend.

We have already pointed out that "thousand" is not *always* to be taken literally in Scripture. God does not own just the cattle on *a thousand* hills, but on *all* of them (Ps. 50:10). Other passages in the Psalms where "thousand" is not literal, but has the meaning "all" or "the whole," are Psalm 84:10, Psalm 91:7, and Psalm 105:8. Those who say that the number must *always* be taken literally—also in Revelation 20—are wrong.

We would point out, too, that there are other things in Revelation 20 that cannot be taken literally. In verses 1 and 2 Satan is not literally a dragon, nor can a spirit, Satan, be bound with a literal chain (see also Luke 24:39). Most, too, would understand the reference to the "pit" in Revelation 20:3 to be a reference to hell, Satan's abode, not to a hole in the ground. Further on in the chapter, antichrist is not in the literal sense a "beast" (v. 10), nor is the book of life (v. 12) a literal book of paper and printed pages.

Numerous things in the rest of the book of Revelation cannot be taken literally. No Christian we know, for example, expects that his reward will actually be a white stone with his name written on it (2:17), or that he will be turned into a "pillar" in heaven (3:12), or that Jesus actually has a sword for a tongue (1:16).

It is striking that those who insist most loudly on a literal understanding of the thousand years and say that anything else is unfaithfulness to Scripture are themselves unwilling to take *literally* the reference to *souls* in Revelation 20:4. They insist that these are not literal, disembodied *souls*, but whole persons.

We would remind our readers that Scripture itself does not demand a strict and rigorous literalism; indeed, it implies that spiritualizing *is* necessary for the interpretation of Scripture. We are told in 1 Corinthians 2:14, "The natural man receiveth not the things of the Spirit of God: for they are foolishness unto him: neither can he know them, because they are spiritually discerned." There are many examples of such spiritualizing in Scripture, Galatians 4:21–31 being one notable example.

The proper way of interpreting Scripture is not a rigid and *impossible* literalism, but allowing Scripture to interpret itself. It does this by showing us that "a thousand" may sometimes be understood symbolically (Ps. 84:10); that the binding of Satan must have taken place during Christ's incarnation (Matt. 12:29); and that the thousand years ends with the end of the world (Rev. 20:7–15). The only possible conclusion, therefore, *on the basis of Scripture itself,* is that the thousand years refers to the whole New Testament age.

Does all this matter? Indeed it does. If there is still a thousand-year age to follow the end of this present age, the heavenly hope of believers and the final judgment become so remote that the calling to watch and to pray and to prepare for Christ's return are all but meaningless. The urgency of our calling to wait and look for the end of all things rests on our assurance that these things are coming *quickly.*

One Resurrection

Revelation 20:5 speaks of a "first resurrection," implying a second resurrection and perhaps others. It is this passage, therefore, more than any other, which is used to support the teaching that there will be more than one resurrection *of the body* before the end of time. Premillennialism teaches two such resurrections and dispensationalism three or four.

For example, premillennialism teaches a resurrection of saints before an expected future millennium and another general resurrection at the end of the world—the two separated by one thousand years of history. Premillennialists say that those Old and New Testament saints who are raised at the beginning of the millennium will reign with Christ on earth one thousand years.

We believe that Scripture teaches only *one* general resurrection of the dead, and that it takes place at the end of the world. Then *all* shall be raised to stand before God in judgment and to receive in their resurrection bodies the reward either of grace or of works. This, we are certain, is the teaching of Scripture as in John 5:28–29, where the word *all* appears in verse 28. Acts 24:15, too, speaks of one resurrection, of both the just and unjust.

In John 6, Jesus *four times* states that the resurrection of believers takes place *at the last day,* not one thousand years before (vv. 39–40, 44, 54). Those words "last day" in Scripture *always* refer to the very end (see also John 6:40, John 11:24, and John 12:48).

What, then, are the first and second resurrections of Revelation 20? We believe that the first resurrection is that of *souls* when they are taken to be with Christ *after death* and when they reign with him in that disembodied state until the end of the world, at which time their bodies are raised in the *second resurrection.* There are a number of reasons why we believe this.

First, Revelation 20:4 actually speaks of *souls.* It is interesting, to say the least, that the premillennialists and dispensationalists, who insist so strongly on a strictly literal interpretation of Revelation 20, are forced in defense of their views of the resurrection to say that these souls are *complete persons* whose bodies are raised one thousand years before the end, and who *then* reign with Christ in their resurrection bodies on earth for one thousand years.

It is true that the word *souls* is used in Scripture to denote complete persons (Gen. 2:7; Gen. 46:26–27), but in every such case, the word *persons* can be substituted for the word *souls* without changing the meaning. That is not possible in Revelation 20. It makes no sense to read Revelation 20:4 like this: "And I saw the *persons* of them that were beheaded for the witness of Jesus."

Second, Revelation 20 also speaks of two deaths (v. 14). The second death is *not* a physical death, a death of the body, but is the eternal suffering of the soul in hell. Why do both resurrections have to be resurrections of the body?

Third, we call attention to all of those passages that speak of the new life of the soul in terms of a resurrection (John 5:24–25; John 11:25–26; Rom. 6:13; Eph. 2:5; Col. 2:12). Why, then, should it be thought strange that Christ's receiving of the souls of believers at death is described as a "resurrection" in Revelation 20?

We believe, therefore, in one coming of Christ, one resurrection of the body, and one everlasting hope.

Death

There is no doubt that death is an enemy—the last enemy (1 Cor. 15:26). We fear death, not simply because it is unknown. No one has ever returned to tell us what it is like to die, but our fear of death comes especially from the knowledge that death is the *wages of sin* (Rom. 6:23), the *judgment of God* upon those who have rebelled against him.

It is no wonder that every attempt is made to cover up the horror and corruption of death. Nor is it any wonder that in the face of death, the majority try to drown their sorrows in reveling and drink. Even when dying themselves, they do not want to think or speak of death, and in many cases they simply deny that they *are* dying when it is clear that there is no remedy or help.

When the ungodly see death in the creation, they speak of "the survival of the fittest"[2] and of "nature red in tooth and claw"[3] in order to cover up the fact that death is *not natural* and that the wrath of God is evident in it. Death is everywhere and always the end of all hopes, the enemy that comes too soon. In death, by God's judgment, all labors and hopes are left unfulfilled and unsatisfied.

It is only by faith that a believer is able to face death, and even then it is not easy. In the face of death, faith must struggle and fight and overcome, though it always has the victory. In the consciousness of his own sins, the child of God must still seek by faith to trust in the sacrifice and victory of Christ over death and to believe with all his heart that death is swallowed up in victory.

Death is conquered for the believer. Death could not hold Christ (Acts 2:24), for the *sting* (the destroying power) of death is sin (1 Cor. 15:56), and Christ had no sins of his own. The sins that he took upon himself as Mediator, he paid for to the utmost farthing. He willingly put himself in the power of death and allowed it to do its worst to him, but it could and did not conquer, for he was the Son of God, the Holy One. His death, as John Owen put it so beautifully, was "the death of death"[4] for all those whom the Father had given him.

That raises a question: "Why must believers die if death is swallowed up in victory?" Or, as the Heidelberg Catechism puts it, "Since then Christ died for us, why must we also die?" The answer of the Catechism is the answer of Scripture: "Our death is not a satisfaction for our sin, but only an abolishing of sin, and a passage into eternal life"[5] (see also John 5:24; Phil. 1:23).

What a wonder! That dark door that only ever opened into hell and

---

2. "Survival of the fittest," from Herbert Spencer's *Principles of Biology* (1864–1869), was borrowed by Charles Darwin to describe his theory of evolutionism.

3. "Nature red in tooth and claw" is from stanza 4 of Alfred Lord Tennyson's poem *In Memorium*, Part 56.

4. "The Death of Death in the Death of Christ: A Treatise on the Redemption and Reconciliation That Is in the Blood of Christ, with the Merit Thereof, and Satisfaction Wrought Thereby" in *The Works of John Owen*, edited by William H. Goold, vol. 10 in Division 3:c Controversiel (London: The Banner of Truth Trust, 1967), 139–421. Originally published 1850–1853.

5. Heidelberg Catechism, Lord's Day 16, Q&A 42.

damnation now opens for believers into glorious heavenly life. Perhaps, therefore, it is not wrong to say that we must die in order to show how utterly Christ has conquered on our behalf. Death is an end of all sin, to be sure, and a door to glory, but also a testimony to the fact that death is indeed swallowed up.

And so believers say, "Whether we live therefore, or die, we are the Lord's" (Rom. 14:8). Will that be your confession when death comes?

The Necessity of Our Resurrection

We have established that there is only one *bodily* resurrection, of both the saved and the unsaved, at the end of the world, not several, as premillennialism and dispensationalism teach. For us, that one resurrection is the focus of all our hopes, as the Word of God reminds us that it should be (1 Cor. 15:12–19). Let us look at Scripture's teaching concerning the resurrection of believers in the last day.

We should see that it is a serious error not only to deny Christ's resurrection, but also to deny the resurrection of believers. If there is no resurrection of the dead for us, then *Christ* was not raised either. There is such a close relationship between the two that one cannot take place without the other. This is taught in 1 Corinthians 15:16–17.

There have always been those who have denied Christ's resurrection. Very often such a denial accompanies a denial of Christ's divinity, his virgin birth, his miracles, and his atoning blood-sacrifice. There have been those also who have denied the resurrection of believers. There were such in the early church (1 Cor. 15:12; 2 Tim. 2:17–18), and there are such around today.

Some, found especially in the Christian Reconstruction movement, having taken a preterist view of prophecy, have resurrected the errors of Hymenaeus and Philetus, named in 2 Timothy 2:17–18. These people believe that much if not all of biblical prophecy is already fulfilled (preterism refers to the belief that the fulfillment of prophecy is past). They have begun to say that the resurrection *also* is past.

Paul, however, tells us that to deny the future resurrection of the bodies of believers is to deny Christ's resurrection and to make faith vain, leaving us in our sins. It is therefore a most serious error. Why is that?

First, the denial of a future bodily resurrection is a denial of Christ's resurrection, because the resurrection of believers is *part of* Christ's resurrection. Believers belong to the *body* of Christ, the church, and have the resurrection life of Christ in them. The result *must be* that they also are raised from the dead with Christ. If they are not, the only possible explanation is that the resurrection life of Christ does not exist—that Christ did not rise and conquer death. The power and victory of Christ over death are proved not only by his resurrection, but also by the resurrection of believers.

A denial of the resurrection would also leave us in our sins, because Christ's resurrection is the proof of our *justification* before God. When Jesus made atonement for sin, he said, "It is finished." When God raised Jesus from the dead, God as Judge also said, "It is finished," so that the resurrection was a declaration of our justification before God. This is what Romans 4:25 means when it says that Jesus our Lord "was raised again for our justification."

Since our hope is of heaven, and since "flesh and blood cannot inherit the kingdom of God" (1 Cor. 15:50), we wait and long for the resurrection. That hope is vain, however, if the dead rise not and if our bodies are not changed in the resurrection. We must, therefore, believe not only in Christ's resurrection on the third day, but also in our own resurrection with Christ, when our vile bodies shall be changed into the likeness of his most glorious body (Phil. 3:21).

The Resurrection Body

There are many questions that cannot be answered now about the resurrection of the dead, about the bodies we shall have in the resurrection, and about heaven, the home of God's people in their resurrection bodies. Nevertheless, Scripture gives us enough information to allow us to believe the resurrection of the body and to know that it is something to be hoped and prayed for.

Scripture says the most about our resurrection bodies in 1 Corinthians 15. There we are told four most precious truths.

First, the resurrection body shall be incorruptible (vv. 42, 52). Not only will we be free from the effects of sin—sickness and death and the grave—but it will never again be possible, as it was for Adam, to be plunged into sin and death. *Incorruptible* means "not able to be corrupted"!

Second, the resurrection body shall be glorious (v. 43). Its glory shall be the glory of Christ himself and of God in Christ. "Our vile body," Paul says, will be changed "that it may be fashioned like unto his glorious body" (Phil. 3:21). That is the glory of heaven and the blessedness of its life.

Third, the resurrection body will be powerful (1 Cor. 15:43). Isaiah 40:31 tells us a little bit about that. To be able to run and not become weary is almost inconceivable, but that is only a small part of what we shall have through the resurrection. Not only will the powers that Adam lost be restored, but we shall have much more besides. We shall have the power to know even as we are known (1 Cor. 13:12). Above all, we shall have the power to love and serve and obey God without sin. What a wonderful thing that will be!

Finally, the resurrection body will be spiritual (1 Cor. 15:44). Here, too, it is difficult to know all that Scripture means, but it certainly means this at least: we shall no longer be "flesh and blood," with bodies adapted to this earth and its life, but we shall be able to inherit that which flesh and blood cannot inherit (v. 50).

The changes that shall take place in our bodies when they are raised from the dust of death are so great that Scripture is forced to use pictures to try to give us some conception of it all. The change between a grain of wheat—a hard, apparently lifeless thing—and the green and living plant that grows from it is a small picture of the way we shall be changed (1 Cor. 15:37).

There are other pictures in creation that help us to understand. The metamorphosis of a caterpillar into a butterfly is one such picture. The Greek word *metamorphosis,* translated as "changed" in Philippians 3:21, is one of the words Scripture uses for the resurrection. From a worm that crawls in the dust to one of the most beautiful of all God's creatures, the caterpillar is changed and is yet the same creature as before.

When we think of these wonders of the resurrection, it becomes the focus of our hopes. Then we say, "My Lord Jesus, come quickly! Come and change these vile, sin-ridden bodies, subject to death and corruption, and make us all, in body as well as in spirit, like unto thyself!"

The Wonder of the Resurrection

The resurrection of the dead is a miracle, a wonderwork of God that is understood and received only by faith. Unbelievers mock when they hear of it (Acts 17:32), and heretics deny it (1 Cor. 15:12; 2 Tim. 2:18), but to those who believe the promise of the resurrection of the dead, it is further proof that God is indeed the true God, the Almighty, the one who does "great things and unsearchable; marvellous things without number" (Job 5:9).

Not the least wonderful thing about the resurrection is that every person's *own* body shall be raised. The bodies of some have long ago turned to dust so that not a trace of them can be found. Others have been eaten by wild beasts and by the fish of the sea. Some, like John Wycliffe, have had their bodies burned to ash and their ashes thrown by their enemies into the rivers and the seas. Yet God, who knows all things, keeps track of each body and gives it back to its proper owner in the resurrection. The resurrection is a testimony, therefore, to the faithfulness of God, who does not forget even our dust.

That this is true is clear from Job 19:25–26, where Job, confessing his faith in the resurrection, does not say, "I shall see God in *the* flesh," but "in *my* flesh." In 2 Corinthians 5:10 we are also reminded of this. There we read that everyone shall receive in *his* body what he has done. Although the word *his* is not present in the Greek, as the King James (Authorized) Version (KJV) shows, the translators nevertheless understood the passage correctly when they added the word *his*. Certainly the passage means that men shall receive their punishment or reward in the body in which they have done the good that is rewarded or the evil that is punished.

That the resurrection is a *general* resurrection is part of this wonder. The thought that everyone shall be raised almost leaves one breathless, for there are billions who have lived and died. To stand in a graveyard and believe that *all* who are buried there will come forth from their graves by the power of God to stand before him (John 5:28–29) can only leave a person amazed at the greatness of God and of all his works.

For believers the most wonderful thing of all is that it will already be seen at the resurrection that they belong to Christ and that they will go with him into eternal glory. They will still have to pass through the judgment, but with a body that is *already* raised incorruptible and glorious

(1 Cor. 15:42–44), that is *already* changed into the likeness of Christ's most glorious body (Phil. 3:21). What great hope that will give them in the judgment!

Those who believe the resurrection do so not only because it is promised in Scripture and because Christ, in our flesh, has already been raised (1 Cor. 15:19–20), but also because the power of the resurrection has already been revealed in them. Already in soul and spirit they are *raised* from spiritual death by the power of the resurrection of Jesus Christ, and they are now waiting for God to finish that work of raising them, soul and body. The resurrection has already begun to happen to them! There is an hour coming in which the dead shall hear the voice of the Son of God and live (John 5:28–29), but there is an hour *already come* in which the dead hear his voice through the gospel and live in him by faith (John 5:25). Having lived by his voice at the hour of their spiritual resurrection, which is their regeneration, they wait now for the hour of their bodily resurrection.

The Immortality of the Soul

We hear Christians speak of the "immortality of the soul." We understand that they usually mean that the souls of men continue to *exist* after death. We agree that the continued existence of the soul after death is biblical and needs to be emphasized over against the teaching of some sects that the unbelieving wicked are *annihilated,* body and soul, after death, rather than being punished eternally in hell.

To call the continued existence of the souls of the wicked "immortal" is, however, a somewhat careless and unbiblical use of the word *immortal.* The Bible uses that word to refer *only* to eternal life in heaven with Christ and to the final blessedness of those who believe in Jesus Christ.

Immortal means "not able to die." Adam did not have immortality since he not only *could* but *did* die, body and soul, when he fell into sin (Gen. 2:17). Fallen mankind is not immortal, since all are dead, body and soul, in trespasses and sins. Jesus says that those who do not believe shall "never see life," because the wrath of God abides on them (John 3:36).

The Bible never recognizes mere existence as "life": "Man shall not live by bread alone, but by every word that proceedeth out of the mouth of God" (Matt. 4:4); "In his favour is life" (Ps. 30:5); "For to me to live is Christ, and to die is gain" (Phil. 1:21).

In 1 Corinthians 15:53–54 the Word of God teaches that by nature men are not immortal, but mortal: "This *mortal* must put on immortality." Only by grace are those who are in Christ immortal. Immortality is the gift of God to them. From Adam mankind receives mortal life. Only through Christ do God's people receive immortality, because he is the Lord from heaven (vv. 45–47).

Are we just quibbling about words? We do not believe so. For one thing, to speak of man's soul as immortal tends to obscure the truth that through sin he has fallen, body and soul, *into eternal death* and needs to be saved, body and soul, from this death by the death of Jesus Christ on the cross. By nature, man is dead, body and soul, in trespasses and sins (Eph. 2:1).

For another thing, the teaching that every man's soul is immortal makes men think that the soul is more important than the body—even that the body is to be despised. In the history of the church, especially in the early church and in Roman Catholicism, that idea led to the practice of abusing and afflicting the body. Scripture teaches that by the grace of God in Jesus Christ, our bodies are not to be despised and abused, but that they are the temples of the Holy Spirit (1 Cor. 6:18–20).

Would it not therefore be better to use the word *immortality,* as the Bible does, to refer only to that wonderful gift of eternal life through Jesus Christ? When we by grace receive eternal life, *then* death is swallowed up in victory, and we shall not be able to die anymore (Rev. 21:4).

The Intermediate State

In theology the doctrine of the intermediate state has to do with the state of the soul between death and the final resurrection. This doctrine answers the question, "What happens to me after death?" What Scripture teaches is, therefore, of vital interest to believers: that after death the believer enters heavenly glory and is conscious of glory and of his being with Christ. How different their experience is from that of the unbelieving and unrepentant, who go into conscious suffering for their sin in hell even before their bodies are raised (Luke 16:22–28).

There are many who deny this. Some teach "soul-sleep": that the souls of those who are in heaven or hell are sleeping and not aware of what is happening to them. Similarly, some Christian Reconstructionists teach that the soul passes out of existence at death. This notion, as Calvin pointed out long ago, is perverse and should not be borne by God's people. It destroys their hope in Christ, renews the terrors of death, and leaves them comfortless in the face of the last of all enemies.

Our hope of glory with Christ is based on Jesus' words to the dying thief: "Today shalt thou be with me in paradise" (Luke 23:43). Does anyone really believe that Jesus meant, "You will be there but will not know it" or that "Your paradise will be that you pass out of existence until many thousands of years have passed and the end finally comes"?

Concerning Philippians 1:23, Calvin says, "Do they think he [Paul] wishes to fall asleep so as no longer to feel any desire of Christ? Was this all he was longing for when he said he knew he had a building of God, an house not made with hands, as soon as the earthly house of his tabernacle should be dissolved? (2 Cor. 5:1). Where were the benefit of being with Christ were he to cease to live the life of Christ? What! are they not overawed by the words of the Lord when, calling himself the God of Abraham, Isaac, and Jacob, he says, he is "God not of the dead but of the living"? (Matt. 22:32; Mark 12:27). Is He, then, neither to be to them a God, nor are they to be to him a people?"[6]

But what about those passages that describe the death of believers as *sleep* (Matt. 27:52; Acts 13:36; 1 Cor. 11:30; 1 Cor. 15:20, 51; Eph. 5:14; 1 Thess. 4:14)? In light of the passages already mentioned, they cannot mean that there is such a thing as soul-sleep. They must refer to the death and dissolution of the body and to the fact that the death of believers, for whom death is conquered, is no more difficult than a falling asleep. Nor is it strange that the death of believers should be described as sleep, for it is through death that they enter *everlasting rest* from their labors (Isa. 57:1; Rev. 14:13).

---

6. John Calvin, "Psychopannychia," in *Tracts and Treatises of John Calvin*, vol. 3 (Grand Rapids, MI: William B. Eerdmans Co., 1958), 444.

Scripture suggests that in the interval between death and the final resurrection, God makes some special provision, so that the soul without the body may enjoy the glory he has promised. "If our earthly house of this tabernacle were dissolved, we have a building of God, an house not made with hands, eternal in the heavens" (2 Cor. 5:1). For this reason, to be absent from the body is to be *present* (literally "at home") with the Lord (v. 8). Thus, though others are unwilling, we are willing to be absent from the body, are we not?

The Great Tribulation

Something much discussed, and a source of many differences between Christians as well as of great concern to God's people, is the matter of end-time tribulation. Is the great tribulation mentioned in Matthew 24:21 still to come, or has it passed? Will there be tribulation when the end comes? If so, will the members of the church be subjected to this tribulation, or will they be gone from the world before the last tribulation comes?

Such questions as these are vital, for they affect our view of the future and of our own calling and the church's calling with respect to the future. These questions weigh heavily as the end approaches and as we ourselves and our children must face the possibility of persecution, if such is indeed coming.

We believe that persecution has been and will continue to be the lot of God's people to the end of time. This is the testimony of such passages as Romans 8:17 and 2 Timothy 3:12. We do not believe, therefore, that the lot of God's people will improve as the end-times come, or that there will be a long period of peace and spiritual prosperity for them in which persecution for Christ's sake ceases. Nor do we believe that the church will be raptured and gone when the last great tribulation comes.

We believe, too, that the great tribulation mentioned in Matthew 24:21 is still to come—that times will not become better, but worse, for God's people. To consign the whole first part of Matthew 24, including verse 21, to the past, as some do, is to consign it to the wastebasket. Nor does the notion that God's people will be away, or that persecution will cease before the end, harmonize with this verse.

Persecution is not something that we must simply endure. It is an integral part of our salvation. Matthew 5:10–12 already indicates this when it speaks of the blessedness and happiness of those who are persecuted for Christ's sake (see also Acts 5:41). Philippians 1:29 tells us that suffering for Christ is a gift of God through Christ, one of the gifts he earned for us by his death on the cross. Colossians 1:24 says that these sufferings are part of Christ's own sufferings, which are left behind for the church's sake (see also 1 Pet. 4:13).

We know, too, that suffering, though never easy or pleasant, is for our good. It is not prosperity and peace that bring us closer to God and purify us, but the fiery trials of our faith. This is the testimony of Psalm 11:5, of 1 Peter 1:7, and of innumerable other passages.

The old saying that "the blood of the martyrs is the seed of the church"[7] recognized the value of persecution. There is nothing in all the life of the church that gives such testimony to the power and wonder of God's grace as the willingness of God's people to suffer all things for the sake of the gospel and of Christ. We must not only expect such suffering, but we must be willing and even happy to suffer such things for our own purification, for the church, and for Christ who suffered all things for our sakes.

The Antichrist

The biblical teaching concerning antichrist has always been of interest because he is pictured in Scripture as one of the great enemies of God's people. There is much disagreement, however, as to who he is and when he arrives.

Antichrist is described in 2 Thessalonians 2:4 as the one "who opposeth and exalteth himself above all that is called God, or that is worshipped." He is *anti*-Christ, because he is "against" Christ, and he puts himself in Christ's place ("exalteth himself above all that is called God").

The name *antichrist* is used only in 1 and 2 John (1 John 2:18, 22; 1 John 4:3; 2 John 7) but is not used in 2 Thessalonians 2. Nevertheless,

---

7. This saying is attributed to Tertullian, a theologian who lived approximately A.D. 160–230.

the correspondence between the name used by John and the description given in 2 Thessalonians 2 leads us to the conclusion that both passages are speaking of the same person.

Notice, too, that while John speaks of many *antichrists,* Thessalonians leads us to believe that he is especially *one man.* This is best understood through the picture that is drawn in Revelation 13; there, too, the name *antichrist* is not used, but a comparison of the passage with 2 Thessalonians 2:4–10 will show that the subject is the same in both.

Revelation 13, which describes a "beast," shows us that this beast is revealed through history. The different heads of the beast represent different kingdoms (Dan. 7:1–8, 15–28). However, all these kingdoms represent one power, finally and fully revealed in one man, who is called in 2 Thessalonians 2 "that man of sin" and "that Wicked [one]" (vv. 3, 8).

These other names are revealing. They show us that it is in this man and in his kingdom that the sins of the human race and all rebellion against God come to their fullest manifestation. He is the one in whom the lie of Satan—"Ye shall be as gods [God]" (Gen. 3:5)—comes closest to being realized. That he is described in Revelation 13 as the beast associates him with Satan also and reveals his true character as the enemy of the church.

The arguments about when antichrist comes, who he is, and whether the pope is antichrist are to some extent defused by what is said in 1 John 2:18: "*Now* are there *many antichrists.*" The final realization of the antichristian kingdom and power may be future, as we believe they are, but we may never forget that antichrists are always present.

While there can be no doubt about it that the pope and the papacy at the present time most clearly fit the description given of "that man of sin" in Scripture, we may not forget that there are many other antichrists. The leaders of the cults and of the charismatic movement also fit the description given. Indeed, all false prophets are antichrists of whom we must beware (Matt. 24:24).

Most comforting for God's people, however, is that antichrist is only a man. For all his enmity and hatred and persecution of the church throughout the ages, he is nothing in comparison to the one he imitates and opposes: the Son of God. There can be no doubt, therefore, who will overcome. and whose kingdom shall endure forever (Rev. 19:11–16).

The Judgment

The final judgment is the event that concludes the history of this present world and ushers in the everlasting kingdom of Christ. Scripture, therefore, has a great deal to say about the judgment day.

That judgment, because it is *one* day and *one* event, will be *universal*. *All* men, angels, and devils shall appear before God to receive from him the reward of grace or unrighteousness, and they shall receive it in the body in which they lived and acted unrighteously or righteously.

The universality of the judgment is clearly taught in Scripture. *All* shall be judged (Matt. 16:27; Matt. 25:31–32; John 5:28–29; Rom. 2:5–6; 2 Cor. 5:10; Rev. 20:11–14; Rev. 22:12). If there are any exceptions, they are the beast, the false prophet, and the devil, who apparently will be cast into the lake of fire without judgment, because their wickedness is already fully manifest (Rev. 19:20; Rev. 20:10).

This judgment will be *according to* works (1 Cor. 3:13–15; 1 Pet. 1:17; Rev. 2:23; Rev. 20:12–13), though not *because of* works. If it were because of works, that would make merit the basis of judgment, and on that basis none could stand. In the judgment the works of every person will show whether or not he is in Christ. His works will be the *proof* either of his justification before God (James 2:14–20) or of his unrighteousness and demerit.

According to those works, therefore, everyone shall receive a proper reward—the reward either of works, which will be eternal damnation, or of grace, which will be eternal life (Matt. 16:27; Rom. 4:4; Rev. 22:12). This reward will reveal the justice of God in the condemnation and damnation of the ungodly and the greatness of his grace to his people.

This judgment and rewarding is the work of *Christ*. To him the Father has given all judgment (John 5:26–27; Rev. 22:12–13). This is necessary, because all, both righteous and wicked, must be judged in relation to Christ. He it is whom the wicked have crucified and slain (Heb. 6:4–6; Rev. 1:7). He it is who has provided a justifying righteousness for his own.

To him the book of life belongs. That book (Luke 10:20) guarantees the salvation of those whom the Father has given to Christ. It is out of that book that some receive not what they have merited, but grace for grace.

For the believer, therefore, the day of judgment is not a day of terror, but the object of his hope and longing. In spite of the fact that he, too, must be judged, his confidence is in Christ and in the righteousness of Christ.

Certainly there is great hope for believers in the judgment. Christ, who is their Lord, their Elder Brother, their Justifier, and their Redeemer, will be the one who sits as their Judge, and when they appear in the judgment, they shall appear as they are in him: raised and glorified with him. That the resurrection precedes the judgment means that when believers appear before the judgment seat of Christ, they shall *already* be in his likeness (1 John 3:2). Their vile bodies shall have *already* been changed into the likeness of his glorious body (Phil. 3:21). What a comfort and foundation for hope! We trust it is yours also.

Only One Final Judgment

In its teaching concerning the last things, Scripture has more to say about the judgment day than about anything else. Let us look briefly at that testimony.

First, Scripture teaches that there will be but *one* judgment. The judgments of the sheep and the goats (Matt. 25:31–46), of the great white throne (Rev. 20:11–15), and of other judgments mentioned in Scripture are not different judgments, taking place at different times in history, but all *one and the same final, public judgment.*

There is, of course, a certain judgment that takes place throughout our lifetimes and at our death, but we are speaking here of the final, public judgment of every man, angel, and devil. There is only one such judgment, not many, as some teach (the notes of the *Scofield Study Bible* teach seven).

It is not our purpose to refute in detail the contentions of the dispensationalists and premillennialists concerning multiple judgments. We give just one example to show the kind of flimsy argument that is used to support such teaching.

It is said that the judgment of Matthew 25:31–46 is a judgment that precedes the end of the world by one thousand years and is a judgment of the then *living nations* in relation to Israel. These nations, so it is said, are judged only with respect to their treatment of Israel during the times preceding this judgment.

Scripture, however, does not speak of *living* nations in Matthew 25, but of *all* nations (v. 32), and it clearly shows that this judgment is not of nations, but of each individual and according to that person's works, just as the judgment of Revelation 20. Matthew 25:46 speaks of everlasting punishment and of life eternal, like the other passages that speak of the final judgment.

This judgment follows the coming of the Son of man in his glory, a coming also described in Matthew 24:30–31, which takes place *at the sound of a trumpet.* That trumpet is the final trumpet mentioned in 1 Corinthians 15:51–52, 1 Thessalonians 4:14–17, and Revelation 11:15–18. According to Matthew 24:29–30, this coming of Christ that is announced by the darkening of the sun and moon is with clouds and is visible to all eyes—all of which describe Christ's final appearance at the end of all ages (2 Pet. 3:10–17; Rev. 1:7; Rev. 6:12–17).

Clearest proof, however, for one final judgment is found in Scripture's teaching that *all* shall be judged when Christ returns, not some now and some later (John 5:28), and that there is but a single *judgment,* not *judgments* (Matt. 5:21–22; Matt. 12:41–42).

Is it important to believe this? We believe it is, not only because it is bound up with our view of Israel and of the resurrection and of the coming of Christ, but also because it is for that judgment, and that *alone,* that we must prepare ourselves, in obedience to 2 Peter 3:10–18.

The Purpose of the Judgment

What is the purpose of the coming judgment? Have you ever thought about that question? It is not so simple to answer as might first appear.

In one sense, the judgment has already taken place. When people die, they go immediately to heaven or to hell. That could not happen unless they had already been judged by God. Thus most people will already be in heaven or in hell when the judgment day comes, and the judgment will not change that. Why, then, is a *day* of judgment needed?

There is also a judgment that takes place in connection with the death of Jesus. He spoke of this in John 12:31, when he said at the time of his death, "*Now* is the judgment of this world." Christ by his death provided eternal salvation for some and not for others (the doctrine of limited atonement). By his death some are excluded from salvation, their eternal destiny sealed, and their judgment determined. Why, then, is there a coming judgment day?

The answer to this question lies in an important theological word, the word *theodicy*. This word means "the righteousness of God" and describes the principal purpose of the judgment day, with respect both to the righteous and to the unrighteous.

The purpose of the judgment is *not* to decide the destinies of men and angels, nor to change destinies. Those are already fixed in predestination and the cross. Rather, the main purpose of the judgment is to show that God is God, righteous and holy, both in the condemnation of the unrighteous and in the salvation of his own.

Today the judgments of God are always called into question. His judgment of the righteous is questioned by Satan, the great accuser of the brethren (Rev. 12:10), and by the ungodly when they accuse believers and say that they are sinners like everyone else. It is questioned even by God's people when they doubt God's work in their own justification.

God's judgments of the ungodly are questioned, too. The claim that God is love and therefore cannot condemn people to hell does this. So do all complaints that are raised against God's sovereignty in the reprobation and condemnation of sinners.

These complaints will no longer be heard in the final judgment. Then it will be evident in the condemnation of the ungodly that God is not unrighteous in sending sinners to hell. Their own works will condemn them. By the opening of the books and the revelation of God's holiness, every mouth will be stopped, and all the world will be found guilty (Rom. 3:19). God will have justified himself forever.

The final justification of God's people will also be found fair and equitable. It will be evident in the judgment that God has not denied his own demands and his own righteousness in receiving them into heavenly glory.

At the center of all this will be Christ. The justice of the condemnation of the ungodly will be shown in their earthly denials and rejections of the *Son of God*, and by the same token, the righteousness of the righteous will be revealed as Christ's righteousness and none of their own, and God will be justified in them as well.

May that day of God's glory and our salvation come quickly!

Hell

Even the word *hell,* standing all alone as it does in the title of this section, has a terrifying sound and makes us shudder. It is no wonder that many today do not want to speak of it.

Like the deity of Christ, the Trinity, and the atonement, hell is a biblical doctrine that has always been under attack in the New Testament church. That attack continues today. It comes not only from those who are "modern" and "liberal" in their teaching. Even the evangelical movement today has in it those who attack this teaching.

The New International Version of the Bible (NIV) illustrates this, since it is very much a product of the evangelical movement. It has banished the word *hell* entirely from the Old Testament. And ten out of the twenty-two times that the word *hell* appears in the KJV, the NIV has re-translated it.

Especially the NIV's banishing the word from the Old Testament is significant. This can be nothing else than a concession on the part of the translators to the idea that people in the Old Testament did not really know about hell, but believed only in a place of the dead to which all went, both righteous and wicked.

To leave the word *hell* out of the Old Testament is bad translating. There are places in the Old Testament where *Sheol,* the word usually translated "hell" in the KJV, *must* be translated as "hell." Deuteronomy 32:22 and Job 26:6 are good examples. Also Psalm 16:10, which is quoted in the New Testament, must be so translated, since in the New Testament (Acts 2:27, 31) Sheol is replaced by the word *Hades,* the usual Greek word meaning "hell."

As disagreeable as it is, the word *hell* may not be banished from our Bibles, our doctrine, or our thinking. It is critical to the preaching of the gospel. Without the doctrine of hell, the command of the gospel to repent or perish loses all its urgency. Even the teaching of "conditional immortality" (punishment for a time, and then annihilation), which is held by some evangelicals, improperly takes away from the truth that we must perish if we do not repent, for it denies that the impenitent will suffer the wrath of God *eternally.*

What is more, that terrible word *hell* is inseparably connected with the fear of God. Jesus says, "Rather fear him which is able to destroy both soul and body in *hell*" (Matt. 10:28). If only men believed in hell today, perhaps there would be more of the fear of God in the world and in the church. It is sadly lacking in most circles, even though "the fear of the LORD is the beginning of wisdom" (Prov. 9:10).

Eternal Punishment

The doctrine of eternal punishment has never been popular. It is troubling, however, that the attack on this doctrine now comes from within evangelicalism. As we have just seen, the NIV has all but eliminated the word *hell* from the Word of God, and many leading evangelicals are teaching what is called "conditional immortality." Promoters of this false doctrine say that the ungodly go to hell for a time but are eventually annihilated, so that in the end there will be *no one* in hell. There is punishment, they say, but it is not eternal. A leading evangelical has said that though their smoke goes up forever, there will be no one burning.

We believe that the doctrine of eternal punishment is not only biblical, but an essential doctrine as well. That it is biblical is clear from such passages as Revelation 19:3, the verse that speaks of the smoke of Babylon going up forever. The reference is to ungodly *persons,* and it takes a very vivid imagination to figure out how Babylon's smoke could go up forever without anyone even being present in hellfire.

That the doctrine of eternal punishment is important should not be difficult to see. For one thing, it leads to a proper understanding of sin. That punishment is *eternal* accentuates the fact that sin is committed against the eternal and most high majesty of God. A denial of eternal punishment belittles sin.

Closely related to this, a denial of eternal punishment calls into question the justice of God. That God should first send people to hell and later end that punishment by annihilating them does not speak well of the unchangeableness or the justice and righteousness of God. It suggests that he changes his mind about their punishment and to some degree relents his wrath against their sins.

A denial of eternal punishment also destroys the urgency of the gospel demand for repentance and faith. The ungodly would not be so terrified of the judgments of God if they knew they would be annihilated. It is the thought of eternal suffering that is so terrifying to them.

It is in the interest of denying their own fears of eternal punishment that men deny the continued existence of the soul, the existence of heaven and hell, and the coming judgment. Perhaps more than anything else it is their fear of eternal punishment that leads them to deny the very existence of God, for to admit his existence and his holiness implies that he lives as a righteous Judge.

That is not to say that anyone is ever saved by being *frightened* into heaven. Nevertheless, it is the terrors of eternal punishment that God often uses to begin the great work by which he brings his people to himself, and the doctrine of eternal punishment is an important part of gospel preaching.

For these reasons, we must bow to Scripture's teaching concerning eternal punishment, as disagreeable as it may seem, even to Christians. We must do so, believing that in Christ we will not be subject to eternal punishment.

Heaven

In speaking of heaven, we must be careful to adhere to what the Bible teaches. There is so much that the Bible does *not* tell us, and so it is easy to indulge in unprofitable speculation and go astray from what we *do* know.

One reason for the lack of information about heaven is that heaven is so wonderful it cannot be adequately described in earthly terms. We get a feel for this when we read some descriptions of heaven: no night, no sun or moon, no sea, no marriage, no temple. Heaven belongs to those things that "eye hath not seen, nor ear heard, neither have entered into the heart of man" to understand (1 Cor. 2:9).

For this same reason, much of what the Bible does tell us about heaven is given in symbols and figures. They teach us that heaven will be wonderful indeed, but they do not tell us exactly what heaven will be like. The description of the new Jerusalem in Revelation 21 is a good example. If we conclude from the picture drawn there that heaven is actually a city fifteen hundred miles long, wide, and high, with streets of gold, gates made of huge pearls, and foundations of precious stones, we are wrong. Revelation 21 itself tells us that that city is "the bride, the Lamb's wife," that is, the glorified church (see also Eph. 5:25–32; Rev. 19:7–9).

We do not mean, however, that there is anything we need to know about heaven that is lacking in Scripture. The Bible tells us everything necessary, though it does not satisfy our curiosity.

Some of the things the Bible does say about heaven are most comforting to us in the world. There will be no more tears, pain, or death there (Rev. 21:4). We will have rest (Rev. 14:13), joy (Matt. 25:23), and glorious liberty (Rom. 8:21). We will be like Christ (1 John 3:2). Even our vile bodies will be changed into the likeness of the body of Christ (Phil. 3:21). Sin, temptation, and all wicked men will be banished forever (Rev. 21:27). We will be in the company of the saints and angels (Heb. 12:22–23).

Yet even these things do not describe the real glory and blessedness of heaven, which are that *God* and *Christ* will be there: "Behold, the tabernacle of God is with men, and he will dwell with them, and they shall be his people, and God himself shall be with them, and be their God." This is what heaven is all about (Rev. 21:3). The blessedness of heaven for believers is that "they shall see Christ's face; and his name shall be in their foreheads" (Rev. 22:4).

So many passages speak of this heavenly blessedness that it is impossible to miss it (Job 19:26–27; Ps. 16:11; Ps. 17:15; 1 Cor. 13:12; Phil. 1:23). Nor *may* we miss it. If we do not desire heaven because God is there and because Christ is there, we do not desire it *at all.* In hoping for heaven, then, our prayer should be that of Philip: "Lord, shew us the Father, and it sufficeth us" (John 14:8).

The New Heavens and the New Earth

Scripture speaks often of the new heavens and earth as the final home of God's people. Just the fact that it is *home* is sufficient to make it desirable to us, for as long as we are in this world, we are pilgrims and strangers. *Here* we have no home, no country or city that we can call our own (Heb. 11:8–10, 13–16). What a great thing it shall be finally to go home after a long, weary pilgrimage, knowing that our Father, our Elder Brother, and all our family will be there, and that we will never again have to leave.

How can it be home when we have never even been there? How can we desire it as home? As in a *true* earthly home, the place is not so important as the people who are there. Them we know and love. We have never seen heaven, but those who are there are our family in Christ, whom we do know and have learned to love.

We might ask, though, why there must be new heavens. The answer lies in Christ's work. Created for him (Col. 1:16), the heavens must be renewed in him and by him so that they are a fit place for him and for those who are in him. That first heaven was affected by the fall of some angels, just as the earth was by the fall of man. Satan, the head of that first heavenly creation, fell from his high estate (Isa. 14:12) and drew many of the angels with him (Rev. 12:4). Thus that heavenly creation must be restored in Christ.

Why a new earth? First, because God does not abandon the work of his own hands. The earth that he created is not cast away and abandoned because of sin, but preserved and in the end restored. And so that Christ may be glorified, it is not only renewed to its first estate, but lifted up to an even higher glory.

Part of that glory is that the new earth is united with the new heavens, when the tabernacle of God comes down from God out of heaven (Rev. 21:1–2). But the great glory of that renewed creation is that righteousness dwells in it. It must be cleansed and renewed so that righteousness may dwell therein, and so that all sin and the works of sin may be destroyed. Nothing may remain of that which the hands of filthy sinners have accomplished. The righteousness that dwells there is Christ's own, the righteousness that we will have in him.

When we speak of these things and realize *what* we are waiting for, truly we count all other things but loss and dung (Phil. 3:8). This world and the life of this world, even the greatest pleasures this world can offer, are but dust and ashes by comparison. A person who knows that heaven is his home will never be at home in this world, and that is the way it ought to be (2 Cor. 5:6–8). Thus our hopes are stirred, and we are encouraged to lift up our eyes, wait for our promised redemption, and live as those whose life is already hid with God in Christ in the heavenlies.

Heavenly Glory

Regarding the glories of the eternal state, or heaven, and of the place every believer shall have there, we should understand that the language Scripture uses to describe heaven and its glories is largely figurative. When we read of a crown of life, of our being pillars in the temple of God, and of receiving the morning star, we should understand that it is not in these things that the glory of heaven consists.

Certainly literal things such as these are of no value to those who have become like the angels and are no longer earthly (1 Cor. 6:13). Revelation 21 and 22 help to make this clear when they say that the city described there is the glorified church (21:9–10) and that the tree of life is Christ himself (Rev. 2:7; Rev. 22:2, 14).

Why does Scripture use such language? It does this because the things of heaven are things that "eye hath not seen, nor ear heard, neither have entered into the heart of man, the things which God hath prepared for them that love him" (1 Cor. 2:9). In other words, heaven is so glorious and wonderful that we cannot even begin to comprehend it except through pictures and figures.

But if the glory and wonder of heaven is not gold and pearls and precious stones, what is it? Revelation 21 and 22 answer this question very clearly. It is *God himself,* and especially God as he reveals himself in Jesus our Savior. God has created all things for himself (Rev. 4:11), and in heaven that becomes a living reality to God's people.

Scripture tells us that God and Christ are the light of that city, its temple, and its citizens (Rev. 21:23–24; Rev. 22:5). These chapters tell us the real glory of heaven when they speak of God's dwelling with his people and being their God (Rev. 21:3; Rev. 22:3–4).

Being with all the believers, being raised and changed into the likeness of Christ, having every tear wiped away, being forever delivered from the presence, power, and possibility of sin—all these are part of heaven's delights. But the best of heaven's glory is none of those things. It is the presence there of God and him only (Ps. 16:11; Ps. 17:15; Ps. 73:25).

This means, of course, that the glory of heaven for us is the realization of God's covenant of grace. Always that covenant has meant that God is our God and we are his people. In heaven this will reach its highest glory, for then all God's people shall live in God's presence, shall see his face, shall know him, and shall enjoy him forever.

For that we wait, but it has application to us now. Those who do not really desire the glory of heaven must not assume that they do. The person who is not interested in God and his glory, who has no delight in the fellowship of God, and who does not above all things desire to see God's face is not interested in heaven, no matter what he may say.

So let us examine ourselves and our lives and see that God is all our desire and all our joy. Then we will not only know what heavenly glory is all about, but we shall be assured of our place and portion in it.

Index to Words in Headings

A

Adam
covenant with, 168
  and human race, 100
adoption, 202
amillennialism, 303
angels, 83
Antichrist, the, 317
antithesis, the, 208
apostolic church, the, 233
atonement
  and justification, 201
  limited, 155
attributes of God. *See* God

B

baptism
  and circumcision, 267
  and entrance into kingdom, 266
  of Ethiopian eunuch, 262
  and faith, 270
  of families, 264
  of infants in N.T., 263
  meaning of, 259
  mode of, 260
  and repentance, 271
  sign and reality of, 257
  symbolism of, 256
baptizing and discipling the nations, 272
Bible versions, 26
bread and wine in Lord's supper. *See* Lord's supper

C

calling, 188
  not an offer, 191
  and preaching, 190

catholicity of church, 231
Christ
  ascension into heaven of, 160
  baptism of Jesus, 262
  body of, and congregation, 218
  burial of, 157
  coming of
    one final, 285
    quick, 291
    signs of, 286
    sudden and unexpected, 289
    various comings, 162, 282–83
    wonder of, 292
  covenant in, 143
  death of, 153
  eternal generation of, 136
  human nature of
    central, 134
    complete, 130
    real, 128
    sinless, 131
    weakened, 132
  lowly birth of, 151
  names of, 119
    Christ, 121
    Immanuel, 126
    Jesus, 120
    Lord, 122
    Only Begotten Son of God, 124
    Son of Man, 125
  and preaching, 249
  presence of in Lord's supper, 275
  resurrection of, 158
  return of. *See* Christ, coming of
  seated at right hand of God, 161
  states of, humiliation and exaltation, 149
  suffering of, 152